Through Gilly's Eyes

Memoirs of a Guide Dog

a novel

Matthew VanFossan

VOLANT PRESS LTD.

VOLANT PRESS LTD.
Pittsburgh, Pennsylvania

Special discounts are available on quantity purchases.
For details, contact volantpress@gmail.com

Cover design by Clark Kenyon
www.camppope.com

Printed in the United States of America
First Edition 2013

Library of Congress Control Number: 2012955466

ISBN 978-0-9886567-0-3 (paperback)

Library of Congress Subject Headings:
1. Coming of age. 2. Biography – memoirs 3. Guide dogs
4. Blind - biography 5. Dogs

Acknowledgments

Thank you to all those who have helped me with this book, especially to Nan Cappo, Beth Miller, Cara Smith, MJ Willard, Aricia Lee, Clark Kenyon, Jennifer Gaidos, my wife, Rita VanFossan, and the staff at Volant Press.

To my mom,
Margaret VanFossan,
for helping me share my story.

Note from the Author

This is a creative retelling of some of the events that Gilly and I experienced together during his career as a guide dog. I've taken on what I imagine to be Gilly's voice and point of view to tell this story for several reasons. First, I discovered that his perspective gave me new space and clarity with which to consider my thoughts, feelings, and actions described here. Second, I found that Gilly's voice added humor and momentum to the unfolding of the story. Third, and most importantly, I took on Gilly's voice in homage to the guidance, companionship, and love that his presence brought to my life.

Chapter 1

For the Love of Kibble

I remember when I first began training to become a guide dog. So many years have passed since then, but from my point of view, it feels like no time at all.

I was considered one of the handsomest dogs at the school. I'm really not trying to brag; I was a good-looking Labrador, that's all. In fact, I almost got diverted into the breeder program. The trainer thought I was such an exquisite specimen of my species that she considered making me a stud. Imagine! A life of uncomplicated sex—all for the good of future generations. But, it wasn't meant to be. I had another calling. I had a human to guide. And what a rewarding job it proved to be. Were there times I wondered if I should have gone into the breeder program instead? Most definitely. If I had a piece of kibble for every time I thought that, I'd have a thirty-pound bag, at least.

Take, for example, the first time I ever met my human. The trainer introduced me to him in what was to become our shared room. He was a wiry, dark-haired, pale-skinned specimen of his species. I wasn't at all impressed. Apparently, he wasn't either.

"Gilcrest? What kind of a name is Gilcrest?" he wondered aloud.

What kind of a name is Matt? I thought. Instead of dwelling on the question, I went about sniffing everything within my leash's range: an unmade bed with Matt's smell, a desk chair covered by Matt-scented clothes, an uncarpeted floor with a faint whiff of disinfectant. Then I found what I had been looking for. Underneath a sink near the bathroom door sat a plastic dog food container. It was shut tight, but I caught the unmistakable aroma of kibble inside. I strained at the end of my leash, sniffing the plastic, searching frantically for a means of entry.

"No!" Matt pulled back on my leash.

Dutifully, I retreated.

"Gilcrest, sit."

I sat.

"Good boy." He patted my head. He felt my long, velvety ears, then the saggy, flexible skin of my jowls.

Having satisfied his sit command, I got up and headed again in the direction of the kibble.

"Gilcrest, no!" He jerked on the leash, pulling me back again. He obviously didn't want me helping myself to an early dinner.

I decided to try another tactic. I sat, looking up at him with my most imploring gaze.

I'm the saddest, most appealing dog in the world, and you can make me happy if you just give me what's in that container, I told him silently. It had worked before, and I figured it would work again. My soulful eyes bore pleadingly into his dark glasses. He was unmoved. Frustrated, I lay down on the floor with a *humph.*

Obviously, I would have to get used to the ramifications of having a blind human. All the other humans I'd known had been sighted, and despite all my preparation, no one had thought to tell me that my human would be unmoved by eye contact.

Matt sat down on the floor next to me and began absentmindedly stroking my soft fur. His disappointment emanated like sour grapes.

Let me explain here that smell is a dog's primary sense. We use our noses to understand the physical world the way that most humans use their eyes. And it tells us a lot. We can detect a spoonful of sugar in an Olympic-size swimming pool. We can learn to sniff out bombs, drugs, and even cancerous tumors. By a person's scent, we can know his heart rate, adrenalin levels, and overall body chemistry. It shouldn't be too surprising, then, that we can smell emotion. Excitement, worry, contentment, anxiety, despair, and joy—they all appear as different blips on our olfactory radar screens. But, our abilities don't stop there. For centuries dogs have been studying human behavior, perfecting ways of coaxing food and devotion from so-called Homo sapiens. We've become very discerning and remarkably intuitive.

Matt had been waiting anxiously to meet me for some time now and had clearly been expecting to receive, in a shower of tail wags and sloppy kisses, my unconditional love and affection. Now that we'd met, he was dismayed to perceive that my interest lay not in him but in the forbidden contents of the plastic container. Of course, this wasn't exactly true. My interest now lay in him *giving* me the contents of the plastic container. Unfortunately, at that moment, he was preoccupied with listening to his roommate, Chuck, through the open partition between their rooms.

"Her name is Zelda," Chuck said. "She's a black lab . . . Yeah, just like Cyrus. I think they'll get along great . . . She seems really cool. When I sat down on the bed, she put her head on the spot next to me, so I invited her up, and she loves it! . . . Well, they told us in class that the dogs were trained not to climb on furniture, but it was up to us if we wanted to let them on the bed."

After a few more exchanges, Chuck hung up. "Hey, Matt," he called. "Did you talk to your family yet?"

"No, not yet. I think I'll wait 'til tonight."

"Well, what'd ya think of your new dog?"

"He's cool," Matt said, but his voice belied his words.

Chuck came to stand in the opening between the two rooms. "Zelda is too. I was just telling my parents how awesome she is."

"Zelda's a great name," Matt said. "Reminds me of the video game. Man, I was addicted to old-school Nintendo as a kid. If I get my vision back, that'll be, like, the first thing I do. Forget sunsets and faces, I just wanna play some freaking Zelda, you know?"

Chuck laughed. "I didn't know you used to have vision."

"Yeah. I mean, I could never see well enough to drive, but I could get around without a cane and stuff like that."

"So when did you become blind?"

"Last year. It was really sudden."

I smelled his anxiety then—just a whiff. He was trying hard to cover it up, but smells never lie. There was something unfinished about Matt's blindness.

Chuck said that he'd been blind since birth. I could tell he was quite comfortable with his situation, even downright happy.

"Hello, Gilcrest," he greeted me. "Gilcrest is sort of an unusual name for a dog, isn't it?"

"Yeah. To be honest, I'm not crazy about it."

"It's not such a bad name."

"Come on, man. Seriously! Gilcrest? What's up with that?"

Chuck burst out laughing. "Well, you could call him Cresty or Gilly. But, you're right. It is sort of a dumb name."

I tried not to take this personally, marveling that a detail like my name could matter so much. I'd never given it a second thought myself. With the advantage of hindsight, I see more clearly that part of Matt's irritation had its roots in his need to express himself, to carve out his own identity. He saw me as his dog, so he thought he should have control over what he called me. For him, it was like being given a new coat and then being told he could only wear it on Thursdays. I felt grateful to be a dog. Life was so much simpler for me.

That evening, after his shower, Matt emerged from the bathroom, his skinny, towel-wrapped form still dripping.

"Hello, Guildenstern!"

Huh? I blinked in surprise.

"It's your new name!"

Guildenstern is the best you could dream up? I thought, but I didn't try to convey my dubiousness. Matt was too caught up in his own idea to listen.

"Hey Chuck—I've just decided! I'm changing his name to Guildenstern!" Matt walked over to Chuck's room.

"To what?"

"Guil-den-stern!"

Chuck laughed. "Where'd you get that?"

"It's from *Hamlet*."

"Uh, okay."

"Yeah, you know, the Shakespeare play. I had to act out a scene in class during my freshman year, and my character was named Guildenstern."

"That's cool. What does Guildenstern think of his new name?"

"I think he loves it. Don't you, Guildenstern?"

That was, I knew, one of those questions that humans ask dogs without really wanting an answer. "Isn't it about time for your bath?" and "How did you get up on the counter?" were similar ones I'd heard from Erin, my human mom. I wagged my tail anyway, thumping it rhythmically against the wall. If the name made him happy, it was fine by me. I didn't care what he called me as long as he kept on dishing out the kibble. That evening's dinner had been as good as any I had ever eaten. My new charge may have cared a lot about silly things like names, but he served up dog food and water reliably enough.

Chapter 2

Enjoy the Ride

Before meeting Matt, I lived in the kennels at the guide dog school. I'd come to train there when I was a puppy, one-human-year old, and stayed until I was two years old and met Matt. The kennel was an exciting place to live. So many other dogs, so many great smells, so much fun! There was always plenty of company and lots of chances to play with my new friends. I remember when I first moved in; I was so excited to be running with a black lab named Sammy that I didn't look where I was going and scraped my belly on a ledge. Youch! I had to go to the medical center and get stitches. Not a fun time.

From that little snafu I learned to be calmer and more deliberate—no more racing around all the time. Instead I would grab a bone during playtime and climb to the highest point in the play area so that I could oversee the action. I realized how silly it was to run myself ragged when I could be perfectly content chewing my bone, watching the others, and taking it easy.

Later, after we got to know each other, Matt teased me that I was lazy. But this wasn't really the case. I just didn't see the point of a lot of unnecessary movement; I preferred economizing my effort. Besides, a lazy dog wouldn't want to do his job. I, however, enjoyed my work as a guide. It gave me a purpose and entry to the outside world. Even during training I was happy to have someone throw on my harness and take me out to learn a new command. Left, right, straight, find the steps. I learned them all without a single complaint. This is more than I can say for Matt.

I remember our first outdoor route together. For several days after we met, Matt had practiced walking with me inside our dormitory. Up and down the halls, I led him at a sedate pace. But we had never been outside. On that day, we waited in a lounge that led to a practice course set up on campus. The early August weather of southern Oregon was a little breezy, but it was perfect for walking outside, enjoying the fresh air and sun. I lay on the floor beside Katie, a fetching golden retriever with a shapely tail. Despite all the training I'd undergone, I couldn't resist giving her a quick sniff.

"Are you nervous?" Cathy sat beside Matt on the sofa. She was a retrain. Katie, I'd heard, was her third guide dog.

"Nope. I just want to get out there and do it."

"Yeah, I know what you mean. I'm ready to go, too." Just then, she was called to the door by one of the instructors.

"Good luck," he said.

"Thanks," she replied, cheerfully, and she and Katie were gone. A few minutes later, the two were back, the dog panting, the woman flushed with pleasure.

"How'd it go?" Matt asked.

"It was great! Katie moves so fast. It's amazing the difference a young guide dog makes."

I see now he didn't quite get what she meant. How could he? I was his first guide dog.

"Matt and Gilcrest," Alice called. "You're up." Matt hadn't gotten the instructors on board to my recent name change yet, having decided to phase it in discreetly.

We met Alice at the door, and she continued. "This is a short course that'll take you about five minutes. There are some ramps, and Gilcrest will slow down as you pass over them. You'll feel him make some slight turns. This is him maneuvering you around the obstacles on the course."

"Sounds good." Matt smiled confidently.

"Okay, whenever you're ready."

"Gilly, forward," he commanded, and we were off. I walked at a brisk trot. I was at home on this obstacle course and intended to show my human what I could do. I pulled him through sharp turns, going up and down slopes, dodging obstacles in the path.

Behind me, Matt stumbled along like a drunken sailor. It was a new kind of locomotion that must've felt totally unnatural. The harness handle pulled him forward in rhythmic jerks that reflected the rise and fall of my body as I trotted. I smelled his clammy skin and felt the tension in his arm gripping my harness. He was terrified. He pulled back on the harness handle to get me to slow down. Instead, I sped up. I couldn't help it. I'd been taught to tug harder against greater pressure from behind. The more he pulled against me, the faster I went. I sensed his growing terror as we whizzed around the course.

Stop pulling so hard on my harness if you wanna slow down, I thought. But, he kept right on pulling, and I kept right on going, my speed mounting. Finally, it was too much for him. In desperation, he let go. I immediately stopped moving.

"Don't let go of the harness handle," Alice called from the door. This was, in fact, rule number one of guide dog school. Letting go of the harness handle was akin to letting go of the rope while waterskiing. At least that's what the instructors always said. I, myself, had never tried waterskiing. Matt stood there, silently torn. Picking up the handle meant plunging back into the obstacle course. Not picking up the handle meant admitting to the watching instructor just how scared he was.

Trust me. I won't run you into anything. I'm a professional.

But he didn't trust me. I saw that clearly. His only motivation for throwing himself back into the guide work now was to save face. He could show his vulnerability and fail to complete the course or continue to get yanked around by a dog and finish what he'd started. Against great resistance, he picked up the harness handle once again.

Attaboy!

It struck me then that his pride might have its usefulness after all. He was following me to save face, but at least he was following me. Hopefully, trust would come in time.

Bracing himself, he urged me forward. We were off again. I took him through the rest of the course and came to a stop in front of Alice, panting happily in the flush of accomplishment. I had completed the course flawlessly despite my jittery cargo.

"Good job, guys."

"Thanks." Matt was apparently in mild shock. His pulse beat rapidly as he stood on wobbly legs at the door to go back inside. He dropped my harness handle, and Alice led us back to the sofa, one contented dog and one dazed human.

"What did you think?" Cathy asked. "Amazing, isn't it?"

"Uh, yeah. It's really . . . different." He didn't say a word about feeling terrified.

Chapter 3

Facing the Music

Like so many new partners, Matt and I continued to have communication issues, and even the simplest undertaking became a challenge. The first time Matt asked me to turn right, he issued the command and twisted awkwardly. I just stood there, confused. I knew he was asking me to do something, but his body language wasn't reinforcing any of the maneuvers I'd learned. He tried again, but the second effort was no better. Like a puppy chasing his tail, he was all over the place.

To ask me to turn right, Matt was supposed to step back with his left foot and pivot his body. Without these essential movements to activate my prior training, I was clueless. As I would discover, body language was not his strong suit.

During those first few days, Matt would come back from routes frustrated and exhausted. It was natural, I knew. Guide work was totally new to him, and some initial faltering and floundering was understandable. What was surprising was how little I heard him voice his frustrations to his roommate, other students, staff, or even his family. He just plowed through the days and let his feelings intensify until he was enveloped in a sour-smelling gloom.

One night he sagged onto the bed as usual, then roused himself and picked up his guitar. He began to pluck the strings, producing delicate harmonic patterns. I listened from the side of the bed, my head on my paw. I was struck by the music's poignancy. What he expressed through the notes was more vivid and intimate than anything I'd heard in his words. Ghostly doubts rode airily on the waves of sound. He felt ashamed and incompetent. I could almost hear the lyrics in his head. *Should I be here? Can I make it? Do I really belong?*

"Wow!" Chuck said, entering the room. "That's really good! How long've you been playing?"

Matt took a deep breath. "Since I was sixteen. I guess that makes six years."

"Seriously, you can really make some music. I wish I could do that."

"You could. It's hard at first, but then it gets easier." His fingers danced lightly over the fretboard. "So, how was your route today with Zelda?"

"It was great! She's like such an expert. It's so cool walking with her. How was Guildenstern?"

"Um . . . he was okay."

Chuck came over and patted my head. I licked my lips and looked at him in appreciation. "Did you use his new name while you were working?"

"No, I've been calling him Gilly."

"Oh, that's good. You can switch it up gradually."

They fell into conversation. Matt talked about returning to his senior year of college that fall, Chuck about his job transcribing braille.

"I learned braille when I was in grade school," Matt said. "Basically, my mom forced me to. My vision was always iffy, and she figured if I lost it I'd have something to fall back on. I hated doing it but I finally got the foundation down."

"That's good." Chuck smiled. "Hard at first, but then it gets easier."

"I guess you're right. The funny part is that I've hardly used it at all since, uh, losing my sight. I mostly use talking computers and audio books."

"Well, technology's a great resource. I still like knowing braille, though."

After a few minutes Chuck went back to his room, leaving a lighter mood behind. Without even meaning to he had lifted Matt's spirits with his infectiously positive attitude. I rolled over and sighed with relief. It felt much more pleasant here now.

Matt dug into his pocket and pulled out a small electronic device. He repeatedly pushed one of its buttons, and the device played messages in his voice. There were to-do lists, song fragments, and phone numbers. He stopped at one of the recordings, a phone number. Someone named Amanda. I felt his pulse quicken as nervousness took hold. With a strange mixture of dread and excitement, he reached for the phone.

"Hi. Amanda? It's Matt." He listened for several seconds.

"Good. How are you? I guess it's been awhile since we've talked. I was just wondering how your summer's going."

There was a pause on Matt's end while I heard a female voice come faintly from the receiver.

"Oh, yeah?" Matt said. He laughed nervously. "Well, maybe it'll be more exciting once school starts up again. Hard to believe it's less than a month away." He seemed to be straining in this conversation.

Come on, just relax, I thought.

"Yeah, I'm with him right now, actually. We just ran a route today. It's been kinda tough, though. I just wasn't prepared for—well, it's a strange sensation. Like nothing I've ever experienced before. Sort of a jerky, up and down movement. It's kind of hard to explain."

He was walking back and forth in the small area next to his bed. "Yeah, maybe like riding a horse. I've only been on a horse once in my life, so I'm no expert. But imagine walking behind the horse blindfolded. It was crazy!"

There was a lengthy reply on the other end.

"Oh, that's cool. Barry's a nice guy." His voice had gone flat.

Matt made a few more polite remarks. He explained that he would be living in a house off campus with some friends and that she should stop by and visit. Was she sure she had his phone number?

He hung up the phone and lay back on his bed, staring listlessly into space. I could see the call hadn't gone the way he'd wanted. Whoever this Amanda girl was, it seemed to me he wanted something from her that she wasn't giving him. I knew what that felt like. Right then I wanted my belly rubbed, but Matt was too wrapped up in his angst-filled girl chasing to notice. I rolled over and fell into a nap.

I'm chasing my old buddy, Helmholtz, around the yard. What fun! He's my best friend. We eat from the same bowl, sleep alongside one another, and play together in the backyard. Right now he's trying to get my bone out of my mouth, but I won't let him have it. It's my bone and it's good to chomp on. Then Erin opens the back door and calls us in for dinner. Ah, Erin. Her voice always sounds so sweet when she's talking about kibble. I race Helmholtz to be the first inside. Erin greets us in the doorway, laughing. I like her laugh. It's so infectious. I sneeze happily, following Helmholtz into the kitchen, drooling in anticipation of what's coming.

I woke up suddenly. The room was dark. Matt was already asleep, his breath rising and falling steadily from the bed. I licked my paw, drowsily. It had been such a nice dream. That first year of my life with Erin and Helmholtz seemed so vivid compared to this confusing guide work, this unhappy human. It's not that I regretted being at the school. I knew I was here for a purpose. But, still, I wondered how Helmholtz was doing. Would I ever see Erin again?

Chapter 4

Escalating Tensions

The next day eleven students, eleven dogs, and two instructors loaded into a bus headed for the shopping mall where the students would practice new commands. Matt sat down in an empty seat, and I flopped at his feet. My large Labrador bulk took up most of the foot room in front of his seat and the empty seat next to him. I wasn't worried. The bus was big, and there was enough room for each student and dog team to sit alone.

"Okay, everyone," Joanne said as the bus driver started the engine. "We're going to practice having the dogs sit in front of you on the bus today. We want to prepare you for crowded city buses where you won't be able to let your dog take up another passenger's space."

Well, so much for my beauty rest, I thought.

Matt had begun allowing me to sleep with him, and I made the most of my new bed privileges. I enjoyed spreading out during the night and would often wake in the morning feeling Matt's feet pushing into my side. It wasn't the most comfortable of sensations, and now seemed like a good time to catch up on my sleep.

"Gilly, sit," Matt told me. Obediently, I sat up. "Good boy."

I sat facing him, my head almost in his lap. I was glad to oblige, but this position was far from comfortable. A minute or so later my head was resting on the seat between his legs. He patted me affectionately. This was a little better but still not quite right. After a few more minutes, I slipped my head off the seat and collapsed in a heap on the floor.

Ah! This was the position I was looking for. I knew that it would be hard for me to practice sitting up while lying down. Still, I couldn't bring myself to break from my comfortable position. Apparently, Matt couldn't be bothered either because he let me be.

Good boy.

The next minute we heard a voice. "Matt." It was Alice. "Can you have Gilcrest sit up for a little longer?"

I looked up, guiltily. I had gotten him in trouble.

"Oh, okay," he said, embarrassed. He told me to sit up.

I pretended not to hear him. It was nothing personal; I just found sitting up so tiresome. Tiresome and pointless, especially when there was so much floor space going to waste.

"Tell him to sit up, and pat your leg for emphasis," Alice said.

He did, and I sat up.

"Good boy, Gilcrest," she enthused.

I graciously received her praise then lay back down again.

"Gilly, sit!" Matt slapped his knee as if it were on fire. This time I didn't budge. I wasn't falling for that one again.

Matt stopped to listen. I think he was straining to hear whether any of the teams around us were having the conflict of interest we were struggling with. From the floor, I noticed that the guide dogs across the aisle were sitting up attentively. Matt was probably wondering how he had been so lucky as to be partnered with the laziest dog in the class. I wasn't being lazy, of course. I was simply practicing an economy of effort. But, at that moment he wasn't seeing the big picture. He wanted me to take him seriously and sit up. I wasn't trying to be disrespectful. All I wanted was to take a little nap.

Alice sat down in the seat next to me and had me sit up. At the first sign of a slouch, she told me to sit, taking my collar and pulling me up to reinforce the command. Matt kept his knees on either side of me to lock me into position as best he could. But I saw no reason to imagine the unhappy predicament of a crowded bus with nowhere to lie down. Our bus wasn't crowded. In fact, there was plenty of room to spread out. Why deny myself the luxuries at hand? Humans could be so stubborn.

After a few more slouches and a few more "sit" commands, we finally reached a compromise in which I leaned against Matt's leg for support, my head resting on his thigh.

"Okay, Matt," Alice said at last. "I think he gets the point. We can let him lie down now." She left her seat next to him and returned to the front of the bus.

I smelled Matt's aggravation at the sudden change of tactics. The goal of getting me to sit up had been declared accomplished with us still only halfway to our destination. Not only couldn't he get me to sit up, but, he had had no say in the sudden reversal in my favor.

I flopped exhaustedly onto the floor with a heavy sigh. It felt good to lie down. I didn't understand the sudden change in bus-riding protocol any more than Matt did, but I let it go. It was just one of many things that was out of my control.

When I lived with Erin, she'd given me a crate that she'd coax me into for naps or when she had to leave the house without me. At first I hated it. I'd whine every time she got me to go inside it. Gradually, though, I got used to the idea. It was a comfortable place, safe and warm. I could stand up and turn around, go to sleep, or chew on my bone whenever I wanted. I was completely free within its limits. I gradually learned that there was a lot I couldn't change about the world. The size of my crate and when I had to go inside it were up to Erin. But, within certain parameters, I was free. Free to lick myself, free to dream.

As I lay on the floor, I watched Matt through one half-opened eye. He was still visibly upset, stewing in his anger over the sitting thing. I guess he probably wasn't crate trained.

Chapter 5

Business and Pleasure

My working relationship with Matt was rocky at best. But off-duty? It turned out that Matt, at heart, was a dog-lover. I had learned that, as a kid, he had played constantly with his grandmother's cocker spaniel. When he got older, his brother's white boxer practically became his niece.

Then, one day, I discovered that playtime offered me the best means of communicating with my new human. I had been having one of my usual dreams, of racing around with Helmholtz, both of us chasing an old tennis ball. Matt was sitting on the bed, playing a few melancholy chords, when I was struck with an idea. I went to the corner of our bedroom where I had left my Kong—a hollow, rubber, snowman-shaped toy which Matt would sometimes fill with several pieces of kibble for me to try to free. I picked up the Kong, and abandoning my usual subdued manner, I pranced over to Matt and dropped it on his lap. Then I opened my mouth in a playful snarl and threw my paws down on the ground. Matt looked up, startled for a second, but then he began laughing. Soon he was on the floor with me, having some much-needed fun.

Every student's room at the school had a door leading out onto a fenced-in patio. My human soon learned the best way to release tension was to grab some toys and hit the patio with me to let loose. Our favorite game was tug-of-war, which we played with a large plastic ring. I would throw my entire body into the game, jerking Matt forward, sometimes almost knocking him off balance. He was still hesitant and didn't let himself get thrown around too much. If he only used one hand, I was often able to wrest the ring away from him. Then, just to tease him a little, I would march a proud victory lap around the enclosure, the ring in my mouth, my tail in the air. Finally, I would bring the ring back to him so he could have another go. Even in the most frenzied moment of play, I was always careful to be gentle with him. And, if at any time he wanted to stop and said, "That's enough," I brought our game to an immediate halt and relinquished the ring. Matt marveled at this product of Erin's good upbringing.

Our off-duty interaction wasn't all fun and games for him, though. Along with play, Matt had to learn another important skill that every human companion must know. He had to pick up after me.

He practiced the technique he'd been taught on a long driveway in front of the school, euphemistically referred to as "the relieving area." When he took off my harness, I knew I was discharged of my guide dog responsibilities. With the magic words "do your business" I began to circle around him, curiously sniffing for signs of other guide dogs imprinted on the pavement. When the leash went slack, Matt would slide his hand unobtrusively down it to gently touch my back. If he felt me quivering under my soft fur, he knew I was leaving something behind.

During the first and second weeks, the instructors picked up after us with shovels. By the third, however, the students were expected to handle the business themselves. Matt learned to slip a plastic bag around his hand to form a makeshift glove. Bending down to feel the pavement in ever-widening circles, he located the remains of my hard work. I observed the face he made as he picked up after me. The smell was clearly far from pleasant for him, and by the way he held the bag afterwards, I don't think he liked feeling the warm lumps inside through the plastic. He was relieved to drop it into a garbage can on our way back inside.

One evening, we were out on the school's driveway, Matt counting the minutes for the relieving time to end. I had done my duty that morning, so he wasn't expecting any more until the next day. Still, school policy dictated the students wait ten minutes with their dogs during each relieving session. To pass the time, Matt chatted with the student to his left. Debbie was twenty, the baby in the class, and newly married.

"I'm trying to decide if I should keep letting Guildenstern onto the bed with me at night," Matt said. "I mean, I like having him there, but he's such a hog! I always wake up in the middle of the night, cramped in one corner with him spread out and taking all the room."

"Aw, let him sleep with you." Debbie smiled. "It's a double bed."

Thanks! I appreciated hearing the feminine voice of reason weigh in on my behalf.

"Yeah," Matt went on, "but if it's cramped now, just imagine when I get back to college and have a single bed again. I don't want him to get used to it now and be disappointed later, ya know?"

She laughed. "Yeah, I'm going to be disappointed if I get back home and Jacob hasn't bought a bed yet."

"You guys don't have a bed?" Matt looked incredulous.

"We've been sleeping on a mattress on the floor since I moved in, and it's been like six months."

"Matt!" It was Alice, the instructor on duty. "Gilcrest did his business."

My human jolted into action. He got a bag and bent down, but since he hadn't caught me in the act and trailed down the leash, he had no idea where it was.

"It's more to your left," Alice called. He swept his hand left.

"More in front of you." He moved forward, still squatting, groping to find the spot.

"Now it's a little behind you. A little more . . . yeah, you got it."

Matt picked up my offering, a few small balls worth, and closed the bag around it. His face was red. I supposed he didn't relish playing Marco Polo with my poop.

He was putting the harness back on me to go inside when we heard Debbie question Alice. "Do we have to wipe the spot when they're done?"

Alice was some distance away. "What?" she asked, coming closer.

"Do we have to wipe the spot on the ground when they finish doing their business?"

Oh, Debbie, don't complicate things for yourself, I thought.

"No, no," Alice said with a chuckle in her voice. "I thought you were asking if you had to wipe the dog's butt when he finishes."

"Sometimes you'll have to." This was Cathy, the retrain, on the other side of Matt. "Tiger used to do his business near the woods in back of our house, and I think he was eating plants back there. Sometimes he couldn't digest them, and I would have to check his bottom to make sure there was nothing hanging out of it before he went inside."

"Yup," Alice said. "That's the reality of having a dog: cleaning up poop, vomit, and everything else."

"Well, it's worth it," Cathy said.

Matt didn't seem to find any of this information edifying. As we went back to our room, his commands were poorly timed and distracted. I guessed he was reliving the embarrassment of groping for my poop. That night he didn't let me up on the bed with him. He could be so temperamental.

Chapter 6

Things Get Intimate

The days passed. The practices I had with my human got worse rather than better. He was clumsy, inconsistent, and unrealistic. I began losing respect for him as a handler. He, too, seemed to be losing respect for me as a guide dog. I think he'd been under the impression that I'd be some kind of robot animal that would follow his every command like it were ones and zeros. But, despite all my training, I was very much flesh and fur. A fire hydrant or passing dog could distract me from the business at hand. It was up to Matt to discern by my pull that I wasn't leading him around an obstacle, but, rather, into one.

After our routes, Matt seethed in frustration as he relived our mistakes, wallowing in self-criticism. It was not a pretty smell. I chewed my bone to discharge pent up energy or went to sleep to escape into happy dreams of my life as a playful Labrador puppy. I would romp with Helmholtz or sniff around in our backyard, looking for something tasty to lick. Erin would talk to me and tell me how great I was. She gave me the nicest belly rubs. Often, I awoke with her familiar scent in my nostrils. Ah, I missed her.

Erin, are you still thinking about me?

One night I heard Matt on the phone talking to his mom. "I think this is the hardest thing I've ever had to do."

He was trying to keep his voice clear of emotion, but I wasn't fooled. I felt as much as I smelled his despair. His mom said some things to him that I couldn't make out.

"I know, Mom. I'll be fine. Don't worry."

I studied him on the phone, listening to his empty assurances.

"I'll call again in a few days. Okay, bye."

I watched him as he dejectedly hung up. I felt for him. He was as removed from the life he'd known as I was, only his training seemed to be going a lot rougher than mine had. I wished there was something I could do to help him. I thought about how I could try to read his muddled directional commands. I could try to respect him more, maybe even force myself to stop sniffing distractedly. In the end, of course, none of these things happened. I see now that as much as I wanted to, I couldn't just give him my respect by sheer force of will. He had to earn it by learning good handling skills. And sniffing was an instinct my species had developed over millennia. Stopping it in one small lifetime was impossible.

I did in that moment the one thing I was able to do. I offered him the support of my company. I went over and lay down at his feet, placing my head on his shoe. He was fiddling with his audio book player and didn't seem to notice. Then, after a moment, he reached down and, almost absent-mindedly, rubbed my furry head. His fingers massaged gently, and I felt a tingling sensation.

"You're a good boy. Even if you don't listen to me."

I sighed. *Go ahead, make me the bad guy.*

Matt stood up—his mood had shifted.

"Hey, Chuck!"

"Yeah?" I heard his response from the other room.

Matt walked through the door to his roommate's side of the suite and I followed behind. "You wanna have a drink with me?"

"Um ... whadaya mean?" Chuck sounded cautious.

"Whiskey! I brought some in my suitcase."

"Really? You know we're not allowed to have any alcohol on campus."

"Yeah, I know, but come on, man. We're here for four weeks. And what harm's a little drink gonna do? It's not like I'm going out on route tonight."

"Yeah, but, we'd get thrown out if they caught us. So, um, no thanks. I think I'll just watch you." It seemed that Chuck didn't possess Matt's daredevil spirit.

"All right, if you say so." Matt disappeared back into his room and returned with a flask and a coffee mug with the guide dog school logo imprinted on it. He poured a drink and then sipped with gusto.

Its odor was offensive. I wondered if he really enjoyed the taste or if it just felt daring to break the rules. Either way, he did seem to be relaxing, becoming chattier than I'd ever seen him. He asked Chuck about his family and talked about his own. We learned he had an older brother and sister. His parents had divorced when he was young, he said, and he barely had contact with his father.

"Do you have a girlfriend?" he asked Chuck.

"No. Do you?"

"No. But there's this girl I hooked up with at the end of last semester. She's really cute. I'm hoping when I go back to school we'll get together, you know?"

"Oh, cool. What's her name?"

"Amanda. She's super smart. She got a perfect on her SATs."

"Dang! That's crazy!"

"Yeah, and she *is* crazy, too. Maybe we're meant for each other." He laughed sarcastically, pouring himself another drink. "God, I can't believe we have two more weeks to go of this training. I don't know if I can take it!"

"Really? I don't think it's so bad," Chuck said.

"Well, no, I mean . . ." Matt blew out a breath of whiskey-scented air, and then tried to clarify. "On the one hand it's freaking incredible that a place like this even exists—a million dollar philanthropic organization that does nothing but train dogs to guide blind people around. And the food is great and the campus is really nice, and they don't charge us a dime for anything! But then on the other hand, you know, it's like the same routine every day, and we're always either in line or waiting for something to start. We're not allowed off-campus, not that I would know where the hell to go. But maybe if I had the chance, I could do something real-life with my dog, and it would matter more to me than getting my technique torn apart by the instructors, you know?"

Chuck laughed. "Yeah, I know what you mean. It is kind of frustrating sometimes."

Matt took another swig. "You know what the best part of having a guide dog will be for me?"

"No. What?"

"It'll be if I get my vision back I won't have to deal with the guide work crap, but I'll go on taking Gilly into restaurants and planes and stuff." He laughed, his scent revealing embarrassment at the confession. "You know, my doctor told me that after my eye heals from the ulcer, I'll be eligible for a corneal transplant. It could bring my vision back to what it was."

"Really? Wow!" Chuck paused for a second as if thinking of that scenario. Then he said, "So, how did you get the ulcer?"

"Well, it was from a virus I got in my eye. My doctor thinks it was from bathing in the river in Guatemala—I went there during January term. A couple days after getting back, I was sitting in my second semester Latin American Politics class. Suddenly the lights seemed really bright. Then it got really painful. By the end of the hour I could barely see well enough to get myself to Academic Services."

"And that was the last time you saw anything?"

"Yep. I spent the next couple months in and out of doctors' offices in Pittsburgh and Cleveland, treating that stupid ulcer." He shuddered and then snorted with amusement. "But the really good part was that the professor gave me an extension on my final paper."

"So you might have a corneal transplant and get your vision back? I guess you really wouldn't need Gilly to guide you after that."

"Well, hopefully not. But, for now I have to go along with it."

He finished his whiskey, and the two said goodnight.

I followed Matt back into his room and watched him get ready for bed. I didn't know quite what to make of this whiskey-induced revelation. If all went well for him, in a year I'd be out of a job. I didn't think I'd mind the subsequent drop off in my guide duties. It would give me more time to sleep and eat. But I didn't know if I liked the idea of posing as a guide dog just so I could go everywhere with him.

Maybe it'd be better for me to go back and live with Erin. She'd be happy to have me back, and I could play with Helmholtz as much as I wanted. That didn't seem like a bad arrangement. Matt could get himself a normal dog, and I could get myself some belly rubs.

That night I dreamt of Erin, of course. She rubbed my belly and told me how much she missed me. I looked up at her with my big, soulful eyes, and with one mournful gaze, I conveyed it all. This new human meant well, but he didn't listen to me the way she had. He didn't study my facial expressions or watch for my subtle tail movements the way she did. And to top it all off, he didn't seem to appreciate my guide work very much.

"Aw," cooed Erin, rubbing under my chin, and in this one word I was completely understood. Communication with her was so easy. I sneezed in contentment.

Chapter 7

Lighten Up!

By the middle of the third week, Matt and I were still struggling. "We're going to try something different," Joanne said as we stood outside the lounge getting ready to run a route. "I know that you've been having trouble connecting with Gilcrest during guide work, so I'm gonna bring this tug ring along. It can break up the routine." She showed Matt the hard plastic ring that we played with when I was off duty.

I wagged my tail happily. I was wearing my harness. So, I knew it wasn't playtime, but I just couldn't help getting excited at the sight of that ring. I could have fun, and it would give me another opportunity to groom Matt in his communication skills. Sometimes when we played, he actually listened.

Matt consented to Joanne with a shrug, and she told him to start the route.

"Gilly, forward." Matt gestured straight ahead.

I was still looking at the ring in Joanne's hand, hoping we could get in a quick tug session before starting.

"He's distracted, Matt. Be insistent with him."

"Gilly, forward!" Matt said again in a mixture of forcefulness and desperation. He gave a jerk on the leash to emphasize the point.

Reluctantly, I tore my eyes from the ring and began guiding him in the direction he'd gestured. We were off, down the block. We crossed one street, then another. At the next corner, Joanne directed us to turn right.

"Guildenstern, right." Matt stepped back as he issued this directive. His movements were still awkward, but I was getting better at reading his body language. I took him right, in the direction of the curb. He probed with his foot but didn't find it. I smelled him getting anxious.

"He's got you close to it, Matt. Tell him to hop up."

"Gilly, hop up!"

Obediently, I brought him closer. His anxiety was growing.

"Just a little more in front of you," Joanne said. "There ya go."

His foot had made contact with the curb, but his pulse continued to pound out a furious beat. He hated not knowing where things were.

"Praise him, Matt."

He did, but in a voice that was flat and insincere. There would be no rejoicing over this small victory. We crossed the street and continued down the next block. Suddenly, I halted.

"Gilly, hop up!" Obviously, Matt didn't understand why we'd stopped in the middle of a block.

Come on. Remember your training.

But Matt wasn't thinking about his training, he was thinking about getting to the next corner. He urged me forward again. I took one cautious baby step then stopped.

"Check in front of you before you tell him to hop up," came Joanne's voice from behind us.

Matt put out his foot. It came into contact with the telephone pole in front of him.

"See, he's looking out for you. I know it's not always easy to recognize that, but he's trying."

There was a softening in my human then. My stopping at the pole spoke louder than any of the other maneuvers I'd executed up to that point. It was a dramatic illustration of my usefulness. We just had to work together.

"Okay, how about some playtime now?" Joanne held up the ring.

So, Matt removed my harness, and I shook myself off, the tension of the route dissipating. Joanne handed Matt the ring, and I immediately grabbed it with my mouth and began pulling. *Lighten up, silly!* I told him with each tug. *Lighten up! It's not that bad!*

I observed with satisfaction as his serious expression melted into a small smile. He tugged back on the ring. By the time we had played our game for several minutes, his whole demeanor had transformed. Levity had taken the place of his anxiety, the stress of the recent past a fading memory.

"See that?" Joanne was triumphant. "You just gotta love a guide dog. He does the work you need him to do, and he's your best friend when it's over."

Well, maybe that was taking things a little far. I knew Matt wasn't ready to call me his best friend, and I had no ambitions on that particular title. I would happily settle for a relationship that was good, both on and off duty. Best friends, if we ever became such a thing, would be a long time coming.

Back in our bedroom later that day, Matt picked up his guitar and began playing. The chords were major, full and forceful. He strummed them with more vigor and enthusiasm than I'd ever heard from him. He was happy, I realized. Gone was his mopey self-reproach. His pounding music conveyed a new optimism. *I can do this,* his playing said. *I will do this.*

I chewed my bone, listening. I wasn't sure what had altered his mood, exactly. Maybe it was my stopping at the telephone pole. Maybe it was our game of tug afterward. Whatever it was, I was glad to see him this way. The skin of my muzzle curled against my teeth as I smiled broadly.

Good boy.

Chapter 8

They're Watching You

We still weren't best friends. But every day, I was growing closer to my human. After all, I was with him twenty-four hours a day. He was my kibble provider, my playmate, my caretaker, and my charge. I was understanding him better and appreciating him more.

One last hurdle remained before Saturday's graduation: a solo route. On all of the routes up to this point we had been accompanied by an instructor, so it was an anxious bunch of students who sat on the bus and listened to directions.

Joanne stood up. "Okay, everyone," she began. "This is the culmination of all your training. In this final exercise you'll be walking in an unfamiliar part of town. We want you to feel what it'll be like to navigate independently with your dogs."

The bus's engine was turned off; only silence filled the air as she paused for a breath. The students listened in rapt attention as she dictated the route's directions. I smelled the tension.

"Don't worry, guys. Instructors will be stationed along the way. If you get stuck, just stand still, and we'll come help you."

I knew this was of small comfort to Matt. He would experience a great deal of shame if he didn't run the route independently.

Matt turned to the student behind him. "Hey, Mike. Are you nervous?"

"Not really. But I think I forgot the directions already."

Matt breathed a sigh of relief. If he messed up, he might not be the only one.

One by one, students exited the bus. "Matt," Joanne finally called. "You're up."

After a deep breath, Matt grabbed my leash. We got off the bus, and he turned to face left. "Gilly, forward," he said, and we started down the block.

"Left off the bus, turn right," he repeated quietly to himself. I slowed to show him we were coming to the first corner. Then I stopped.

Matt put out his foot but didn't feel the curb. "Gilly, hop up!"

I didn't move. I was as close to the street as I could get.

"Damn it, Guildenstern. Do you have to do this to me now?" He stretched his foot out further. Still nothing.

I'd been trying to tell him what was happening, but he wasn't getting it.

"Gilly, hop up," he said again, trying to keep the frustration out of his voice.

I didn't budge. We were at the corner, but he didn't realize it. He wasn't understanding me, and there was nothing I could do but wait.

Matt stood there, frozen in uncertainty. He wanted to be sure we were at the first corner so that he could tell me to turn right. In desperation, he bent down and touched the sidewalk. His hand passed over the smooth line where the street began, and his face lit up. This is where the curb should have been! I had been right all along, and Matt had just discovered the proof.

He stood up and with a deep breath said, "Sorry, Gilly."

Taking a half step back, he commanded me right. I crossed in front of him, and we were on our way.

At the next intersection, Matt listened for cars. He heard one idling at the corner, but there was no other traffic. He commanded me forward. As I stepped off the curb, the car's engine revved, and it started towards us.

Whoa! This guy's gonna hit us! Before Matt had time to react, I stopped on a dime. I had been trained not to walk into the line of a moving car, even if commanded.

Matt and I stood frozen for several seconds. He seemed a little shocked, still not understanding what had just happened.

"Good job, guys." It was a voice from the car that had now stopped. "Go ahead."

I had been right again. I realized then that this was part of the course, that the instructors wanted the students to feel what it was like when the dogs overrode their commands. I was wondering how Matt felt about this when I was rewarded with a hearty "Good boy!"

We finished the last few blocks accompanied by Matt's sweet-smelling relief and made it back to the lounge successfully.

"Come on in and have a seat. There're just a few more students to go," Alice said.

I heard Matt exhale in relief. I don't think he'd ever been so glad to hear her voice.

When everyone had finished, Candice, the head trainer, gave the group debriefing.

"Okay, guys, good job. You all completed this successfully. Larry, excellent praise for your dog. Debbie, you looked like a natural. When you guys had problems, you persevered. I'm glad to see that even if you have to get down on the ground and feel the curb with your hands, you'll do what it takes to be successful. But," she paused, and looked directly at Matt, "I don't recommend this as a technique to be used frequently."

Well, at least the other students couldn't see Matt's red face.

For me, the whole thing had been kind of amusing. There had never been any real danger. An instructor had been near us the entire time. The only thing really on the line had been my human's pride. Still, I was pleased with him. He had completed the solo route with me as his guide. It was the first of countless trips we would take together. Maybe it hadn't been perfectly smooth, but he'd have plenty of chances to redeem himself in the years to come.

Chapter 9

Hi, Mom!

C lasses were finished. Looking back now, I see that the pendulum swing of Matt's expectations had begun to come back to center. He had started the training believing that I would be a graceful, intuitive guide who would whisk him around smoothly and with ease. Then he'd realized that our movement could be jerky, that sometimes I preferred to sniff posts instead of follow his instructions. It took him weeks to appreciate just how much skill and effort were required on his part to keep us on track. In his disillusionment, he'd fallen into doubt, questioning the value of my help and his ability to work with me. Now he was starting to accept us for what we were, striving to meet me at the place where my helpfulness stopped and his work began. He didn't always get there, but he was trying.

Graduation day arrived, and so did the puppy raisers. That morning we gathered in the dining room of the school, prepared to meet them. The buzz of conversation swirled around us as students, guide dogs, and surrogate parents were matched up by the instructors. Matt sat with several others and waited, fiddling nervously with my leash. I lay at his feet, out of harness and off-duty. The students had been told that it was better for the volunteers to meet the dogs without their harnesses so that they could interact with each other more freely.

In spite of the commotion surrounding us, I wasn't really excited or nervous. I was a little sleepy and a bit hungry. But then, I was always a bit hungry.

"Matt." It was Joanne. "I'd like you to meet Erin, your puppy raiser." He stood up, and Joanne quickly excused herself.

Here she was. Erin. I leaped joyfully into the air, once, twice, three times. It was all I could do to keep myself from making contact with her. But, I knew she wouldn't like that.

"Hi, Gilcrest," she said in that soft, familiar way. "Hi."

"Hi, Erin, great to meet you," Matt said, sticking out his hand. I could feel his discomfort. It was strange, I imagined, for him to realize just how much attachment I still had to my human mom. Then, after a pause, Matt said, "Here, why don't you take this?" and handed my leash over to her.

I nuzzled her legs, sneezing happily, my tail pumping like a jump rope in a children's game.

Mom! It's so good to see you!

"Yes, it's good to see you, too!" Erin said, as if she could read my mind. She bent down to pet me. After another minute or so, she gave my leash back to Matt and they sat down to talk.

I was calm again. The moment of excitement had passed.

"Gilcrest was one of my favorite dogs," Erin began.

"Aw." Matt gave me a pat on the head. "I remember hearing you've raised a lot of them."

"Twenty-one."

"Wow! How did you manage so many?"

"I just love doing it," she said simply. Then she added, "Thirteen of them have become guide dogs."

I listened to Erin's soft voice with pleasure. She had turned out so many dogs! None of the others had been considered for the stud program, I felt sure, but some of them were probably attractive, almost as good-looking as me.

Matt interrupted my reverie. "You must be really good at raising guide dog puppies by now. Have you been doing it for a long time?"

"Ten years. I started when I was sixteen."

"Really! I didn't know you could start so young."

"Well, a representative from Guide Dogs came to my high school looking for volunteers, and I signed up. I've loved being a puppy raiser ever since." She reached down and stroked my back. "I'm hoping to get hired as a trainer."

"Cool," Matt said. "Will that be tough to do?"

"Very." She sighed. "You have to have some veterinary training, and there are always lots of applicants."

"Well, if Guildenstern is any indication, you should be a shoo-in."

"Thanks. Uh, what did you call him?"

Matt laughed. "Sorry. I've been calling him Guildenstern. It's a character from *Hamlet*." There was a moment of silence. "I had to study it freshman year."

"Oh," Erin said, but she made no further comment about my new name.

The two talked some more. Matt shared where he was from and what he was studying at college, and Erin talked about some of the other puppies she had raised. I lay on the floor, using her foot as a pillow. It was so good to smell her again. Her scent brought back memories of potty training, trips to the mall, and kibble—lots and lots of kibble. I drooled a little on her shoe.

The conversation ended with Matt and Erin exchanging e-mail addresses and agreeing to talk again after the ceremony. Then she walked us back to our room.

The graduation was held in a large lecture hall and was attended by trainers, volunteers, donors to the school, students, family, and of course, guide dogs. Matt's family was back in Pittsburgh and I knew from listening in on phone conversations that, because of the distance, they were waiting to meet me when we flew home. Of the eleven students who started the program, ten were graduating. Betty Lou, a seventy-four-year-old woman, had been the eleventh student.

She had referred to her dog as "a noble beast" and told Matt she couldn't wait to show him to her grandchildren. Unfortunately, her macular degeneration had still been in a preliminary stage, and she hadn't resisted the temptation to use her sight to guide her dog rather than letting him do the leading. After three weeks of pushing and pulling with the harness handle, she had been asked gently to consider leaving the program. She could enter in another class down the line and try again.

The ten graduates sat together in front with their guide dogs sprawling beneath their chairs. Introductions were made, and then speeches began. I dozed on the floor of the chilly, air-conditioned hall. During intermittent periods of waking, I heard students offering heartfelt poems and expressing outpourings of emotion—thanks to their puppy raisers. I wondered briefly what my human would do. He wasn't the type to emote or recite poetry. Suddenly, there was a tug on my leash, and Matt and I were led up on stage.

"Hello, everyone," he began.

His voice sounded strange projected over the sound system. His heart was pounding, and his smell was of clammy nervousness even though he was trying to appear confident. He took a deep breath and plunged on.

"Uh, this is a really intense moment for me. A lot of things were going through my head as I listened to my fellow graduates speak just now. I was thinking about how lucky we are to be the recipients of such hard work and generosity on the part of the puppy raisers. I was thinking about what a great job the trainers and instructors have done during this whole time. And, I was thinking about going back to my room to get a coat because it's so incredibly cold in here."

There was an awkward silence as he paused.

I was shocked. *What was he thinking?*

This wasn't a time to be glib. People had poured out their hearts on this stage, and now he was trying to make a joke out of it. Of course, looking back, it made perfect sense. A dumb joke was just the thing for him to distinguish himself without showing any real emotion.

Then, miraculously, the sound of laughter came from someone in the front row. Some more people joined in, and the laughter gradually spread through the room. It was a beautiful sound, a sound of people who were kind enough to entertain a student's dubious attempt at humor.

It's not even that cold in here, I thought. But then I noticed Matt's bare arms covered in goosebumps and decided that my fur coat was coming in handy.

When Matt finished giving his thanks, we were guided back to his seat by an instructor. Soon, the last student went up to receive her diploma, and it was the puppy raisers' turn. One by one, each volunteer that had come to the graduation took the stage and shared what it was like to see the fruits of his labor enjoyed by a worthy student. Before we knew it, I heard Mom's voice over the microphone. She described meeting Matt for the first time that morning and said that she thought he was an excellent partner for me. She added that I was one of her favorite dogs.

"But Matt didn't tell you," she went on, "that Gilcrest has another name." Matt's face broke out into a big, silly smile. "His other name is Sweet Darling."

A collective "aw" arose from the audience. Matt sat back in his seat, the smile gone from his face. I guessed he wasn't a fan of that name either.

At last, the ceremony came to an end. Erin appeared and walked with us back to our room. As we made our way through the crowd, I was heeling at Matt's side when, suddenly, Firefly appeared. I stopped to get in some good-bye sniffing. Matt hesitated, probably reluctant to correct me in front of Erin. I imagine he didn't want to seem like a tyrant.

Mom felt us stalling and looked back. "He's being bad."

"Yeah," Matt agreed, giving me a quick jerk. I ignored him.

"Here, let me try," she said, taking the leash. She gave a massive yank, and I shot to her side in an instant. "Sometimes you have to be stern with him."

Matt was clearly impressed. I wasn't, but I sheepishly did my best to ignore the other dogs we passed. We reached Matt's room and stopped.

"Here ya go," Erin said, handing Matt back my leash.

"Thanks. Thanks for everything."

"Well . . ." Erin began.

Matt shifted his weight awkwardly, unsure of what to do.

I looked up at Mom with an "I'll miss you" look. I knew there was something else she wanted.

"Do you mind taking off his harness so I can say good-bye?"

"No, of course not." Matt bent down and quickly undid the buckles. I wriggled with the pleasure of freedom.

"Good-bye, Gilcrest," Mom said, with a tremor in her voice. "Take good care of Matt." She bent down and gave me a hug.

I love you, I thought, feeling her arms around me.

Matt was moved, I could tell. But, he didn't know what to do with his emotions. All he could manage was to stand there and hold the leash.

Mom let go of me and stood up. "Bye," she said.

"Bye," Matt echoed, standing in the doorway.

Her footsteps sounded through the hallway as she walked off. I sadly watched her getting farther and farther from me. Then she stopped and turned. "He's watching me go," she said from a distance.

It was true. I was giving her my best "I'll never forget you" gaze. Then she was gone.

I followed Matt into our room and watched him begin to pack his suitcase. We were leaving for Pittsburgh the next morning, and from there we would be off to college. I had a strong feeling that I might not see Erin again for a long, long time.

In this world of dogs and humans, comings and goings, hellos and good-byes, nothing is constant but constant change. The pangs of emotion that accompany each new shift are felt by people and dogs alike. We dogs trust instinctively that behind the twists of fate and fortune there's a greater purpose. What that purpose is, we don't attempt to articulate. We leave this to others.

As Matt came to grapple with understanding the bigger picture in his own terms, I would be there to help guide him. He, in turn, would give me something just as valuable to a dog as all the wisdom in the world is to a human. I'm referring, of course, to kibble.

Chapter 10

Home

I slept curled up at Matt's feet in the bulkhead of the airplane for the majority of the trip back to Pittsburgh. At his request, the flight attendants had moved his seat to the front so I'd have more space to stretch out on the floor. He knew from past experience my refusal to sit up on long trips.

I wasn't nervous. I'd been taken flying by one of the instructors as part of my training at guide dog school, so I knew what to expect. But it was Matt's first time in the air with a guide dog, and he observed the fuss I caused. Flight attendants cooed at me. Passing passengers gawked, and children pointed and exclaimed. The woman sitting next to us reverently asked my name and age while the man across the aisle spoke nostalgically about the Lab he used to have who never would've made the cut to be a guide dog.

Matt was pleased with all the attention. He answered all questions politely, and he even showed off to the man on the aisle by saying that, "Only half the dogs trained to be guide dogs are actually selected."

At the gate, a slender, blonde-haired woman greeted Matt with a quick peck on the cheek.

"Hi, Mom!" he said, cheerily. "Good to see you."

"Hi, honey. It's great to see you, too. And this must be Guildenstern," she said, looking down at me while offering her arm to her son. "He's a really good-looking dog. You said he was a Lab, right?"

"Yep."

Changing the subject, Matt's mom asked if he'd used the bright red ribbon she'd given him to make his suitcases stand out from the rest. He'd forgotten.

I followed along behind them as we clipped down the corridor toward baggage claim and was surprised by his mom. She hadn't cooed over me the way the flight attendants had. Then again, she hadn't cooed over her son, either. She didn't seem to be the cooing type.

She did take him out to lunch at Panera on the way home, though, and when he seemed unsure whether or not to get a dessert from the display of decadent treats, she insisted. While she described in detail the various yummy-looking choices, I looked at them longingly, drooling just a little. It was one of those rare moments I wished I were human.

"We need to fatten you up, boy."

At first I thought she was talking to me, and for a second I couldn't believe my luck. But, no, she was talking to Matt. I found out later that his family called him "boy" as a term of endearment. His brother had started it, taking it from their favorite TV show, *The Simpsons*.

"You look skinny. How was the food at guide dog school?"

"Really good, actually," Matt said between bites of an enormous oatmeal cookie. "I ate really well. I just never seem to put on weight."

"Just like Grandpop says. It's in the genes. Speaking of which, do you know there's a hole in your right pant leg? On the knee."

Matt winced. "Yeah, I know."

"Maybe we can get you some new jeans before you go back to school."

"That's okay, Mom. I have enough."

"How many pairs do you have without holes?"

"I don't know, Mom. Enough."

I smelled his rising defensiveness. I think his mom could smell it, too, because she let the matter drop.

They lived in a comfortable, two-story brick house at the end of a cul-de-sac in the suburbs. It had a well-kept front yard with bushes and flowers where I could do my business—a huge step up from the paved relieving circle back at school.

In those two weeks before going to Matt's college, we didn't run any routes together. When we left the house, it was always with his mom. I lay stretched across the back seat of the car, and Matt sat up front. We went out to eat and to huge stores where they bought last-minute supplies for the upcoming college year. I noticed they didn't buy any new jeans, though.

One trip we took stood out from all the rest. They called it "the appointment with Dr. Malhotra." To get there, we drove for about thirty minutes and parked inside a huge garage stinking of exhaust and filled with the sounds of echoing car engines. We made our way through elevators and corridors until we finally entered a reception area. A pungent scent of impatience lay heavy in the room. Humans of all kinds sat in the large living room-styled space, a TV on the wall blaring a program that nobody seemed to be watching.

After an incredibly boring wait, a woman in a lab coat entered and called Matt's name. The three of us followed her into a small examining room where Matt was led to a stiff-backed chair in the center.

"Have there been any changes in your vision since last time?" After Matt told the woman there hadn't, she asked him to take off his sunglasses.

"Can you count how many fingers I'm holding up?"

He couldn't.

She picked up a small flashlight and flicked it off and on. "Can you tell whether the light is on or off?"

"On," he said. Then, once the light had winked out, "Off."

"Okay. Dr. Malhotra will be in shortly." As she got up to leave, her gaze lingered on me sprawled by Matt's chair. "Your dog is so adorable."

I blinked in agreement. *Why don't you see if my taste buds are working by giving me some kibble?* But no such luck. She was out the door and down the hall in a flash of white.

"It's funny," Matt's mom said. "They always ask if there have been changes in your vision, and then they go ahead and measure it anyway."

"Yeah. Maybe they think I got my sight back and didn't notice."

About fifteen minutes later, a dark-haired woman entered the room. Her white lab coat contrasted with her olive skin complexion. I detected the smell of hand sanitizer.

"Hello, Matthew," she said in a soft, unaccented voice. "And who do we have here?" She smiled down at me.

"That's Guildenstern. He's my new guide dog."

I raised one eyebrow slightly upon hearing my name.

"Oh, he's just beautiful! And he's so well-behaved."

Obviousy, this doctor knows her stuff.

The formalities over, she began the examination. "How's your vision been since your last visit?"

"Pretty much the same," Matt said.

Dr. Malhotra then proceeded to flash a light, duplicating the steps just carried out. Matt again identified it as off or on. Next, the doctor gently pried Matt's right eye open with her thumb and forefinger, tilted back his head, and inserted a drop. I sensed a stab of pain shoot through him. He dabbed his eye with a tissue.

"I know how sensitive you are to light," she said, pivoting a machine to hang suspended in front of Matt's face, "but I need to get a look at how the ulcer is healing. I'll be as quick as I can."

Matt brought his chin to rest on the metal bar of the machine. Dr. Malhotra flicked a switch, and a bright light shone into Matt's eye. Again, there was the stabbing pain, this one sharper than the last. I saw Matt squeeze his lids shut immediately, tears streaming down his cheeks.

"My goodness," clucked the doctor. "Has his light sensitivity always been this pronounced?"

"It has," his mother said. She sat tensely in the corner, seeming to be as pained by the light as her son. "We used to put blankets over the windows after his eye surgeries."

"Photophobia," the doctor said. "It's often associated with congenital eye disease. His glaucoma has been since birth, right?"

"Yes. Well, he was born with cataracts and developed the glaucoma when he was a few months old. Actually, we found out that he has no hearing in his right ear when he was four, but his doctor thinks that was probably from birth, too. Anyway, he had about twenty surgeries in his first couple of years—you know, to try to control the pressure in his eyes. They couldn't save the vision in his left eye, but they did save some in his right one."

"Matt, it sounds like you've had your share of doctor and hospital visits. Okay, let's try this one more time. See if you can open your eye, please."

Since he couldn't, the doctor pried it open again.

Matt's body tensed, his hands gripping the sides of the machine. The pain was back, coursing through him. But, he didn't pull away. Instead, he continued pressing his chin against the machine's lower bar, tears gushing now.

He'd been through this routine many times, I could tell.

"Just a little more," Dr. Malhotra said, turning a knob. Finally, she withdrew her hand. Matt's eyelid snapped shut, and he sat back in exhaustion.

I let out a deep sigh of relief. I'd been experiencing this pain along with Matt, feeling it not as he did, but in my own empathetic way. It occurred to me this must be what his mother had gone through during each of those twenty surgeries.

The doctor pressed tissues into Matt's hand, and he wiped away the tears. "Well, it looks like the ulcer is healing very nicely."

Matt didn't respond. He rested his forehead in his hand, his elbow propped up on the arm of the chair.

"Last time you told us he would be eligible for a corneal transplant once his eye was healed enough." Matt's mom got to the heart of the visit.

"Oh, yes, absolutely. The ulcer did cause a lot of damage to his cornea. In fact, there's so much scar tissue there now that I can't really see to the back of his eye. But I think if we can get a new, clean cornea, it could help things a lot."

"And you think that would improve my vision?" Matt murmured without lifting his head.

"Well, as I said during the last visit, there's no way to be sure, but I think it has a really good chance."

"How much of my vision could it restore?"

"It's hard to say," Dr. Malhotra said slowly. "I really can't predict what will happen."

"Well, would it be possible for him to get back what he had before the ulcer?" his mom asked.

"Yes, that's possible."

I felt an excited charge pass through Matt at these words, though he didn't let on. Outwardly, his position in the chair remained the same. It wouldn't be for another year, the doctor explained. She wanted to give any lingering effects from the ulcer's trauma a chance to heal. Plus, she said, in a year he would be finished with college and would have time to dedicate to the surgery and recovery.

We rode home. Matt sat with his car seat reclined to a near horizontal position and used his hands to shield his eye from the August sun. His eye, it seemed, was still very light-sensitive.

"Do you want something to keep out the sun?" His mom looked over at him as she drove.

"No, I'm fine."

"Really? Are you sure?" She reached over to the glove compartment and withdrew a small hand towel. "Here, honey, just in case you change your mind." She put it on his lap. "What did you think about what Dr. Malhotra said?"

"About what?" If he knew what she was talking about, he was in no mood to let on. He reached down and took the towel, placing it over his face.

"About having a corneal transplant in a year or so. Do you think it's worth it?"

"Of course it's worth it. I don't know why we have to wait a whole freaking year, though. Seems like she's being way too cautious."

"You're right. A year is a long time. But, hopefully it'll be worth the wait."

I listened with rapt attention from the back seat. I was realizing just how important Matt's vision was to both of them. So important that for the chance of keeping it, they'd gone through twenty surgeries and who knew how many painful doctors' visits. So important that they were already pinning their hopes on a procedure that was a year away.

I rested my head on my paws. I could coast through a year's worth of guide work without too much trouble. The corneal transplant would be win-win. Matt would get his sight back, and I'd get an early retirement. If I got bored with just sleeping and eating, maybe I could become a therapy dog. I'd heard about other retired guides doing that. I liked the idea of going into hospitals and retirement homes and lifting peoples' spirits. Whoever went with me could tell my incredible story—how I selflessly served a human for a year. He miraculously got his vision back, so I courageously threw myself into another line of work. Yawning, I turned over on the back seat. All this thinking about the future made me tired and hungry.

Chapter 11

Back to School

We cruised slowly down the street, Matt's mom scanning the house numbers while her friend, John, drove. Matt and I rode in the back. I had sprawled luxuriously across two and a half of the three seats for most of the car ride, my head resting in Matt's lap. His shorts were still damp with my drool. Now, as heightened expectancy wafted from the other passengers, I sat up to look out the window. Students were flooding the college town of Oberlin, Ohio. The roads crawled with cars, and on close inspection, all seemed filled with stuff—suitcases, boxes, piles of clothing—not to mention the people. Many of the cars had assorted belongings tied on top. Obviously, these kids were not leaving home unprepared. I even saw one small truck with a refrigerator and microwave in the back. Now that was thinking ahead!

I'd gathered from his conversations with his mom and John that Matt was entering his final year here. The semester before he'd arranged with four friends to rent the top part of a house. I wondered what they'd be like.

"Two-oh-five," Matt's mom read. "What's the number again?"

"Two-two-five." Matt sighed. His boredom with the last two and a half hours of cramped confinement was beginning to show.

"There it is," John said, and we pulled into the driveway.

We had made it.

While his mom and John moved some of our things onto the porch, Matt gave me a chance to christen the front lawn. I took in the rich scents of my new home as I searched for a good spot to let loose. The air was fresh and laden with the pollens of late summer. There were at least three cats living nearby. I could also make out the faint fragrance of burning hemp leaves coming from a neighboring house.

Matt's mom came over to us. "So, Matthew, would you like me to walk with you anywhere on campus before we leave? Maybe we could help you learn the route from your house to the cafeteria." She stopped. "It's just a suggestion," she added, seeing the grimace on his face.

"No, that's okay."

"Well, how're you going to get around campus? Won't it be hard for you and Gilly to get used to things, at least in the beginning?"

"No, Mom, it'll be fine. I already have a good mental map of the college from before. Don't worry—I'll just ask for directions if I get lost."

Personally, I thought his mom was probably right. I remembered the difficulties we had at guide dog school when everything was new. But, Matt didn't seem to relish wandering around the campus with his mom or John.

"Okay. But how about you ask the college for a few sessions with a mobility instructor just until you—"

"Mom," he interrupted, "I won't need it."

I knew about mobility instructors. Apparently, Matt didn't want a licensed professional guiding him around campus any more than he wanted his mom to. He definitely had his pride. Matt's budding argument with his mother was interrupted by a lanky, blonde, long-haired male emerging from the front door of our new home.

"Hey, Rutiger!" The newcomer came down the steps toward us.

"Clay! How's it going?" Matt took a couple steps in his direction.

The spice of excited reunion was in the air. Matt and his old friend gave each other fierce hugs and then began talking in animated tones.

Several feet away, John turned to Matt's mom and asked, "What did Matt's friend call him?"

I looked at the two real adults with interest. I had been wondering the same thing.

"Rutiger. He decided to go by Rutiger when he got to college."

"But why? Does it mean something?"

"It's from *The Simpsons*." She rolled her eyes.

John laughed. "I should've known."

Matt finally remembered his manners and introduced his parents to his roommate, Clay.

Then, Clay turned to look at me. "You got your new pooch."

"Yep!" Matt said, sounding like a proud parent.

"Oh, well, hello dog!" Clay spoke in an exaggerated, high-pitched voice, bending down to pat me.

I wagged my tail, my whole body wriggling along with it. I could detect the tang of ginger-flavored beer on his breath.

"You're a real pooch! Yes, you are! Oh, yes you are!"

I liked this human. He had a funny voice and an eagerness to demonstrate his clear grasp of the obvious.

Clay turned to Matt. "What's his name?"

"Guildenstern."

"Guildenstern? Hmm ... Where have I heard that before?"

"You know. It's from *Hamlet*."

"Right, right! Rosencrantz and Guildenstern. Heh, that's a funny name for a dog."

I was thinking then that Rutiger and Clay were funny names, but I said nothing.

"We should let the guys take it from here," John said, closing the trunk and coming over to stand next to Matt's mom.

"Yeah," Matt agreed, a little too eagerly. "You two have done your part."

"Okay," his mom said. "I guess we'll be going." She gave him a hug and kissed his cheek. "Call me when you get settled in, will you please?"

"I will, Mom. Thanks."

Matt shook John's hand and thanked him for the help. The two students and I watched the car pull out of the driveway. Everyone but me waved good-bye.

I smelled Matt's relief. It was mixed with a kind of giddiness, similar to what I experienced when he took off my harness. Dog pups are usually weaned from their mothers in less than eight weeks, and they're ready to run with the pack not long after. I knew that human babies nursed for much longer and continued living under their parents' protection for years and years. Maybe the sheer magnitude of all this time explained why maturing humans were so sensitive to parental interaction and so eager to strike out on their own. Time would tell if my human was up for the challenge.

I was brought out of my reverie by Clay, who was bending down to pat me. "You're a dog! Yes, you are!"

Very good, I thought, looking up at him indulgently. *You're a human, and a very nice one.*

"He reminds me of my dog, Jedi, back in California. Except, Jedi's not nearly so well behaved. If he were here, he'd be running around the yard eating plants."

"Well, Gilly's been really well trained," Matt said, feigning modesty.

"One time Jedi ate so many plants that he took a shit in the yard while he was walking, and the shit just kept coming out of him and made one long shit-stripe." The two laughed hysterically.

"Shit-stripe!" Matt repeated. "That's great. Guildenstern would never do that, would you, boy?" He bent down to give me a pat.

I had already lain back down on the grass, my muzzle resting flat on the ground, my floppy Labrador jowls spread out on both sides of my lower jaw. I would much rather be eating plants than listening to these two clowns talk about it.

A few minutes later, leashed to the porch, I watched them moving Matt's things into the house. I knew with calm certainty that it was only a matter of time before one of these goofballs gave me a chance at exploring this place unleashed. Matt wasn't the only one eager to strike out on his own. I surveyed the yard, wondering which of the vegetation to sample first.

It might just lead to a shit-stripe, I mused.

Chapter 12

Hello, Good-Bye

The next day I lay curled up on the padded chair in our new bedroom. I had claimed it as mine when I found out I would not be sharing the single bed. The owner of the bed now sat plucking his guitar, producing music, unfocused and nervous. Riffs trailed off into nowhere, arpeggios stopped and started at random. But even without the music, I knew what was up. Matt had just talked to Amanda on the phone. She was coming over any minute.

Self-doubt continued to pour from the fretboard. What was he going to say to her? What would they do together? It had only been a hook up during commencement week. Would she still want to be with him? Had she met someone else during the summer?

The questions and the music were finally interrupted by a faint knock at the front door. Matt stood up fast, his heart pounding. He had my leash on me and we were down the steps from the bedroom in a few quick seconds.

"Hi, Rutiger," the girl said in a high, thin voice. She was petite, with short, dark hair and the sweetness of grass on her clothes.

"Hi, Amanda." His voice was strained in his attempt to hold it steady. He opened the screen door. "Do you wanna come in, or . . ." He stopped uncertainly.

"Let's sit out on your porch. It's such a nice day."

"Oh, sure." He opened the door, and we went out to meet her. He gave her an awkward hug, and they sat down on the steps. I sniffed around in the grass until I'd reached the end of my leash, then lay down to sunbathe. I had a feeling this wasn't going to be pretty, so I figured I may as well get comfortable.

"So, how was your summer?" she asked.

"Okay. I got Gilly here, so it wasn't a total loss. I talked to you from guide dog school, remember?"

"Right, I remember. You said it wasn't going so well."

"Yeah, but, I eventually whipped him into shape." He cleared his throat.

Amanda tittered. "He seems like a nice dog."

"Oh, he is. We'll have to take him for a walk together sometime."

"Yeah, sure."

Why not now? I thought, but neither one made a move.

"So where're you living this year? You never did say on the phone."

"Well, I was gonna live at Harkness, but I think I'll probably end up in Keep. A couple of people I was hanging out with this summer are living there, and I think it'll be good for me, you know, to have friends around."

"Oh yeah? Who's living at Keep?"

"Oh, you know." She paused. "Stacey's there, and Barry. You remember Barry, right? He did that diner exco last year."

"Right. I never did understand how someone could teach a class about diners."

Amanda laughed. "We basically just drank coffee and smoked the whole time and got credit for it. Oh, and now he's talking about taking us on a road trip to Austin to see his grandmother during fall break!"

"His grandmother?"

"Yeah, I really wanna meet her. I bet she's as crazy as he is!"

"I bet she is." The scent of jealousy coiled up.

"What's wrong?"

"Nothing. What do you mean?"

"You just seem pissed off all of a sudden."

"I'm not pissed off. I might be a little bummed, that's all. I thought you were gonna live in Harkness. That's where I'm eating lunch this year, and, you know, it's so much closer. Keep's on the other side of campus."

"Rutiger, it's not that big of a campus. Anyway, I'll come by and see you, don't worry. We can take your dog for a walk. What's his name again?"

"Guildenstern. You know, like in Rosencrantz and Guildenstern."

"Oh, yeah, right. Did you ever read the Tom Stoppard play *Rosencrantz and Guildenstern Are Dead?*"

"No."

"Oh, it's really good. It's like a spin off of the Shakespeare play. Really funny."

"I'll have to check it out."

"Hey, do you know what time it is? I told someone I'd meet them in front of the library at 4:20."

"I don't know. You guys gonna smoke pot?"

Amanda laughed. "Well, yeah, of course. Why else would we meet then?" Another even more bitter whiff reached my nostrils.

"Okay, then. You better get going. It was nice seeing you."

"Yeah, you too, Rutiger. I'll be back to visit soon. I swear."

And she was gone.

Matt got up slowly from the porch steps and tugged on my leash. I stood up and shook myself off. I could see that my walk wasn't going to happen. Most likely, I was in for some angst-filled guitar playing instead. I sighed and followed Matt up the porch steps. I wanted to tell him not to worry, that he had me, and with my animal magnetism he was going to meet any number of girls who would fall right in his lap. I could have conveyed this to him with tail wags and a wet nose on his face. But, at this point, he wouldn't have believed me.

Chapter 13

Counting Steps

Matt and I made our first solo foray onto campus. I had no idea where we were going, and Matt, it turned out, had only a vague one. The two of us made an extremely awkward team.

As we started off down the block, he began counting his steps in a low voice.

Smart boy, I thought. I wouldn't be able to find our house on the very first return trip. He'd be able to cue me on the way back.

Unfortunately, walking and counting at the same time didn't seem to be one of his strengths. I distinctly heard him say the number "sixty" twice. Then, I heard him curse. Finally, we reached the intersection.

"Two hundred and fourteen," he announced.

Give or take a few dozen.

After a few blocks, we found ourselves walking down a promenade, past storefronts and restaurants. This was the town of Oberlin at its most urban. Students were out in full force, making up for a long summer away from their friends. They congregated in clusters all over the sidewalk.

It was a stressful series of starts and stops for Matt. Each time I halted, he had to assess the situation and how best to negotiate the path. He had learned at guide dog school to probe with his hands and feet in order to identify the obstacle and the reason for the stop.

But, if the obstacle was a student, this meant he would end up unwittingly groping someone.

I've noticed how uncomfortable many humans are about making physical contact with strangers. It's funny to me. As a dog, when I'm able to make contact with strange dogs, it's about the best thing that can happen. I want to sniff them all over, especially in their most intimate places.

Matt didn't share this eagerness—quite the contrary. He reeked of embarrassment every time we came near other students. I could tell that if he would inadvertently bump into someone, he'd be mortified. So, I tried my best to steer clear of the groups. It wasn't easy, though, especially since a lot of people were staring at me, some girls making cooing sounds as we passed. Finally, the clusters of students fell behind us, and I came to a halt at a small side street.

"Hop up!" Matt urged me forward. I didn't budge. He hadn't probed to find the curb like he was supposed to.

"Gilly, hop up!" he repeated, growing impatient. I took one cautious step forward. Matt moved with me and stepped down into the small alleyway, just barely catching his balance after the surprise step.

"Oh, good boy!" Sheepishly, he motioned us across the narrow street.

I didn't bother saying I told you so. Nor did I demand an apology or withdraw in silent disapproval. Like other dogs, I knew instinctively that it was better to be gracious than to be right.

We crossed two more streets, and then began walking down the block. Matt slowed our pace.

"Gilly, left, left, left," he repeated as we walked. Immediately I turned left and led Matt to a series of steps leading up to a building. Matt felt the contour of the stairs with his foot.

"Nice try," he said, sighing. Then, he turned us back onto the main sidewalk. After a minute, he again began asking for a left turn. I kept walking, seeing no obvious turn. After about twenty paces of repeating "left, left, left," Matt stopped us, and we did an about face.

"Gilly, right, right, right," he said as we headed back in the opposite direction. I wasn't dumb. I knew what he wanted. I just couldn't find a turn for the life of me.

Finally, exasperated, Matt stopped us. I heeled alongside him as he angrily walked the length of the sidewalk, trailing his foot in the grass, feeling for the turn. Students passed us by. If they thought he looked funny walking with one foot in the grass and one foot on the sidewalk, they were right. They didn't say anything, though, and I didn't, either.

At last, he found it. It was a narrow passageway branching off diagonally left. Indignantly, he jerked me into position and got me going forward down the path.

"It was right there, dog," I heard him grumble to himself.

I saw that my demonstration of the "better to be gracious than right" principle just moments earlier had been lost on him. I considered sitting down to get his attention but then decided against it. I knew he was in no mood for canine wisdom.

I led him around the back of a gothic-style building. He slowed.

"Gilly, right inside, right inside." He was asking me to find the entrance, I knew, but in this unfamiliar territory, it was easier said than done. I kept walking. Then I noticed someone coming out of a door in the building. There was an "umf" as the door was pushed open. Matt cued in on the sound and urged me in its direction.

"Hey!" he called to the footsteps now drawing closer. "Excuse me!"

"Yeah?" It was a young, male student.

"This is the entrance to Peters, right?"

"Uh huh, it's right there." The young man pointed. "You need some help?" he asked, realizing his mistake.

"No, thanks, I'm just trying to get my dog to find it." Matt directed me towards the entrance.

"A little to the left," offered the student. Finally, I'd guided Matt to within inches of the door and he found the handle.

"Thanks," he said, turning to the guy still watching us.

"Sure," he replied. "Man, your dog is so amazing. I wish mine was that smart."

I recognized my human's bubbling rage just below the surface as he forced a smile and turned away. I guess he knew by now it was pointless to protest people's high opinions of me. In a popularity contest between the two of us, my Labrador charm would win out every time—and, rightfully so. Anyway, I was doing my job. Finding places the first time, even when Matt already knew, more or less, the layout of the route, was going to be tough. There was no way around it, and he knew that as well as I did.

I felt for him. I knew it wasn't easy. It was as much a battle with his fierce ego as it was a lesson in mobility. He was too quick to judge our mistakes and too ready to dismiss the difficulty of the challenges we faced. He was going about things the hard way, too. Getting lessons from a mobility instructor or asking for assistance from among the many passersby was not an option for him. Unfortunately, he was still hindered by the idea that he had to do things himself, to prove his worth, to establish his independence. He would learn the value of taking the easy road in time.

But, I mused, *how much time?*

Chapter 14

We All Need to Be Free

A manda didn't come back for a walk. I walked plenty with Matt as it was, so I didn't mind. Given the heavy thoughts of loss that pervaded his guitar playing in the following days, I knew Matt minded a lot. He didn't show his melancholy to any of his house-mates; he didn't talk about it on the phone with any of his family. He only let me see it in those most private of moments when he sat strumming away on his guitar, feeling abandoned and alone.

Nobody loves me, mourned the minor chords. *I guess I'm not good enough to have a girlfriend. I'll never be attractive to anyone. I'd better just get used to being on my own.*

Of course, he wasn't on his own. I was right there with him. All he had to do was tear himself away from his self-pity and give me a belly rub. Then we might both feel better. But, he didn't. His angst-filled music continued day after day. It was hard for both of us.

Finally, a bright spot appeared. I heard him on the phone, mak-ing plans with a friend for a whiskey-drinking, guitar-playing session on our front porch. His voice was enthusiastic and conveyed interest and anticipation. Maybe this experience would snap him out of it.

The expected knock finally sounded at the front door. "Mateo?"

"Hey, Collin, come on in!" Matt called.

I went to greet the new human who was now coming up the steps. He smelled faintly of beer and unwashed denim, and I wagged my tail in welcome.

"What's up, man?" Matt asked as he came out of our room.

"Not much, bro." Collin put a hand on his shoulder in greeting. "So, this must be your new pooch, huh? What's his name again?"

"Guildenstern."

"Hey, Guildenstern." Collin patted my side, and I sneezed happily. "I brought two friends along with me. They're out on the porch. I didn't think you'd mind if they joined us."

"Nah, man, the more the merrier. Come with me to the kitchen so we can get some glasses for the whiskey."

On the porch Collin introduced Matt and me to his friends, Amber and John. They both accepted drinks.

"Mateo and I were in Guatemala together," Collin said, sipping his drink. "We had like the most amazing month of our lives."

"What were you doing there?" Amber asked.

"It was a human rights delegation," Matt said. "We lived in a couple of resettled refugee communities with people who had been displaced by the Guatemalan Civil War."

"They were really tiny, rural villages," Collin added. "They didn't have electricity or anything."

"Wow," Amber said. "That's so cool."

"Yeah, man," John added.

Matt was encouraged by this reaction. "It's amazing when you think about how the vast majority of people in the world live like that. The way we live here is the exception."

The four students talked and drank, enjoying the cool, late summer night. I lay under the table and sniffed for something edible between the old wooden planks of the porch. Matt, I could tell, was intrigued by Amber, who sat to his left. He laughed at everything she said and agreed with her a lot, a lot more than with the other two. Then, prompted by Collin, he got his guitar and began a song.

"*I get high as I see you go by,*" he sang with whiskey-fueled enthusiasm. He finished playing, and the three clapped.

"Remember when you played 'Yesterday' in Spanish for the language school in Guatemala?" Collin snickered. "*Ayer,*" he intoned.

Matt laughed, embarrassed. He passed over the guitar to his friend, then sat back to listen.

Collin began to sing, softly. *"If you turn the porch light off and let the marble night withdraw . . ."*

"Does your dog ever get to run around?" Amber asked during a break in the singing.

"Well, the guide dog school says I'm supposed to keep him on a leash all the time, unless he's in a fenced-in area."

"Aw, that's too bad."

It certainly is, I thought.

"Yeah, but sometimes I break the rules a little." Matt reached down and unhitched my leash. "You're free, Gilly!"

I stood up and sneezed happily. The moment I had been waiting for had arrived, and all it had taken was a cute girl and some alcohol. I made a beeline for the steps. An enticing selection of plants was waiting for me in the yard.

"Uh, hey Collin, can you just make sure he doesn't wander off?" Matt asked quickly.

"I gotcha covered, Mateo."

Mateo sat back, relieved.

I went to town out in the yard. So many delicious smells! I was having my own party.

After a few more songs and more than a few more sips of whiskey, I heard Matt turn to Amber and ask, "So, how's my pooch doin'?"

"He seems pretty happy. He's just sniffing around in the yard."

"That's great! See, I think every rule has its exceptions. I mean, if we go around following everything everyone tells us, we'll make ourselves miserable."

The girl was giggling then. Matt must've thought she was giggling at him; he went on comically about "the slavery of convention."

"Your dog's peeing," she interrupted. Amber had been laughing at me, of course. I hadn't been trying to steal the limelight, but I guess there was no denying my appeal.

"Good boy, Guildenstern!" Matt called to me. Not to be outdone, he got up from his seat and found his way down the porch steps and into the grass. "Guildenstern is a role model for us all," he proclaimed, turning away from the porch in the direction of the empty yard next door. There was a zipping sound, and a second later a stream of urine cascaded into the grass.

"Oh, good grief!" Amber exclaimed. "He's peeing." The three laughed.

"Good boy, Mateo," Collin called out, and they laughed even harder.

"We all need to be free," Matt said, making his way back to the porch and his seat.

I sniffed the grass near where Matt had left his mark. The smell betrayed that he had gone overboard on the whiskey, but you didn't need a canine's nose to figure that out. Aside from wanting attention from the pretty young lady, he had obviously been suffering from a case of pee-envy.

In any case, he'd certainly attracted Amber's attention. The two flirted with each other the rest of the evening. And yet, when the time came to say good-bye, neither one made a move—no phone numbers were requested, no e-mail addresses were exchanged.

All that showmanship for nothing.

I was mystified as we went upstairs. I knew Matt was frustrated, and I knew he'd wanted more from Amber. So why hadn't he been more assertive? She'd seemed to find him funny, and she definitely thought I was cute. He'd had plenty of opportunity to make a move.

It was confidence, I realized. Or, lack of it. Underneath his playful exterior, I'd sensed his uneasiness. It was most likely a fear of rejection. Just where it came from—bad experiences he'd had with girls in the past or a negative self-image—I couldn't say. With my charm, I could attract lots of girls for him, but whether or not anything happened was out of my paws, so to speak. Either my human would work up the courage to make a move by himself, or a girl assertive enough to do it for him would have to come along. Until then, Matt was flying solo, and I was his one-engine Labrador.

Chapter 15

Rigors of Academia

We went to classes. Apparently, they were the reason we had moved to this small town in the middle of cornfields. And yet, for both of us, they were the far less memorable part of college. During those first few weeks, Matt spent more effort learning how to get to them than learning the subject matter once we arrived.

He developed an ad hoc approach for finding our destinations. First, he directed me to the appropriate building. Then, he would go to the floor of his classroom. Stairwells were generally easy to locate during peak times because of the number of students using them.

Once we made it to the floor, we would take up a conspicuous position in the middle of the hallway and look distressed. This wasn't hard for Matt to accomplish, anxious as he was about arriving on time. It was even easier for me. I adopted the most forlorn expression possible and fixed my soulful gaze on passing students. Sometimes, I pretended they carried kibble in their backpacks and that persuading them to stop and help us was the only chance I had at getting some.

Sooner or later someone would stop, and Matt would seize the opportunity to ask where room such-and-such was. He received a variety of reactions, ranging from "I think it's down that way" to "Would you like me to take you there?" He preferred the latter response; that was obvious. But, I noticed he resisted asking for help outright. I think it was the fear of inconveniencing someone—and that damnable pride.

Female students were best about offering help. Perhaps their feminine sensibilities made them more susceptible to my doggy-in-distress act. Of course, male students stopped, too. So did professors, visiting prospective students, and the occasional maintenance worker. It took a village to get my human to class.

Once we reached the room, Matt would walk cautiously forward until he found an open seat. Unfortunately, I hadn't been equipped with a "find the chair" command, so he had to do that himself.

When he finally sat down, I wasted no time flopping onto the floor, sometimes near his seat, sometimes sprawled in the middle of an aisle. It didn't matter to me where I lay since students were always careful about stepping around me.

As professors began lectures, I took advantage of the quiet time to catch up on my beauty rest. I had many interesting dreams. Sometimes I was gnawing on delicious, kibble-flavored bones. Sometimes, I was chasing my old buddy, Helmholtz, around Erin's yard. Sometimes, however, the dreams weren't so nice. In a particularly vivid nightmare during one political theory class, I was pursued by a massive cat with huge teeth and razor-sharp claws. I awoke with a start, a yelp still caught in my throat. We were in the front row, just a few feet from the professor who was looking at me, an amused expression on his face. The students, too, were all staring. Matt shifted in his seat nervously, his embarrassment strong in my nostrils.

Then, in that moment of awkward silence, the professor seized the chance to quip, "It seems Guildenstern shares d'Tocqueville's misgivings about a tyranny of the majority."

The room erupted in laughter.

I rolled over with a deep sigh. *Political theory was so boring.*

As we crossed the campus to and from classes, Matt and I struggled over the issue of how and when I would relieve myself. Ever since the first time I had done my business on the sidewalk, he'd been careful to give me a bathroom break before running a route.

But even this wasn't foolproof insurance against accidents while working. Regardless of my status as a guide, I was a dog, and marking territory was what I did. Besides, peeing in the same yard every day was boring. And I didn't always have to go when he gave me the chance.

During bathroom breaks, Matt acted like a mother trying to persuade her four-year-old to use the restroom before resuming a car trip.

"We're not stopping again until we get there," he would tell me, putting on my harness after an unproductive attempt. But, we both knew it was an empty threat.

One morning, we were rushing to his ten o'clock class when I stopped short and began to squat in the middle of the sidewalk. I didn't actually let loose. I'd learned during the past few weeks that if I stopped and squatted, Matt would take off my harness and guide me into the grass where I could proceed with my business. This time, however, he was having none of it.

"Why didn't you go in the yard when you had the chance?" he said, furiously.

I offered no explanation. Some things he just didn't understand. I took a few hesitating steps forward, then stopped and squatted again.

"Guildenstern, no! Hop up!"

Reluctantly, I resumed walking down the sidewalk. After about ten steps I stopped again. This time, there was no holding back. I relieved myself on the sidewalk as the bells in Finney Chapel began to toll. It was now ten o'clock, and we were officially late for class.

"Great! Right on time!"

I knew sarcasm when I heard it. Matt hated being late. Even so, he pulled a bag from his pocket and cleaned up after me. There was actually a large metal trashcan a few feet away, but he didn't know this, so he twisted the bag shut as tight as he could and stuffed it into his jacket pocket.

When we arrived at the lecture hall, class had started.

We entered the room at the front. "Gilly, forward," Matt whispered. Obviously, he didn't want to disturb the lecture that the professor was now conducting a few paces away. Rows of students sat at attention, looking down from their stadium seating.

"Gilly, find the steps."

All eyes were on us as I guided him across the front of the room, passing just a foot away from the podium. Matt, I could tell, was extremely uncomfortable in this performance of Johnny-come-lately. The professor had stopped his lecture. I think he was unsure of whether or not to help us. As we finally reached the steps, however, someone else did.

"Right here." It was Amy, the student who took notes for Matt during the class. She led us to the empty seat next to hers, I found a cozy spot near the two, and the professor resumed speaking.

After a minute, my nose began to twitch. I detected the pungent odor of something familiar, something that was usually outside. Uh oh. It was the poop in Matt's pocket. I looked up at him. By the way he was wrinkling his nose and shifting nervously, it seemed he could smell it.

I looked over at Amy typing away on her laptop. *Could she smell it, too?*

Finally, class ended. As the students began to trickle out of the lecture hall, Amy closed her laptop.

"Hi, Matt," she said, in her usual, forward way. "How's it going?"

"Hey, Amy. It's good. How are you?"

"Good. I've got tons of reading to do this week, though. This is the only class I'm caught up in. It's nice the college is paying me to take these notes for you. I just wish they'd pay me to take notes in my other classes." She smiled and Matt laughed. "I'll e-mail them to you this afternoon." She stood up and picked up her computer and textbook. "Do you want to walk out with me?"

Matt hesitated and I saw his dilemma. If he accepted the offer, she would almost certainly notice the stink from the bag in his pocket. On the other hand, if he said no it would seem standoffish.

Not that Amy would mind. She was the kind of girl who said what she thought and didn't mind other people doing the same.

"Hey, what's that smell, anyway? Did you step in dog crap or something?"

"Uh, that's pretty close." Matt explained what had happened.

"Eeew! I was smelling that during the lecture and wondering what the hell it was."

Matt tried not to betray his discomfort. "Yeah, you might not want to walk with me after all."

"Don't be silly." She offered him an arm. "We'll find a garbage can outside."

Matt tugged on the leash, and I got up, giving a big stretch. "He's acting like he has no idea what trouble he caused this morning."

"Well, he's doing a great job of it. Those puppy-dog eyes of his are pure innocence."

Amy found a trashcan outside the building, and Matt deposited the stinking bag. She pointed him in the direction of our house, and they said good-bye. I was glad it had been her sitting next to us during class. She was cool about things—like bags of stinky crap.

Matt was still mad at me, though, and gave me the silent treatment for the next few hours. Luckily, his anger cooled by dinnertime.

I was coming to appreciate that while his mood might change from hour to hour in any given day, his loyalty to me would remain strong. It was the way of a human, I supposed, to get upset about things that wouldn't faze a dog. I couldn't hold it against him.

Chapter 16

Matt Turns Up His Nose

We got in the habit of sitting next to Amy during politics classes and walking out with her afterwards. One day, she asked Matt how he was doing with his readings.

He was holding her arm as we walked down the hall toward the building's exit. "Oh, I'm kinda behind."

"You should come over to my house. I could read to you."

"You don't have to do that. I have them all scanned. I just haven't gotten around to listening to them on my computer yet."

"No, really. It would help me, too. I think if I read them aloud, I'll retain the material better."

"Yeah?" He seemed happy to be convinced.

"Yeah. And it'd be fun, too, you know, to have a study partner."

"You're right. It would."

That Thursday we made our way to Amy's house on north campus. They sat on the couch together while she read from one of their politics books. Matt listened attentively.

While they were both absorbed in this, I seized the chance to wander around in search of something edible. My reward was the half of a peanut butter sandwich I found in Amy's backpack in the bedroom.

Delicious.

We went over to Amy's semi-routinely during the next few weeks. She read to Matt while I sniffed for food. I liked these visits, almost always finding something tasty. Matt seemed to enjoy them, too. I could tell he was comfortable with Amy. He never smelled nervous or seemed on guard. They would chat after their reading sessions and got to know each other better.

One evening, Matt told her that he was studying Portuguese for his trip to Brazil during Oberlin's winter term.

"Wow, Brazil! I'd love to go there."

"Yeah, I know! I studied abroad for a semester in Argentina during sophomore year, and that's where I first got interested in Brazil. The two countries have this big rivalry going, but all the Argentines I met were like, 'Yeah, Brazil is incredible—you gotta go there!' My guitar teacher most of all. He was teaching me to play tangos and other traditional Argentinian stuff, and then he switched to Brazilian sambas and bossa novas. I just about fell in love when he played me that first bossa nova. The chord forms are so intricate, and the rhythm, God, it's like nothing else I've ever heard!"

"That's so cool. Maybe you'll get to learn more of it when you go in January."

"I hope so. But honestly, just being in that country, learning the language, experiencing the culture, that'll be the best part of all. I just love to travel. You get to see how different the world is in other places. And it forces you out of your comfort zone, you know? You leave all the boring old routines you had back home and just open up to whatever's coming. It's so freeing!"

"I know what you mean. I love being out of the country. I lived in China for two years when my dad was working there."

"Wow! Did you learn to speak any Chinese?"

"Yeah. Actually, I'm a double major in politics and Chinese."

"Oh, cool! I guess that explains why you're in a class on the Maoist revolution."

"Sure does." She paused for a moment. "I learned to make some authentic Chinese recipes. Want me to cook us something?"

"Really? Sure!"

Matt never turned down food, I'd noticed. He may have been human, but he wasn't dumb. I think he liked eating almost as much as I did. He was just more finicky about what it was.

A few nights later Matt and Amy ate a fragrant-smelling stir-fry dish while I lay under the table, salivating.

"Isn't it about time for Guildenstern's dinner?" Amy asked.

My ears perked up. *Matt, you need to marry this girl.*

"Yeah, it's getting close," he agreed around a mouthful of rice and vegetables.

"Want me to give him something? There's a little more stir-fry here."

"No, thanks. He only eats dog food. If I give him people food, it'll be harder for him to work when we go to restaurants and stuff."

I let out a deep, agonized sigh. He could be such a tool sometimes.

As they finished dinner, I saw Amy give Matt a quizzical look. "So you must get a lot of girls hitting on you because of Gilly."

Matt laughed. "I wish. Plenty of girls think Guildenstern's cute, but I can't say the same for me."

"I think you're cute."

Instead of seeming pleased, Matt suddenly looked embarrassed. "Well, thanks. I guess what I mean is, like, just because I have a guide dog doesn't mean I can get a girlfriend so easily."

"Why not? You're a nice, good-looking guy. And you're smart, and you have a cute dog. What's the problem?"

"I don't know!" His answer came out sounding plaintive. "I guess people just get caught up in games, you know? Like who likes who, and who will make the first move, and all that. It'd be so much easier if when someone liked someone else they could just say, 'I really like you, and I wanna try being with just you.'"

"Well, okay," Amy said, taking a deep breath. "Here goes. I really like you, and I wanna try being with just you."

Matt was silent then. I could smell his stunned surprise and confusion. He'd had no idea this was coming and seemed to have even less of an idea how to react.

Go for it! I thought. *You've been waiting for something like this since I met you. This girl can make a mean stir-fry, and she might even let me try some of it without you noticing. Tell her you're interested!*

"I, huh, I really don't know what to say."

"You don't have to say anything if you don't want to." Amy seemed nonchalant, though I sensed that underneath she was feeling more emotion than she let on.

"Well, okay. Let me just think about that one then."

Under the table, I let out a disgusted sigh.

"Sure. Do you want any more stir-fry?"

He didn't. They talked a little more, and soon we were on our way home. I didn't understand. A nice girl practically throws herself at him, and all he can do is "think about it." What was holding him back? They'd had great conversations. She was smart and down-to-earth. He seemed at ease around her—not the way he'd been around Amanda, nervous and awkward, desperately seeking her attention. Maybe that was it, I thought, as I stopped at the street corner before our house. Maybe he wanted to feel nervous and awkward around someone before he decided to be with them. This seemed totally senseless, but it was all I could come up with.

Back in our kitchen, Matt placed a bowl of kibble and water in front of me. With pleasure, I sunk my face into it. I was so grateful to be a dog then. I had to wait for Matt to get around to feeding me; it was true. But, at least when he finally did, I knew it would be satisfying. Matt had been waiting for a girl to get around to feeding him, but when one did, he still wasn't satisfied.

Go figure.

Chapter 17

A Very Cold Walk

Fall gave way to winter, and with it came snow—lots of snow. I liked finding the white, wet powder waiting for us in the morning when Matt took me out for relieving. I sniffed it curiously, sneezing and snorting with pleasure. Matt experimented by making small snowballs to see if I would eat them as low-calorie snacks. I think he reasoned that since I liked to chew ice cubes in the summer, I might enjoy snowballs in the winter. It was a nice try, but I wasn't into it. I was holding out for kibble. That was the good stuff.

One snowy evening we were leaving Matt's course on the Chilean coup. For some reason, the class was held in the science center. Matt, being a social sciences student, had very little familiarity with the natural sciences, and even less familiarity with the science building itself. This probably explained why we wound up going out the wrong door of the building and heading in the opposite direction of home.

About twenty paces out into the cold night, he stopped, realizing our mistake. He turned around, about to direct me back into the building, when he seemed to change his mind. He turned us back again and away from the building.

He must be deciding to take an easier way home, I thought.

We followed a sidewalk as it cut across a huge, snow-covered quad. Matt asked me for a right turn, but I saw no path branching off in that direction. Maybe it hadn't been plowed. Soon, the path we were on disappeared under snow and we were traipsing through unmarked territory. Matt's shoes crunched on the white powder underneath. The snow made it impossible for him or me to tell if we were on sidewalk or grass. I felt his whole body tense. We were totally and completely lost, and he was beginning to freak out.

He halted our progress abruptly. I heard his breathing in the quiet of the night. It was coming out in frosty, shallow puffs. He seemed to be listening for movement, for someone he could ask directions. But, no one was around.

"Gilly, find the path." His voice was shaking. It wasn't so much that he was afraid for his safety, I realized. We probably weren't going to die out here on north campus, after all. No, his voice was shaking with anger, anger at himself for directing us into this cold, snowy confusion, and anger that we were wandering around at the mercy of some passer-by to direct us towards home. Added to that was humiliation at the situation we were in.

I couldn't find any path, so I decided to take us to a building instead. Maybe Matt and I could go inside and warm up a little. And, he could calm down. I stopped at the doorway of the next building we came to. I thought it was a dorm, but I wasn't sure. Matt reached out and felt the door handle. There was no flash of recognition, no glimmer of gratitude. He wanted to go home, and this wasn't it.

"No, Gilly," he said in frustration. He turned us around and gestured for me to leave.

Just then a thin, female voice cut through the stillness. "Rutiger, hi!"

Matt stopped, listening.

"Rutiger, it's Amanda! How've you been?"

His shock turned to barely repressed anger. "Well, hi, Amanda. What a pleasant surprise."

"I've been wondering how you've been."

"Oh, really? You've been wondering how I've been? Well, let me tell you. I've been getting lost and wandering around this freaking campus, and my dog's been taking me to dorms where I haven't wanted to go, and you are the last person in the world I was hoping to run into right now because I'm dealing with enough other crap, and I hope that satisfies your curiosity about how I've been."

"Maybe we could talk sometime," she said in a wounded little-girl voice.

"Yeah, maybe so. But now is sure as hell not that time. I'm really upset as you can see, and I just want to get home. Now have a lovely evening."

We were off again. I don't think Matt had even the vaguest idea which direction we were going, and I don't think he cared. He just seemed to want to get away from Amanda.

It was too bad. He'd been so mad that he hadn't even asked her for directions before telling her off. I hadn't realized just how much resentment he'd been holding onto in relation to that girl. Now we were on our way to who knew where, our ticket home further and further behind us.

Would he ever learn to choose the easy way?

We eventually found our way back onto a main sidewalk that was cleared of snow. Matt managed to attract the attention of a passer-by who wasn't someone with whom he had an emotional bone to pick.

We finally made it home. It was warm and cozy again. Matt took off my harness and went to bed soon after. It was the best thing for him, I thought as I curled up in the cushioned chair. Tomorrow he'd feel better.

And, I was right. The next day he awoke refreshed and recovered. He never did call Amanda, however. I guess he preferred to leave that sharp stone unturned.

Chapter 18

Winter Break

A s we closed in on finals at the end of the semester, our routes around campus became more infrequent. Matt holed up in our room where he pecked away at his talking computer, slavishly pushing to finish the papers he had due. I sat in the cushioned chair and served as a very bored supervisor. I often groaned loudly to express exactly what I thought of all this extra academic work. I guessed he shared my opinion but felt responsible for finishing the semester he had started.

It proved to be no easy task. He was a slow writer and even slower researcher. Like his housemates, he didn't spread out his assignments into even intervals but raced to finish in long, laborious stretches leading up to the deadlines.

He showered less frequently to gain an extra fifteen minutes of writing time, and he stopped grooming me almost entirely. His efforts to vacuum the room earlier in the semester were now a distant memory, and the floor became carpeted with my fur.

One afternoon, Clay came in to give me a belly rub. I rolled over happily and basked in the massage. "Geez, Rutiger, I can hardly see your carpet underneath all the dog hair."

Matt sat at his computer, as usual, chipping away at one of his papers. "Yeah, I know. It's Guildenstern's fault. He's shedding all over the place."

"Why don't you vacuum?"

"I will, I will, just as soon as finals are over."

"Seriously, Rutiger, it's kinda disgusting how much hair is in here."

Matt finally stopped typing and turned around to face his friend. "Come on, man, you sound like my mom. I'm just trying to get these papers done, and then I'll have time for other stuff."

"Fine," Clay said. "But I'm not coming back in your room until you clean."

Matt seemed stung by this, but I saw he had no intention of caving in. For the rest of his finals time, I made a point of lying in the hallway so Clay could still give me belly rubs. There was no reason to deny us both this pleasure just because Matt was frantically struggling to climb out of the hole he'd dug.

Finally, it was all over. Matt handed in his papers, vacuumed our room, and gave me a thorough grooming. We headed back to Pittsburgh to spend the holiday with the family. I was as glad as Matt for the change of scenery.

For Christmas, I got a new plastic bone. My old one had been chewed into deformity. I also got a squirrel hut—a large, felt tree trunk full of stuffed squirrels that squeaked when I chomped them. I loved that gift! I had never been allowed to chew on stuffed animals before because of the danger of choking on the stuffing. But, the humans were all so charmed by the way I happily carried the squirrels around in my mouth that Matt let me play with them under close supervision. It was so satisfying to hear those little critters squeak.

Matt's Christmas gift didn't make any funny noises, but he was just as excited. It was a plane ticket to Brazil. He'd use it to fly to the city of Salvador and live with friends of his family for the month of January. His study of Portuguese would fulfill Oberlin's winter term requirement.

A whole month—a month without me! The Brazilian family had told Matt that guide dogs were very rare in Brazil and that it would be better to leave me at home. I couldn't believe it! A country without guide dogs? I wondered why Matt didn't just take me along anyway and let the Brazilians see what a good idea I was. Maybe he didn't realize that my Labrador appeal would win them over. Maybe he was afraid that I would get in the way. Whatever it was, I was getting left behind, and I was none too thrilled about it.

Before he left, Matt made arrangements to stop off in Florida and leave me with his aunt and uncle for the month. Even though I was glad to escape the cold winter weather, this seemed like a terrible idea. Without my expert guide work and animal magnetism, there was no telling what trouble my human would get into.

On the two-hour plane ride to Orlando I spent most of the time sleeping at Matt's feet. I dreamed that I put him in a huge crate and told him to wait for me while I went off to play with Helmholtz. He whined, but I wasn't having any of it. He was a person, I explained, and Helmholtz would have thought it strange if I brought him along. It was better for everyone if he stayed behind.

In the airport, I met Aunt Beth and Uncle Mike, who immediately made a big fuss over me. Matt's aunt gushed and his uncle told me how handsome I was. This was nice, but what really intrigued me was their smell. They had a dog, I could tell, another Labrador about my age. I snatched eager sniffs of their pant legs before Matt jerked on my leash to get my attention.

We arrived at the house, and I met him. He was a yellow lab, not quite as handsome as me, but still pretty good-looking. Cousin Ben, they called him. Ben and I became instant friends. We chased each other around the fenced-in yard, we peed over each other's scent, and we ran through the house together. It reminded me of the good old days with Helmholtz. When Matt left the next morning for Brazil, I was sad to see him go, but not all that sad. Ben got me playing chase with him, and soon I was having a great time.

While Matt spent the month learning how to turn his fluent Spanish into broken Portuguese, I spent my days eating a generous supply of dog treats and playing tug-on-the-rope with Ben. We even rode in the minivan to and from Aunt Beth's law office where we played chase in the enclosed yard. One time Uncle Mike fed me breakfast, went off to work, and a few minutes later Beth came downstairs and fed me breakfast again. It was heaven!

Matt eventually came back. I jumped up in the air the moment I caught sight of him coming through the front door of the house.

"Guildenstern! Hey, boy!" His face was flushed, and he looked happy. His hair was a little longer, and his sunglasses were ones I hadn't seen before, but it was Matt.

I leaped into the air again. Then I nudged him with my nose and sneezed happily. It was so good to see him!

That night at dinner he told his aunt and uncle all about his month in Brazil.

"It was awesome! I studied *capoiera*—it's this Brazilian martial art. I didn't know what I was doing but the capoiera master was so cool. He was like, '*Positividade*, my brother' and guided me through all these different positions. I learned a ton of Portuguese, too. I really wanna go back there. It's such an interesting country, and I feel like I haven't even scratched the surface."

"Oh, I'm sure you will." Aunt Beth smiled. "And when you do, you know Gilly is welcome to stay here for as long as he wants. We loved having two Labs around."

"Aw, thanks Beth, but I don't care what Brazilians think. Next time, Gilly's coming with me. It just wasn't the same without him."

My tail twitched as I lay listening on the dining room floor. I was glad that our time apart had helped Matt to realize the value of my company. Next time he left the country, I'd be with him, and that was that.

Still, I wasn't going to rule out taking Aunt Beth up on her offer of a vacation with Cousin Ben sometime. Guiding Matt could be stressful, and a little visit to Florida would be the perfect way to relieve some of my tension during the challenging times ahead.

Chapter 19

Infinity Forever

We returned to Oberlin in early February, and so began our last semester there. It was still the dead of winter. The sun that we had soaked up during our respective trips would have to hold us both until spring. We plodded back and forth to a new batch of classes. Learning the different routes wasn't easy, but it was much easier than it had been six months earlier. We still got lost from time to time, and Matt still got frustrated, but our first semester experiences made a big difference.

Matt was learning we wouldn't always find the building he wanted on the first try, and he became better at asking for help sooner, rather than later. I, in turn, became better at anticipating his commands and reading his particular body language. Instead of puzzling over his footwork, I could tell when he wanted to go left just by the way he turned his body. I knew that when we clipped down our home street on the way back from town, he wanted us to turn into our driveway. I would make the move without him asking me. This saved him the trouble of counting steps, and it never failed to earn me a hearty "Good boy!" as we headed toward our front door.

We were coming into our own as a team. As we did, the confidence my human derived from our successes encouraged him to push forward in another area of his life. Music.

He'd been playing guitar for as long as I'd known him, but never had I seen him collaborate with anyone. One afternoon in late February, that all changed. Matt's friend, Greg, came over for a visit.

In a flash of inspiration, Matt showed him a song he was working on, one I'd heard him practice more times than I cared to remember. Greg responded enthusiastically by taking the guitar and playing a song he had written while studying abroad in Germany. It had a unique, descending chord progression that led into a rocking chorus.

Matt was lit up with excitement. "We gotta start a band!"

And Greg agreed.

Wasting no time, Matt said, "So when's our first practice?"

"Uh, Rutiger, don't we need a drummer?"

"I don't know, we'll figure that out. If nothing else, Guildenstern can thump his tail in time with the music."

I lay on the floor by Matt's desk since Greg now occupied my cushioned chair. I didn't mind contributing to the music, but I did mind having to give up my comfortable seat.

"Two people and a dog isn't really a band," Greg said. "Is there anyone else you know who would want to be in on it?"

Matt thought for a minute. "Well, all my housemates are musical. Leif and Ivan both play guitar. Clay plays the diggeridoo, and Adam does throat singing in the shower. I'll ask around."

He did ask around. I witnessed several of these awkward conversations with his skeptical friends. The rejections began piling up.

"So, it would just be you and Greg and me? That's not really a band, Rutiger."

"I don't think so, Rutiger. Diggeridoo is more of a solo instrument."

"Um, no offense, Rutiger, but I think I'd rather play on my drum machine."

He didn't appreciate getting turned down, I knew. It was his pride again. But his enthusiasm for the idea overrode his dislike of rejection. Each time he talked about the band with Greg, he became excited, almost giddy.

His housemate Ivan, a soft-spoken, art history student, protested initially that he didn't play guitar well enough. Through sheer relentlessness, Matt finally convinced him otherwise.

And so the band was born. The absence of a drummer persisted, but Matt seemed completely unconcerned. The next week they had their first practice. The following few weeks were spent arguing over the band's name. It was a war of attrition that Greg finally won with the name *Infinity Forever*. Why he had come up with this wasn't clear to anyone, including Greg himself, but what was clear was the vision that had come to him while he'd been drinking.

"I saw this race car with an infinity sign on the hood," he told the others excitedly during practice. "We can make t-shirts with Infinity Forever in big letters and the race car underneath!" Although the t-shirts never got made, the name stuck.

After the next practice, Matt convinced the other two that the band was ready for a show at our house. They each invited a couple of friends who they thought were loyal enough to sit through the band's repertoire of three songs. The gig went down in Ivan's spacious attic room. The onlookers were indulgent, even laughing at some of the between-song banter. I had a great time, going from person to person, soliciting friendly pats and the occasional belly rub.

The show was such a success that a few weeks later they decided to have another. The difficulty, I saw, lay in expanding the list of people beyond those who had been to the first show. As Matt put it to Greg, he'd run out of people who could be counted on to come hear his three-piece band with no drummer. He would have to go outside of his small circle of close friends, and this, I knew, was going to be difficult for him.

For good or for bad, Matt was not very assertive. He still hadn't found a girlfriend after nine months with an incredibly attractive Labrador, and finding new people to come to his band's shows wouldn't be much easier. Still, I resolved to step up and help.

Chapter 20

The Goddess of Faith

One afternoon we were walking to campus with Ivan. He and Matt were discussing how gender roles varied from culture to culture with respect to romance. Matt said that in his experience in Latin America, the male was expected to play more of an aggressive role than in the United States.

"I think that goes for most Mediterranean countries," he added, "but that's just my impression. I've only ever been to Spain."

"I was in Italy for a summer," Ivan said. "I think men had a tendency to put women on a pedestal there more than they do here."

"Oh, right, like how they tell women how beautiful they are when passing them in the street."

"Yeah. The biggest compliment you can give a girl there is telling her she's a goddess."

"I guess that's all any woman really wants . . . " Matt's theory was interrupted by a shapely female with dark, curly hair. She had the fragrance of perfume and an air of intrigue.

"Hi, guys."

From his expression, I gathered Matt didn't recognize her.

"Hi, Faith," Ivan said.

As Matt heard her name, his face lit up. "Faith," he exclaimed. "You're a goddess!"

She giggled. "Hi, Matthew. How've you been?" The group stopped walking. "Your dog is really cute."

I batted my long, golden eyelashes at her in agreement. *Come on, human! Tell her she's even cuter.*

But, all Matt said was thanks. Obviously, he was still inexperienced in the concept of flirting.

"You know what?" she asked, undeterred.

"What?"

"I see you eating at Dascomb all the time. I always want to come over and say hi, but I never think you'll remember me."

"Faith! How could I forget you? We did a biology project together, and you're a goddess."

Atta boy! Now we're getting somewhere.

She giggled again. "Next time I see you at the cafeteria, I'll come over."

"Hey, please do."

No! I thought. *Get her number and invite her out to lunch!*

But, it was too late. They were saying good-bye.

Once we had moved out of earshot, Ivan speculated, "I think Faith was into more than just your dog."

"Yeah? I guess that 'goddess stuff' really works."

"Sure it does. Why else would Italians use it?"

A few days later while Matt was eating lunch in the cafeteria, Faith sat down next to him and started a conversation. While I licked some salty bits of french fry off the floor, the two reminisced about freshman year biology. Then, Faith talked about how much she loved animals and how I reminded her of her pet hamster, the fat one, who had devoured its companion and been found alone in the cage with a bloated stomach. I had put on some weight over the last few months, yes, but I found the comparison unflattering.

"That's a nice thing about dogs," Matt said. "They don't usually get eaten."

Under the table, I rolled my eyes. *These two are clearly meant for each other.*

As they finished eating, Matt invited her to Infinity Forever's next show. "Bring a friend. We could really use more audience."

Faith came, as it turned out, and she brought more than a friend.

By the time the ten o'clock start rolled around, three people had turned up for the group's second show: two mutual friends of the band from down the street and Greg's girlfriend. Ivan had been too embarrassed by the whole affair to invite his own girlfriend. The three decided to go ahead with things since at least as many people would watch the show as would be performing.

After five original songs, a few recycled jokes, and some disparaging comments from Ivan, the performance came to an end. The three band members and three audience members left the attic and went to the kitchen to mingle. I followed close behind, hoping for some post-show refreshments.

A few drinks later, people began to file out. It was at this moment that Faith showed up, accompanied by her friend, Jennifer. Matt welcomed them both. I think he was pleased that they had decided to come but perplexed that they had shown up so late.

"Sorry, guys," he said. "I'd ask the band to play an encore for you, but Ivan already left."

"Aw, I'm sorry we're late," Faith said. "I really wanted to hear you guys play."

The girls decided to stay for a drink anyway. Greg and his girlfriend soon left, leaving Matt and me alone in the kitchen with the newcomers. It turned out that Jennifer had studied abroad in Brazil. Matt told them he had spent the past January there, and the two swapped stories.

"I had sort of an awkward first impression," he told the girls. "In the airport, when I showed my passport to the customs official, he said some stuff to me in Portuguese that I didn't understand. But by the tone of his voice, it didn't sound good. Then I was taken out of the line and led somewhere to wait. Another guy looked at my passport and spoke some more Portuguese to me. Then someone took my hand and pressed my fingers into this soft material. So then I felt my fingers being pressed one at a time against a piece of paper. I didn't know what the hell to make of it all."

"They were fingerprinting you!" Jennifer seemed excited to figure this out.

"Exactly, but I only realized it later."

"So, did they arrest you?" Faith asked.

"No, after that they gave me back to the guy from the airlines, and he went with me to get my luggage."

"That's weird," Jennifer said. "They didn't take my fingerprints when I went there."

"Yeah. Turns out that after 9/11 the United States was making all foreigners coming into the country give their fingerprints. Brazil has a policy of reciprocity, so all Americans entering Brazil had to do the same thing."

"Crazy," Jennifer said.

"Why is the world so screwed up?" Faith asked.

The discussion turned to the reactionary politics of the United States after 9/11. Under the table, I sighed deeply. Unlike Matt and his Oberlin friends, I didn't care much for politics. Deciding how to carve up an imaginary pie of resources was for the humans. For me, it seemed like an exercise in futility. The only pie I cared about was the kind that might fall to the floor and be eaten in sweet mouthfuls of fruit and sugar. Now that was provocative.

The three talked and drank for a while longer. Finally, Jennifer said she needed to get going. Faith told her to go ahead and that they would catch up tomorrow. This left Faith with Matt in the kitchen. I was falling asleep on the floor, the prospect of food now a faded memory.

"Do you mind if I smoke some pot?"

"What? Oh no," Matt said. "You brought some with you?"

"Yeah. I have a little pipe. Wanna see?" She put the tiny glass pipe in his hand. "His name is Sammy."

"You name your pipe? That's a riot."

"Of course I named him. You named your dog."

I was nonplussed as I listened to their conversation. Just a few days before this girl had compared me to her cannibalistic hamster, and now she was comparing me to her drug paraphernalia. She obviously wasn't giving me much credit.

"Do you want some?" she asked after taking a drag. Matt accepted, asking her to light it for him. After a few attempts Faith got her lighter lit and in the bowl of the pipe. Matt breathed in then coughed as he exhaled.

"Are you okay?"

"Yeah," he said, in between coughs. "I just—I always cough when I smoke."

He got up and got a drink of water. Faith took another hit as Matt sat back down. An awkward silence fell between them. I wondered if they were both too high to think of anything to say. Maybe the pot hadn't been such a good idea.

Then, Faith broke the silence. "You have such elegant fingers. Can I feel them?"

"Sure." Matt extended his hand.

"It looks like you should be a painter or a pianist or something."

"Thanks."

I noticed that when she was done admiring his hand, she held onto it, wrapping it in both of her own.

Nice move. This girl obviously knows what she's doing.

"Let's go to your room," she said.

I blinked. *Damn.*

Matt readily agreed. It seemed he didn't need his arm twisted, and he led the way down the hall.

I followed close behind them, marveling at this unexpected turn of events. Faith was the most forward girl I'd ever seen. I was pretty sure I knew what was going to happen next. Faith may have wrongly compared me to her hamster and her hash-pipe, but she did know a thing or two about the direct approach. Well, good for them. I was glad that she was finally giving Matt some of the attention he'd been wanting for so long. I only hoped that they would stay off of the cushioned chair. It was past my bedtime, and I was getting ready to turn in for the night.

"You know, people can't believe I do some of the things I do." Faith sat on the bed next to Matt. "I think it's because I have such an innocent face."

"Oh, really? How does it look innocent?"

"I have dimples, and people say I have a sweet smile. Do you wanna feel?" At that moment I suspected Matt was more interested in feeling things other than Faith's dimples, but he went along with it. She guided his hand to her face. Her skin looked smooth, and her cheeks were round and full.

"Yeah. It's a very nice face."

"I told my friends that I have a crush on you. They don't really think I should."

"Whadaya mean?"

"Well, it's just, you know, I'm black." She paused a moment. "Did you know that?"

Matt laughed. "Of course I knew it, Faith."

"You did? How?"

"Well, first of all, when I met you freshman year I could see your skin color. I had a lot more vision then. But, second of all, I can tell by your voice."

"Are you saying I have a black voice?" she asked; then laughed at her own question.

"Well, a little bit, I think. I don't know, maybe I'm just biased 'cause I already knew."

"Nah, you're probably right. I never really thought about it. Well, my friends are all black. It's the same clique of like nine people that I've hung out with since freshman year. There's a lot of pressure for me to date other black people."

"Really? I thought a place like this wouldn't have that as much."

"Oh, it does. Believe me."

"Okay, I believe you. It's too bad, though."

"Well it doesn't matter because I think you're cute."

"Thanks." I caught a whiff of his embarrassment.

"Do you mind if I close the door?" She stood up.

"Uh, no."

Faith shut the door. Then, to my astonishment, she began taking off her clothes. Just taking them off right there in the middle of the room without a word of explanation. First her shirt, then her pants, then everything else. Matt, obviously, had no idea what was going on. He just sat there, waiting for her. Finally, she sat down on the bed next to him. Stark naked.

He reached out and touched her arm. I saw his expression turn to surprise as he felt her bare breast. Cautiously, he traced his hand down her body. "You're naked!"

"Yeah," she said, giggling. She kissed him on the mouth.

From my spot on the chair, I watched the two go through the motions that preceded human mating. It was the first time I had witnessed Matt engage in such activity. I was relieved to see him take careful precautions before they started.

As things got more animated on the bed, I lifted my head to watch more closely. They were moving around an awful lot and certainly seemed to be having a good time of it. I admit that I felt just a little left out. Matt hadn't played with me with that much enthusiasm in quite a while. Then Faith's naked behind came just inches from my nose, bouncing hypnotically as she moved. I stood up to get a little closer.

Faith let out a frightened gasp. "Your dog! He just sniffed my butt!"

Matt laughed. Reaching out, he found my head, now resting on the bed. I was asking politely for an invitation to join them.

"No, Guildenstern," he told me, pointing away from the bed.

I took the hint. If they didn't want me in their game that was fine with me. I circled, then lay down with a *humph*.

The two finished what they had started, and soon, they were asleep. Now that the commotion was over, I, too, quickly fell asleep. Matt, I imagined, would be in a good mood the next morning. Maybe he would be up for playing with me then.

Chapter 21

How About Putting Out?

The rest of the semester flew by. Matt's spirits were higher than I'd ever seen them. He thoroughly enjoyed his late night playtimes with Faith. They saw each other only in that context and for that implicit purpose, and he seemed satisfied with the arrangement. Gone was his notion of romance from last semester. Faith had led him to discover that a girl didn't have to make him sick to his stomach before he could enjoy playing games with her.

Faith, it turned out, had her reasons for wanting to keep their interactions purely recreational. During a rare moment of sincere discussion, Faith shared that she had no intention of getting married. She had watched her parents fight too often and live too unhappily, and the only way she would ever have kids, she said, was if she raised them herself. Matt seemed perplexed by this logic but didn't try too hard to talk her out of it.

When her visits stopped as suddenly as they'd started, he didn't show any sign of distress. There was no real break-up to speak of, just as there had been no real relationship. Faith just stopped showing up for slumber parties, and Matt didn't call to ask why. He continued to focus on his music and the band. That, I sensed, was where his real passions lay.

Infinity Forever continued to have practices and shows. Sometimes it was difficult to distinguish between the two since Greg's girlfriend sat in on practices and was sometimes the only one who came to shows. Nonetheless, Matt continued to revel in it all. He played guitar and sang with such enthusiasm that it seemed as if the three musicians were playing to sold-out amphitheaters rather than sparsely attended gatherings at our house.

Their creative output was nothing short of bizarre. They started out playing love songs. Then, when Ivan complained that the sixties were over and they should be able to write about other things, they experimented with songs designed to make people laugh. "I Bought Your Mom on E-Bay," "East College Rap," and "How About Putting Out" were the most dubiously distinguished titles. The songs were met with mixed success in their attempts at humor. Matt and Greg thought they were hilariousl. Ivan rolled his eyes a lot. Audience members were similarly divided.

But, Matt didn't care. Playing music with his friends seemed like the highlight of his young life. There was an incredible vitality and a blissful feeling of freedom coming through his guitar and voice that gave me a whole new view of him.

"Now this is what college is about! I'm finally getting to do what I love! I don't care who's watching or what they think; I'm gonna have fun with this!"

These messages were louder and clearer to me than any lyrics he sang. His enjoyment was infectious and aromatic. I loved listening to the band play just for the effect it had on my human. The songs, well, on that I discreetly chose not to comment.

The downside to starting a band in the last semester of college was that its days were numbered from the outset. Not that it would've lasted much longer, anyway. Ivan was increasingly dissatisfied with the performances. He opted out of the last show, which Matt and Greg played on the roof of the neighbor's house to a crowd of eight people gathered below. It was the most impressive turnout in the band's history.

And then, after the show, Matt and I received an unexpected visitor.

"Rutiger?" The cautious call came from the doorway to our bedroom.

I looked up and saw the familiar figure. I jumped off the chair where I'd been curled up and went over to greet her, wagging my tail. I couldn't believe she'd come.

"It's Amanda. Do you mind if I come in?"

"Amanda? Whoa, what a surprise!" Matt smiled. "Sure, come on in."

She crossed the room and sat down in the cushioned chair. They hadn't seen each other since that night we'd gotten lost in the snow all those months ago. On the surface she seemed the same. I even caught the scent of grass on her clothing just as I had at the end of last summer. But underneath that was a smell I hadn't noticed before, a pungent anxiousness, a whiff of desperation.

"So what can I do for you?" Matt was in his element. He had just played a show with his band and he projected confidence and ease.

"I've been wanting to talk to you for a long time," Amanda began. "I just ... I thought you were mad at me, so I didn't come looking for you."

"Really? I'm not mad at you."

"But that night when I ran into you in the snow ..."

"Yeah, I'm sorry about that, Amanda. I was really having a tough time, you know? I was lost and frustrated, and then seeing you brought up all this emotion. I guess I still ..." He faltered for a moment; then he continued. "I guess I still felt rejected by you."

"I know!" She moved from the chair and sat down next to him on the bed. "Rutiger, I'm so sorry! I don't know what I was thinking!" She sounded ready to cry.

"Hey, it's okay, really. I'm totally over it."

"I know!" she said again. "I'm just so mad that I missed the chance to be with you."

"Aw, don't say that. Maybe it wasn't meant to happen."

"No, it's 'cause I was chasing after Barry. Stacey and I were both interested in him. And you know what he did? He invited us both on a trip with him during fall break, and we both went! God! It was the most awkward thing ever!"

Matt flinched. She had touched a sore spot. It was an old wound, scabbed over now, but still sensitive. "Yeah, I had a feeling you had a thing for him. I just needed to keep my distance, I guess."

"Well, now when I see him, I just laugh. I can't believe I thought I was in love. He's just a big jerk who wants girls to fawn all over him."

"I see."

It was obvious to me that he was trying to hide his satisfaction with this remark.

"Yeah, but, what about us?" Amanda's tone was plaintive.

Matt laughed, a little too loudly, I thought.

"What about us? There's like two weeks left before graduation. I'm going back to Pennsylvania, and you've got another year to go, right? I don't see how anything—"

Amanda interrupted him. "Rutiger, why do you have to be so rational about it?"

"What? I'm just saying. It's not a lot of time. That's all."

Amanda leaned toward him just enough so that her head rested lightly against his shoulder. "I know, but what if we just enjoyed the time we have together for what it is."

"Uh, well, we could do that."

Her head on his shoulder, I noticed, seemed to have stopped any rational thought from getting in the way.

"But only if you want to." She lifted her head again to look at him, moving closer so that their arms touched.

"Well, sure. I guess we've got nothing to lose." He put his arm around her.

She leaned into him. "You know, I heard your band playing up on the roof."

"Yeah? What'd you think?"

"It was good. Just that one song made me a little uncomfortable."

"What song?"

"How About Putting Out?"

"Oh, come on! It's just a joke song."

"Yeah, but it seemed like you wrote it about me."

Matt laughed. "No, I wrote it just for fun."

"Well, that's good," she said. An awkward moment passed. "So whadaya wanna do now?"

"Uh, I don't know. It's up to you."

What he wanted to do was obvious to both Amanda and me. "How About Putting Out" may have been a joke song, but like many jokes it had been built around a kernel of truth.

Amanda turned her face up towards his, and they began kissing, slowly at first, then passionately. She responded to the unexpressed question that hung between them with an emphatic yes. I got up on my chair and turned my head away from the scene, preferring not to watch. I knew from experience this playtime wasn't going to include me, so I was better off ignoring it.

They were making up for lost time, it seemed, and for the rapidly approaching graduation which now threatened to end their blossoming love fest. I couldn't say if what they were doing was smart in human terms, but from my point of view, it seemed like a great way for Matt to end his senior year.

He was going to be a college graduate soon, and it was high time he learned to think less rationally. Human intellect could only go so far, after all. Besides, when he was happy, I was happy. And, I foresaw myself doing a lot less work during the next two weeks. Matt had a person to guide him now, however temporary.

Chapter 22

Graduation

Before we knew it, graduation was upon us. Matt spent his last night with Amanda. He told her she was special, that he wanted to continue seeing her, regardless of the distance. It had been a very irrational two weeks, and this dramatic declaration was the icing on the cake. They talked about visiting each other over the summer. Though they both spoke passionately, I think each of them held doubts.

The following day was the graduation ceremony. The college had a policy that made caps and gowns optional. This left many students opting out of the traditional attire for something more personally expressive. Some wore suits, some wore dresses, some wore camouflage, and some wore sparkles. Matt went with shorts and a t-shirt. His message was clear: I have no intention of dressing up for this event.

He did, however, dress me up for the occasion. I was less than thrilled. But, as Matt pointed out, I was the one who would be drawing the attention as we ascended the stage to receive his diploma. There were nearly three thousand students graduating, but I was the only dog making an appearance.

Matt's Aunt Beth had come through by making me a graduation cap, which she mailed to us. It fit perfectly. This surprised no one since she had tried it out on Cousin Ben first. It had a strap that tucked under my jowls to hold the square top securely on my head, and it gave me a decidedly accomplished appearance. I wasn't crazy about articles of human clothing, but I had to admit that I looked good.

The big event had been moved into to the gym at the last minute to avoid the threatening thunderstorms, and the cavernous space was less than ideal. It might have been great for basketball games, but sound bounced off the walls making it difficult to understand anything that was said. Matt fidgeted and squirmed in his seat, eager for the whole thing to end from the moment it started.

When his name was finally called, Ramona, from academic services, came and guided us up onto the stage. Matt accepted his diploma to some of the most enthusiastic cheering heard all morning. I knew that my presence had a lot to do with this, but I didn't let on that I'd noticed. There was no point in bragging.

At the end, a reporter from a local paper came to talk to Matt. He asked him what he had majored in, how it felt to graduate, and what he would do next. He then got Matt's permission to use a picture of us for his article. When the paper came out, it contained a close-up shot of me looking bored, my graduation cap askew. It was right on the front page. There was also a short blurb about Matt. His last name was spelled wrong, but my name was letter perfect. I could tell he was a little bitter.

"They just interviewed me because of Guildenstern," he told his mom, who bought copies of the paper to send to all the relatives.

This was true, of course, but so was the reverse. I was only interviewed because of Matt. We were a team. This last year had driven that point home for me in a very real way. I'd been relying on him now for so many breakfasts and dinners, for bathroom breaks and directions on where to take him, for playtimes and belly rubs. The idea of me succeeding without him was inconceivable. He wasn't my best friend as many people assumed. He was more like an extension of myself—a somewhat temperamental, less-adorable extension, but an extension nonetheless.

He had grown attached to me, too. A year spent relying on me for guidance, for cuddle sessions, and for attracting the attention of girls had made sure of that. If his ego still protested when outsiders overemphasized my importance in our teamwork, this didn't lessen the deep-seated feelings I knew he had developed for me. I was confident that these feelings would only grow stronger as time went on. How could they not? I was an amazing dog!

While the graduation ceremony at guide dog school had marked the end of an era in my life, the graduation ceremony at Oberlin marked an end in Matt's. He had struggled, learned, and thrived in the bubble of a private college. It had given him opportunities and freedoms he had desperately needed. And yet, I sensed in him a readiness to move on. Exactly what we were moving on to wasn't clear to me, however. I don't think it was clear to him, either. He had no job lined up, no definite plans on where we would go or what we would do.

Only one thing sat squarely on our post-college agenda: the corneal transplant. We had been to the eye doctor together during Christmas and spring breaks, and each visit had been a poignant reminder for Matt of the possibility of sight. It was his chance to rejoin a world of color and shape and gain greater freedom of movement. It was my chance at less work and longer naps.

As time passed, Matt's eagerness for sight grew. I could tell he was thinking about it more. At first, he hadn't discussed it at all, but now he talked about it more openly with friends and family. I think in his mind it became a golden opportunity, looming large and beautiful.

I began to realize that Matt had never really let go of this hope. He had made huge strides in adapting himself to his blindness, yes. He learned to walk with me around campus, use a talking computer to write papers, and rely more on his other senses. Still, he had done so in the context of overcoming a temporary difficulty. As I listened to his hopeful talk, I understood intuitively that he'd never given up on regaining his vision.

Perhaps he'd been reluctant to talk about this at first as it might have distracted him from the challenges at hand. Perhaps he'd been afraid of letting his expectations soar, only to be dashed in disappointment. Whatever the reason, Matt was now opening himself up to this long-held possibility of being able to see.

I was as eager as Matt. My early retirement wouldn't impede the flow of kibble. Nor, I'd decided, would it mean our separation. I had given up the idea of returning to live with Erin and Hemholtz as well as any ideas about another line of work. Matt and I were a team now, whatever the circumstances. He could continue to enjoy my companionship and I, his. Maybe he would put the harness on me and take me into restaurants and on plane trips for old times sake, the way he'd fantasized at guide dog school. That was all right with me.

Chapter 23

Into the Swing of Things

T hat summer I accompanied Matt to an interview. He wore a jacket and tie. I knew how much he disliked dressing up and figured that whatever it was that he hoped to be picked for, he wanted it pretty bad.

"So what sets you apart from the others applying for this scholarship?" The questioner, a woman smelling of Siamese cats, sat at a table across from Matt with five other adults, also dressed in their best clothes.

I lay under the table, listening for what had to be his obvious answer. *I set him apart! I'm the X factor that's sure to win him this thing. Cute, intelligent, charming, whatever the scholarship is, I'm perfect for it!*

"I'd say it's my experience living abroad." Matt went on then about his time spent studying in Argentina, Guatemala, and Mexico.

I sniffed. His answer was okay, I supposed.

In the end, to Matt's great excitement, he was awarded something called a Rotary Ambassadorial scholarship. We would spend a year studying in Brazil. But, that year didn't start for another eighteen months. So we returned to Pittsburgh to stay with Matt's mom.

She lived in a nice house in a nice neighborhood. It was a nice place to raise a family, but perhaps not the nicest place for a young man fresh out of college to spend his days. His corneal transplant had been scheduled at the University of Pittsburgh Medical Center for October 8, so a number of anxious weeks still separated him from this moment of truth.

Matt languished amid feelings of restlessness and impatience. He had no place to go and little to do with himself while he waited. His mom worked as a teacher during the day while he stayed home. Listening to recorded books, playing guitar, and browsing the Internet were all things he enjoyed, but they weren't keeping him sufficiently occupied. He began a part-time job with his aunt MJ's telecommunications company, which gave him a paycheck and something else to do. But he still wasn't happy.

It was tough. I knew that like any human, Matt needed something that stimulated his curiosity and utilized his talents, something that tapped into his passion and challenged him. Instead, he was sitting around waiting and obviously bored out of his mind.

I was just as bored as he was—maybe more so. While he sat typing at the computer or listening to a book, I lay listlessly drifting in and out of dreams. I became nostalgic for my brisk walks around the college campus and I missed the attention from my many admirers.

In addition to being bored, I was getting fat. Labradors neutered as I'd been have a strong tendency to put on weight, and without exercise, my once defined figure had become a mass of flab and bulges. Not only was I weighing more, but also, I was eating less. At a veterinarian's suggestion, Matt had decreased my kibble ration to try to slim me down. Though I hadn't gained any more weight, I hadn't lost any either. I felt sluggish and unattractive, and, worst of all, hungrier than ever.

As Matt stroked my soft fur and encountered the flabbiness beneath, I saw that it finally dawned on him that he needed to get us both out of the house. The problem was that even a simple route around the neighborhood was not possible for him at that moment.

Looking back, I understand the problem better now. He knew his neighborhood well enough by sight, but he hadn't learned to navigate it since becoming blind. If he'd tried to blaze us a trail through suburbia on his own, we would've gotten hopelessly lost.

I've learned that humans generally don't like to ask for help. They enjoy the feeling of accomplishment that comes from figuring things out on their own. Many believe on some level that depending on others for assistance shows weakness. Matt was no different. He had a fierce streak of personal pride. Being a member of the "stronger sex," living in a country that celebrated rugged individualism, and being of an age when most young adults begin to come into their own, well, they were all reinforcers of that aversion to assistance. And yet, somehow, he found the courage to ask his mother for help. Maybe it was the vivid memory of all the times we'd gotten lost at college. Maybe it was my simple canine presence that relied on him for food, affection, and bathroom breaks that helped to convince him that showing a little vulnerability was okay. Or, maybe it was just the beginning of an inner shift. Whatever the reason, Matt asked, and, of course, his mom was happy to oblige.

One evening in early September, Matt, his mom, and I began the process of reacclimating him to his neighborhood. First, we needed a route. Matt held his mom's arm as we walked together up the steep hill from the cul-de-sac where our house sat. I trotted along at his side. It felt good to breathe in the flavor of late summer. Several dogs lived in our neighborhood, and I hoped for a chance to mark some territory.

"Do you want to walk down into Laurel Gardens? You used to walk through it when you were in high school."

"I was thinking I'd walk around where I used to deliver papers," Matt said as we reached the top of the hill.

"Well ..." she paused, thinking. "Then you'd have to walk on Scharz Lane for a while, and it can get really busy with traffic off the highway."

We descended a small slope, passing the entrance to what looked like a park. "That's okay," Matt said. Obviously the prospect of traffic bothered him much less than it did his mother.

"I really think Laurel Gardens would be better. It has less traffic from the highway, and you can make a big circle."

Matt gritted his teeth. "Fine, Mom, whatever." We turned left towards Laurel Gardens.

"Let's just see what we find. If you don't like the route, we can try a different one."

Matt said nothing. We walked to the end of the next street.

"Here's where you'll turn left onto Scharz. You won't be on it for very long, but you'll have to listen carefully here because cars come pretty fast down this way."

I could tell by his bitter smell that Matt wasn't enjoying the instruction on traffic flow. We turned left on Scharz and walked to the next street.

"This is Jefferson. It's the street that you turn on to go to the high school."

"I know, Mom."

"So we'll follow Jefferson for a few blocks and then turn right to start making a circle. Does that make sense?"

"Not really," he answered, irritated. "How am I supposed to know where to turn right?"

"Let's see. Maybe we'll find a good landmark."

We walked on. We passed the turnoff leading to the high school. People were out on their porches enjoying the crisp early evening. Traces of neighborhood pets wafted to me on the breeze.

"Oh!" His mom stopped walking. "This is perfect! Here's a little park with a fountain. Can you hear it?" The sound of gushing water was clearly evident. "And look at this—a garbage can where you can throw Guildenstern's poop bags if you need to."

We turned into the small park and walked a few paces. "Put your hand out, and you'll feel the garbage can." Matt did. It was large and metallic. "And the best part is," his mom continued, "the park is right across the street from where you can make your right turn."

She sounded much more enthusiastic than Matt probably felt at that moment. I couldn't tell, however, because I was busily sniffing some weeds by the garbage can. A male spaniel had been there a few hours ago.

"Gilly, no!" Matt jerked on my leash much harder than usual. "Let's go," he said to his mom. I think if he'd had a leash on her neck, he would've jerked that one, too.

We crossed the street, and then followed the new street as it curved around to the right. Now we were heading back in the direction from which we'd come. After passing two more intersections we were back to Scharz Lane.

"Sorry if I'm repeating myself, but just be really careful on this street. I know it's harder to tell where the traffic is coming from because of your hearing."

Apparently, that was more than Matt could take. He exploded. "You know what? Maybe I shouldn't even go on Scharz at all. Maybe I should just stay home and do absolutely nothing all day, and then I'll be so much safer. That should make you happy!"

His mom looked stricken. "Honey, I'm sorry." Her voice quavered a little. "This isn't easy for me either."

We walked in silence for a minute. "That's why they have mobility teachers to help with this," she said, finally. "It's too emotionally charged for a mother and son."

"Yeah," Matt said. "Maybe I shouldn't have asked you in the first place. Better to have a specialist come in to tell me how to walk around my own friggin' neighborhood."

Thankfully, his mom didn't respond. The two were quiet the rest of the way home.

I trotted along beside Matt. It was easy to see they were both hurting. But I knew there wasn't much I could do. I was a dog, and what I gave them was the gift of my being. My thoughts turned to the poodle I'd smelled at the park, and I wondered if we'd run into him sometime.

It had ended badly, but the task had been accomplished. Matt now knew, more or less, a route that he could walk with me. The next step was managing to do it on our own, and this step proved to be as difficult as the previous one.

During the next couple of weeks we lost our way again and again. Matt got confused along various parts of the route, but one intersection proved particularly challenging. It was an oddly shaped, four-way intersection. Each time we crossed, we ended up somewhere different, but never where Matt intended. This threw him off completely. Try though he did, he rarely managed to pick up our route.

Each time, totally disoriented, he was forced to flip open his cell phone and dial his mom's number. We ran the route at night so that she would be home. And while she was always willing to come find us, he hated having to call her. Each time was like a defeat, and Matt would ride home in his mom's car in silence.

I often took the blame for these mistakes. I didn't mind. I knew it wasn't my fault, of course. It wasn't anyone's fault. It was just a thing we had to learn, and rarely are things learned correctly the first time. Though not always patient with himself or me, Matt was determined. We would manage to finish the route without having to phone home, or we would die trying. Well, that wasn't going to happen. I had many bowls of kibble yet to eat.

One unremarkable night in September, Matt and I completed the circle, and we found ourselves back on our own street. Sweet relief washed over him. We had finally done it. It wasn't a victory he could brag about to anyone—not to his mom, not even to himself. I don't think he even quite recognized it as a victory. What had he done but walk around his neighborhood, after all? Still, we had done it, and the perfume of accomplishment was there whether he chose to recognize it or not.

Carried by the tide of his good cheer, Matt steered us into the park at the top of our street. It was deserted and full of shadowy outlines in the night. But I could tell it was large, complete with baseball diamond and playground equipment. He removed my harness and let me sniff a while in the grass lining the parking lot. Besides the usual earthy smells, I caught the scent of a visiting German shepherd.

Matt put my harness back on and urged me forward, down the path leading to an imposing set of swings. His excitement grew as we approached. He must have recognized the gravel under his feet, for he walked slowly forward, hands outstretched. Then, his fingers made contact with the heavy chains of a hanging swing. He attached my leash to one next to it, sat down, and began to pump his legs. I lay down on the gravel and watched him take off.

Soon, he was flying. The breeze passed deliciously over me as he cut through the air. His joy was a sweetness that had been missing for a long time.

Matt swung back and forth, back and forth, exhilarated with his freedom. He leaned back into the motion, laughing. He was a child again. Now, maybe, it was okay to be living at home, to get lost in his own neighborhood, to have no idea of what lay ahead. I saw clearly that his only care, his only responsibility in that moment was this innocent pleasure. He swung, and swung, and swung.

Chapter 24

A Special Snack

Our walk around the neighborhood became a welcome escape from the daily routine at home. I got to stop at the park with the fountain and leave my mark on a territory thick with the scents of other dogs. Matt got to stop at the park with the swings and lose himself in the hypnotic movement.

Matt had one more, though less frequent, way to escape from his life in waiting. This was through his long-distance relationship with Amanda. True to their promises, the two had been keeping in touch through phone conversations and visits to Oberlin.

I liked the trips. I slept at Matt's feet on the rumbling Greyhound buses that wound us into and out of Ohio. Back on campus, I recognized familiar territory from which my smell had, distressingly, all but faded. These trips were happy interludes for Matt, too. He was always excited to see Amanda and particularly enjoyed their playtime together. He reconnected with old friends in coffee shops and at the town bar. It was as if he'd never graduated, except that we weren't going into class buildings anymore. Neither of us seemed to miss that. I found other places to take naps, sometimes at his friends' houses where we spent the nights.

Matt brought along lots of snacks in his backpack that held provocative, stimulating smells. One snack he always brought was a plastic bag of homemade cookies that he'd share with his friends. Inevitably, after munching on these treats, the humans would begin laughing hysterically while devouring bags of chips and salsa and dazedly watching movies or listening to music. I would observe them sadly, wishing that, just once, one of them would share some of the food with me. One little cookie couldn't hurt, could it?

Finally, during one of our Oberlin trips, I got my chance. Matt decided to go with some of his friends on a quick run for more beer. The only problem was that the cramped space in the driver's Volkswagen left no room for a Labrador, so, somewhat regretfully, Matt left me in the bedroom where we were staying.

At first, I was incensed. How could he choose a stupid car ride over me? Didn't my constant companionship mean anything to him? Then, as I began sniffing around the room, my nose caught a familiar scent. Sure enough, I quickly found the plastic bag of homemade cookies. Mmmm, intoxicating butter and sugar aromas with herbal overtones. I had planned to eat just one, but the taste of that first cookie left me no choice but to devour the entire bag. I didn't feel mad about Matt leaving me anymore and lay down for a nap.

I am a tiny speck in the middle of an ocean of fur. I make my way over ripples of flesh, then stop and find myself biting into the softness beneath me. The hot liquid that trickles out tastes wonderful! I bite again and drink my fill. Suddenly, the world around me shakes! Everything is turned upside down. I run to escape something huge and terrible. Whew, it's over! I'm safe now, but for how long? I find myself questioning the nature of my life—could there be something greater? I begin to contemplate the existence of Dog.

"Hey, Guildenstern!" It was a voice I knew, waking me from my dream. For a strange moment, I couldn't remember where or who I was. I opened my eyes and lifted my head, but things began spinning so fast that I quickly put it down again.

"Uh oh." This was a different voice. "He got into your backpack, Rutiger. Oh, and I think he ate your—" The voice broke out into a nervous laugh. Then, hands were stroking me.

"Guildenstern! Are you okay, boy? Oh, man, I can't believe I left my backpack right here! I'm so sorry, Gilly! Are you okay?"

His familiar presence snapped things into focus. It was Matt. I was Guildenstern.

Soon, I was standing, rather shakily, in the long grass of the front lawn. The cool night air was bringing some clarity to my scattered senses. I lifted a leg and peed. I was okay. Whatever was in those cookies would eventually wear off. For the rest of the night, however, I was even more low-key than usual.

Our visit to Oberlin in late September was little more than a week away from Matt's upcoming surgical procedure. We spent the last night of our trip in Amanda's dorm room. The two lay pressed together in her small bed. I knew it would be fruitless to even try to get in with them, so I made myself comfortable on a pile of laundry on the floor.

"Can you believe that when we see each other the next time, I might actually really see you?"

Matt's voice held something I couldn't quite place. Amazement, I thought. Awe.

"Yeah," Amanda said.

"You don't sound all that excited about it."

"I am excited for you. It's just, you know, a big change."

"Yeah! That's an understatement. I'll be able to see again! Why would that be anything but great?"

"I just wonder how it'll be for us, you know?"

"Well, you won't have to lead me around as much, that's for sure. I'll be able to see your face again, and any other part of you." His hand traced the curve of her body then, emphasizing his point.

"Yeah," she said, taking his hand and holding it in hers. "I mean, like what if things'll be different when you get your vision back." Then she added, "Forget it. It's stupid."

"No, go ahead."

"I'm just worried that if you have your vision again, you won't be interested in me anymore."

"Why would you think that? I already know what you look like from junior year. I thought you were cute then, so why would now be any different?"

"There'll be other cute girls, and you'll be able to do everything yourself. You might not, you know, need me as much."

"You think I need you now and that's why we're together?" He pulled his hand away.

"Hey, I told you it was stupid! You're the one who wanted me to say it!"

"Okay, okay. But, listen, it's not like that. And when I have my vision back things'll just be easier for us both. Trust me."

I stood up and turned around a few times on the mound of clothing, digging at it with my paws to find just the right spot. I lay down again, thinking.

It had never occurred to me to wonder if Matt would still want me around after he got his vision back. I'd considered going back to live with Erin, but Matt not wanting me? It seemed like a silly idea. No, like Matt, I was looking forward to him being able to see again. It was going to be easier for everyone. If Amanda didn't get that yet, I thought, she would understand soon enough.

Chapter 25

October 8

The day of Matt's corneal transplant finally arrived. It was to be done in a surgery center rather than a full-fledged hospital, and as Matt discussed this fact with his mom, it seemed to bring some relief to his obvious anxiety. There would be no overnight stay. I was almost as glad as Matt to be spared a night in the hospital. I had been in one a couple of times as a puppy, and the fumes of sickness, fear, and regimented procedures had been almost more than I could handle at that young age.

Matt's mom took the day off from work, and early Wednesday morning she drove us to Oakland, not far from downtown Pittsburgh, where the procedure would take place. I sat sprawled out in the back seat. The car was quiet, the pregnant possibility of the day hanging in the air.

After signing in at the desk, we sat down in the waiting room. It was crowded with people and reminded me of Dr. Malhotra's reception area. It smelled the same. The TV on the wall showed an episode of Judge Judy. She was chastizing someone about being irresponsible.

Matt's mom started leafing through a magazine she had found on a rack. "Matt, do you want me to read something from *Time* magazine?"

I was sure what Matt really wanted was to get this procedure over with and his vision back. Still, he accepted his mom's offer. I guessed he figured anything was better than Judge Judy. His mom read from the table of contents, and he picked out an article on stem cell research. She flipped the pages and began reading in a quiet voice near his ear, his good one. At the end of a sentence about scientists growing organs in test tubes, she paused.

"It's amazing how technology just keeps getting better and better. Who knows? Maybe someday you'll be able to get a whole new eye."

"Yeah, who knows."

I don't think he cared much about the possibility of a perfect eye in a distant future. He'd be happy getting back the imperfect vision he had a year and a half ago.

"Matthew VanFossan," the receptionist called. Matt took his mom's arm and my leash, and we were off. In the examining room, Matt sat down in the patient's chair. The armrests looked hard and uncomfortable. The footrest was tucked under, and his feet barely touched the floor. I lay down beside him and shivered a little. Maybe it was the coolness of the tiles.

An assistant came in for a preliminary screening. "Oh, isn't he just darling!" she exclaimed, seeing me spread out on the floor. She stepped past me and sat down at the desk to begin the standard procedure.

To the obligatory, "What's the purpose of your visit?" Matt replied with a note of enthusiasm that he was there for a corneal transplant. It was strange to see him excited, looking forward to a surgical procedure. The assistant did the perfunctory vision check. Matt could see the change in light when she turned a flashlight on and off; but, as usual, when she asked him to count fingers, he was at a loss.

"Okay," she said, getting up from the desk. "The doctor will be in shortly."

Ten minutes later Dr. Malhotra entered the room. After smiling her greetings to the three of us, she got down to business. "We're putting in the alpha core today, Matthew. Now this is a very new technology, but I think in your case it offers less risk of rejection than a normal cornea."

She had explained this to him before. The alpha core was a piece of clear plastic that would replace his scarred and opaque cornea.

"The surgery should take about twenty minutes," she went on. "I'll cut a hole in your cornea, remove the damaged area, and place the alpha core in. Then I'll put a piece of plastic over your eye which I'll remove when your eye has healed and things are stable."

"How long will it take to heal?" This was the first it had occurred to Matt to ask about the recovery process.

"About three months."

Matt's scent changed immediately then, betraying how stunned he felt. I think he'd been expecting three days, maybe three weeks. But three months?

"Will I be able to use my eye during the three months?" His voice was flat.

"You'll have to keep it bandaged. And you'll want to keep it closed as much as possible. It'll heal faster that way."

He tried to conceal the disappointment washing over him, but I wasn't fooled. He obviously hadn't imagined this was going to be such a lengthy, two-step program. I think that in his mind he had pictured himself walking out of the office after the transplant, a seeing man.

"So we'll have to wait three months to know if it works or not?" His mother was also having a hard time digesting the news.

"Yes, the plastic covering I'm putting in over the alpha core isn't transparent, so we won't know about his vision until after it comes out."

I empathized with my human. I knew a lot of his energy had been invested in waiting for this day. But, there was no turning back now.

Dr. Malhotra left the room to prep for surgery. An assistant came in soon after to take Matt to get ready. He wanted to take me with him; I could tell by the reluctant slowness with which he handed my leash over to his mom. Unfortunately, there were limits on where even I could go.

I anxiously watched him leave. I didn't see why I couldn't go too, so I could provide the comfort my presence offered. I would certainly behave myself. I might even fall asleep. And I was definitely clean enough. Matt had just given me a bath a few days before. People could be such germaphobes.

I followed Matt's mom into a separate waiting room where she distractedly flipped through another magazine, and I lay waiting on the floor. I knew Matt was okay. Still, I had a feeling he was going to experience some pain, and the sooner I had him back, the better. Usually, I didn't mind being away from him. I wasn't one of those dogs who whines and cries when separated from his human. After all, I had spent a whole month in Florida without him, and I'd been fine. But, this was different. I knew how vulnerable he was, so I wanted to be with him. Finally, I did what any good dog does when experiencing a moment of stress. I lay my head on the floor, closed my eyes, and went to sleep.

Things would be better when I awoke. Hopefully.

Chapter 26

The Strangest Dream

I had a dream then—the strangest dream.

I'm sitting in a chair. Never sat in one of those before. Arms pressing against hard armrests—are those really mine? Dr. Malhotra is there, her smooth, soothing voice in my ear. She lifts my head, splashes medicine in my eye. Then a needle pierces through my eyeball. It doesn't hurt, really, but seems profoundly disturbing.

The chair begins whirring; the backrest slowly reclines. Then I am flat. Stretched out. A cold, hard object enters my eye, pressing against my upper and lower lids. No more blinking. My eye is wedged open.

Suddenly, there's a bright light. It pierces through the shadows into my being. Pain shoots through me. Tears flood my eyes. The sudden piercing stab becomes a dull, constant throb. My eyeball rolls instinctively back but can't escape the invasion of light. There are hands, mine, I think, and they clench at my sides.

"I know you're light-sensitive," murmurs the doctor. "I'll try to be quick."

I've heard that before.

She's talking to her assistant, now—a confusion of medical jargon. There's a tugging at my eye. "I'm making an eight-millimeter incision." The doctor's voice isn't soothing anymore.

Suddenly a patch of the brightest light imaginable appears. It has a white, clear quality. My fists clench even harder as tears stream down my face.

"How are you doing, Matt?" Dr. Malhotra dabs at my face with a tissue.

A low "okay," finds its way through my tense throat, past my dry lips.

There's pressure again. The doctor says something about the alpha core. "We're almost done, Matt," she says after a few more terribly long minutes. "You're doing great."

Then a large object enters my eye. It's strange and foreign. Every impulse calls for its immediate removal, but it stays. Her fingers dance on my eyeball, pressing it firmly down. Finally, the metal wedge is removed. My eyelid closes at last.

"Okay," she says, sounding satisfied. "We're all done."

My clenched fists begin to relax. My head turns; my cheek rests against the cool, flat chair. Exhaustion mingles with relief. It's over.

I woke to his smell. Opening my eyes and catching sight of Matt in the waiting room, I stood up, my body wriggling with excitement. As he was led over to me, I pressed my nose against his hand in greeting. He smiled faintly and patted my head. Dr. Malhotra soon joined us in the waiting room.

"How did it go?" his mom asked, nervously.

"It went fine. Come back in a week so we can make sure everything's okay." She gave her some drops and instructions on how often to use them. Matt didn't seem to catch any of it. He was obviously too exhausted to pay attention.

"Was it very painful?" We walked through the parking garage to the car.

"Yeah. I'm just glad it's over."

"Oh, honey, you did a great job. It'll all be worth it if you can get some vision out of this."

We drove home in silence. I watched Matt resting the whole way, covering his eye to keep out the light. When we got home, he went to rest in the cool darkness of the windowless downstairs bedroom. I guessed he was too tired to notice he had closed the bedroom door and left me on the outside.

"Do you want anything?" His mom opened the door a crack. I seized the opportunity to push my way inside and lay down near the bed.

Matt said no. As his mom closed the door, I heard him mumble, "Just wake me up in three months."

Chapter 27

Jake

Three months was a long time to spend waiting in a dark room. Matt soon abandoned the downstairs bedroom and resumed the pattern we had been following before the transplant: a few hours of work for his aunt's company in the morning, an afternoon of playing guitar and listening to books, and a walk with me around the neighborhood in the evening. It wasn't the worst routine in the world, but he was still restless. I knew he needed something else to do, some outlet for his creative energies.

Then, miraculously, something else did come. I first caught wind of it listening to Matt's end of a phone conversation.

"Hi, is this Lifesaver Studio? . . . Ok, well, how much do you charge? . . . Oh, okay. . . . No, it'll just be me recording. . . . Well, I play guitar and sing. . . . That all sounds great. The only thing is, I don't know how I'm gonna get out there. Is there a bus I can take? . . . Oh, you can? Really! Great!"

Matt gave his address and set a date for 10 a.m. on November 15. I'd heard him talk about recording some of the songs he'd written over the past few months. Now, it seemed, he'd found a way to do it.

During the days leading up to his recording session, Matt practiced a lot. I was a captive audience of one. His mom was at work—I think this was intentional on his part. Music was the only avenue he had allowed his pent-up emotions to travel recently. Each of his songs was a tiny, hyper-personal diary of rhymed couplets and chord changes. I don't think he could've stomached having any of them criticized or under-appreciated. They were raw and open wounds that he couldn't show off.

The songs he had picked for recording weren't bad. They didn't redefine pop song craft or shake the foundations of rock music, but one of the three was pretty nice. Of course, I didn't tell him that. I just listened quietly, sometimes drifting into a light nap while he played. I knew that was all the feedback he wanted.

By the time the recording day arrived, I think Matt was as ready as he'd ever been. At a little after ten, the doorbell rang.

"Hello there, it's Jake from the studio." A tall man in a leather jacket stood in the doorway. He was older than Matt, although it was hard to tell by how much.

"Hi, come on in." Matt held the door open.

Jake moved past him into the entryway. "Sorry I'm late—had a kinda long night last night." He coughed, an exaggerated, hacking noise from the depths of his throat.

"No problem." Matt smiled.

"Hey! You have a dog." He had spotted me sitting on the landing overlooking the front door. Even from that distance I caught the rank flavor of beer and chemicals. I descended the last flight of steps to greet the visitor, my tail wagging.

"Hi, Killer." Jake gave a goofy, exaggerated laugh as he petted me. "I called him 'Killer.' But this dog wouldn't hurt a fly."

"Yeah, he's my guide dog. His name's Guildenstern."

"You gonna bring him with you?"

"Yeah, if it's not a problem."

"Naw, we'll make him all cozy in the studio."

"Should I bring my guitar?"

"If you want. We got plenty of 'em there for you to use."

As Matt began harnessing me up, Jake, still in the entryway, took a look around at the modest surroundings. "This is a nice house. You live here with your mom?"

"Just temporarily." Matt sounded a little defensive, and it was my turn to smile.

"She must be rich. Mind if I walk upstairs and look around?"

"Uh . . . no, go ahead."

Jake gave himself a one-minute tour of the rest of the house while Matt put on his coat. "Yeah, this is nice all right. What does your mom make, like six figures?"

"No. She's a teacher."

"What about your dad?"

"They're divorced. He lives in Florida."

"Well, your mom does pretty well for herself then."

"I'll tell her you said so."

It was hard to take offense at Jake's invasion of privacy. He did it with the innocent charm of a five-year-old who asked questions he didn't know he shouldn't.

In the car, Matt sat in the front passenger seat, and as usual, I settled myself in the back. As Jake drove up our street, he looked around carefully.

"This is a nice neighborhood—one way in, one way out. I bet the cops like never come down here."

"Yeah, it's pretty safe."

"I've been to jail, so I always think about this stuff."

"Oh." Matt hesitated, and I could tell he was considering whether or not to ask why. But he didn't have to.

Jake went on. "It was 'cause I got caught smoking pot. Then, when I got out and was on probation, they caught me doing it again. They came to the house and arrested me right in front of my mom. It was terrible. She was crying and everything."

"Oh, man," Matt said.

"You smoke weed?"

"Well, sometimes."

"Good, mind if I do?" Jake laughed. It was the same goofy laugh as when he had called me "Killer."

"No, go ahead."

There was the flick, flick of a lighter and Jake's loud inhale. He rolled down the window, spit, and rolled it back up. A sharp, nose-tickling smell filled the car.

After a few more minutes, we had reached the highway that led to the small town where Jake's studio was located. The car began to pick up speed, and before long we were flying. Jake's car ate up the miles. Then, suddenly, we turned off onto a side road with a swerve that had Matt gripping the door handle and me digging my claws into the back seat.

"Aren't you going a little fast?" Matt straightened up, and I tried to resettle myself. We flew around another bend in the road, and this time I was pressed against the door.

"Nah, there aren't any cops out here this time of day."

Hello! We're worried about the car crashing! I thought, but Matt didn't press the issue.

We reached the house, car and passengers intact.

As we entered, a male terrier yapped loudly at us, perturbed by the strangers in his territory.

"Down, Boo!" Jake shouted. "This dog's way better 'an you!"

Matt snickered at the backhanded compliment, but as I strained against the leash trying to get a whiff of Boo, it was his turn to give a reprimand.

"This is my mom. Mom, this is Matthew VanFossan. He's recording in the studio today." Jake waved a hand at an older woman in a wheelchair sitting in the living room.

"Hi, Mrs. Patel," Matt said, and she returned the greeting, the television blaring in the background.

"Jake, I need you to go to the store for me." After the pleasant greeting to Matt, Mrs. Patel's voice had turned angry.

"I'll do it later, Mom. I gotta get recording. My client's here."

Jake guided us upstairs, then up another flight of stairs and through a heavy door. We were in the attic. He turned on a space heater and went downstairs for coffee. Matt waited, seated on a couch that looked like it had been ripped from the back seat of a car. After giving the place a quick sniff-down, I sprawled out on the cold, thinly carpeted floor. I licked my lips. I hadn't found any crumbs, but the sour scent of beer and pot smoke clung to everything, including the computer chair, desk, and large speakers.

After a few minutes, Jake came back and handed Matt a paper cup filled with hot coffee.

"I got a blanket for your dog." Jake came over and tossed a small blue blanket over me. "I put it on him. He looks like a ghost dog." He laughed the goofy laugh, then reached down and adjusted the covering so I could see. He laughed again. This time it wasn't goofy but filled with an affectionate tenderness.

"I'm just kiddin' around with ya, Killer."

My head now poked out from under the heavy blanket and I was snug and cozy.

From my warm cocoon I watched the two go to work. Jake guided Matt into a soundproof recording room he referred to as "the booth." He sat him down and carefully positioned two microphones near his guitar.

"Here ya go, Lou Reed." He shoved a pair of earphones over Matt's long hair and dark glasses.

First, Jake listened to Matt play his song on the guitar. Then, after punching away at his computer, he explained to Matt that he'd hear a metronome beat in his earphones so his playing would be in perfect rhythm. Matt played the song again and Jake recorded it. Next, he went back into the booth and adjusted the mikes so Matt could sing standing up.

"It's better this way. You'll get more outta your diaphragm."

Matt was obviously nervous. But, there was no way out at this point. He had to sing and Jake would be listening in, whether he liked it or not. On the computer, Jake hit some more keys. Through the speakers came a countdown cue.

"Three, two, one, and . . ."

Matt made it through the first verse before forgetting his lyrics. Without comment, Jake played it back to him.

"Um, let me try that again." Matt sounded embarrassed at his shaky vocals.

"Relax, Lennon, you're just getting warmed up."

After a few more takes, the first verse was much better, but hardly perfect. "That's good," Jake said. "There're just a few little things, but I think the computer'll fix 'em." He punched keys and played back the recording. It was perfect.

"How'd you do that?"

"It's an auto-tuner. The computer puts your voice in tune."

"Isn't that kinda like cheating?"

"Don't worry, everybody uses this thing. Even the professional singers do. It's just easier. Almost nobody sings absolutely perfect, but that's what people wanna hear."

I could tell Matt remained apprehensive about digitally altering his voice, but he agreed. Maybe he saw that it was the quickest way to achieve the best result. After all, he was paying by the hour.

The two finished the lyrics to the first song. Jake suggested some vocal harmonies to add. Inspired, Matt offered some of his own ideas. It was sounding better and better.

Then Jake recorded the bass. He quickly came up with an arrangement and Matt suggested a couple of additions. Jake went into the next room and pounded out a beat on his drum kit. Finally, they added some guitar riffs, some electronic sounds, and other stuff that sounded great. It was probably everything Matt could have ever wanted in his songs but had never been able to put there himself.

He was in heaven. A sweet-smelling euphoria surrounded him as he listened to his ideas take shape through the speakers. Jake's pounding drums and energetic bass nicely backed up Matt's guitar playing and digitally perfected voice. The beautifully textured music was proof that his songwriting efforts during the past few months had not been in vain. He had poured his insecurities into his music, and Jake's studio had transformed it. I was thrilled to hear the polished results.

Jake was a goofball, but he was a professional. When he was on the clock, he went to work with a driving ethic. It had to be exactly right, or he wasn't happy. Over the five hours of recording, he punched out only twice—once to use the bathroom and once to eat a quick lunch.

He didn't forget me, either. He casually dropped a leftover piece of his chicken while Matt was in the booth singing. I scarfed up the meat. It would be our little secret.

Finally, they finished. Jake had been hitting his hash pipe continuously throughout the session. And Matt, now that he was done, took a celebratory drag.

"You sure do smoke a lot of weed."

"I have to, man. I hear the same thing repeated fifty million times in a day. If I didn't burn, I'd freak."

Matt didn't argue the logic. I, too, saw no reason to object. I was so impressed with what he had accomplished that I didn't care if he smoked all day and all night.

Matt recorded two more times before the year was out, and we would return periodically over the following year. Jake never critiqued the songs. He simply accepted them for what they were and used his talents to improve and nuance them. He never deleted anything, only added to what Matt had brought. With each session the songs got better, the recordings more intricate.

As the music reached new depths, so, too, did their relationship. Jake learned about Matt's chance to have his sight back. Matt learned about his mom's rapidly worsening MS. Matt met Jake's girlfriend, his truck-driving dad, and three of his four brothers. Jake met Matt's sister and mom, commenting to him later that his mom was hot.

After the recording sessions, Matt shone with an intensity that I rarely saw at other times. He exuded purpose and deep satisfaction.

In this climate of celebration, he accepted an acrid white powder that Jake particularly enjoyed snorting. "I'll try anything once," he said.

I watched him with concern. I could understand his curiosity. I liked to try eating things I found on the ground, and many of the substances that Matt thought were disgusting, I found tasty. But this stuff had the stink of poison.

My distress deepened when I saw him try the white powder a second time, but there was nothing I could do. I was only his guide; the choices were his. Then, he agreed to try one particularly foul-smelling chemical that he breathed in through a pipe while I looked on in disgust.

"Man, this is a good high," he said.

No, this is definitely not good, I thought. But after several more minutes I heard Matt mutter, "Damn. I better quit now 'cause this is how suckers get hooked."

I breathed a sigh of relief—finally, some sense. During future sessions I saw him make good on his assertion. After a while, he turned down the white powder, too. In the end, I saw, the drugs were irrelevant. Music was his only addiction.

Matt poured out his heart to Jake on several occasions, telling him that recording with him was the best feeling in the world and that their partnership was magical. He vowed that if he ever made it big with the songs, he would give Jake half. I could tell he meant it. He was clearly grateful for his friend's technical ability to transform his simple songwriting efforts into digital masterpieces. But, more importantly, I knew he valued having someone hear his music and listen without passing judgment. It empowered my human in a way nothing else did at that time in his life.

"Naw, man," Jake would protest after an outpouring of Matt's gratitude. "These songs are all you. I'm not doing anything, really. I just push the record button, and you pay me for it."

Like any good partnership, each one valued the other's efforts as much as his own, and neither one could fully explain the depth of what they were accomplishing together. The songs never topped any charts, but looking back, I see that something more important and long lasting was accomplished. They had helped each other by their mutual appreciation. The money exchanged and the music produced were only convenient by-products of their collaboration. The food that Jake let fall to the floor—well, that was just icing on the cake.

Chapter 28

My Beautiful Face

The decisive day for the unveiling of Matt's eye had been scheduled for January 25. It wasn't three months after the transplant as his doctor had said. It was three months and seventeen days, a nominal difference to those who weren't counting. But we were.

Christmas morning, one month from the big day, Matt and I joined the rest of his family in the living room. Jeff, his older brother, was sprawled on the love seat. He'd been the last one up and still seemed to be only half awake. Ghostmutt, Jeff's beloved white boxer, lay near his feet. Matt's older sister, Cara, was perched on a low stool near the Christmas tree. She was obviously delighting in the job of handing out presents, one by one, while Matt's mom took pictures.

"One for me—aw, Little Brother, you got me a gift!" She held the small box up to her ear, shaking it.

"Might as well thank me now," Matt said. "You're gonna love it!"

Cara tore off the wrapping paper. "Hey, Metroid!" She held up a small box. "And Zelda II. Wow! Where did you find these?"

"EBay," Matt said, grinning foolishly. "When you told me you'd found that old Nintendo, I thought I'd see what games they had."

"Thanks, boy. I can't wait to try these. Remember how we used to race home from school to see who got to play first?"

"How could I forget? You were always hogging the games."

"Yeah, right!" Cara threw the now empty box at his feet. "Well, since you were so thoughtful, I'll let you come visit me and play these—after I've had my turn."

"January 25, baby. Mark it on your calendar. I'll be paying a special visit to you and the Nintendo."

I realized then that Matt might have been planning this visit well before Cara opened the video games. In fact, it was probably a large reason he bought the games in the first place—to make up for lost time.

Almost a month later, Cara came home to visit us instead, and she brought the Nintendo with her. As she explained to Matt the day before the all-important appointment, "I want the first thing you see to be my beautiful face."

"Well, it'll be the second thing, for sure. I already promised Guildenstern his would be first."

I was happy to see he had his priorities straight.

The next day, Cara and Matt sat in the waiting room of the doctor's office and I lay beside them. The place was packed, as usual. Matt nudged me with his foot. I was flat on the floor, spread out like a dead horse, busy thinking how overjoyed he'd be to see me for the first time.

"Matthew VanFossan." Once again, we were led into an examination room.

"Someone will be in shortly," our escort said, leaving. Someone was in shortly, but it wasn't the doctor. Matt answered the medical tech's questions with the indulgence of one who held a winning lottery ticket. His excitement was heady.

A few minutes later, Dr. Malhotra entered. "Hello, Matthew."

I was glad to hear her. She had the most reassuring voice.

"And who is this lovely young lady?" Matt introduced his sister. "And hello to you, beautiful."

I looked up in silent greeting.

"Let me just take a look at your eye before we take out the lens." She was now all business and rolled her chair carefully around my outstretched paws to arrive in front of Matt. Gently lifting his eyelid with her finger, she shined the flashlight in.

Matt teared up instantly, and I felt him wince in pain.

"I know it hurts, but I won't be too long." After directing him to look up, down, right, and left, she let his eyelid close. "Well, the surface seems great. I'm going to take off the plastic protecting the alpha core, and we'll be able to take a look."

She gave him a numbing drop and they began their familiar dance of light and tears, once again.

Tense moments passed, but not quickly enough for me. I could tell all Matt's powers of concentration were focused on what was happening to him and the pain it involved. His sister's face was pale and she had turned away. I watched, wishing I could help.

Finally, Dr. Malhotra sat back. "Okay, it's out."

Matt leaned back gratefully against the chair, his eye shut tight, damp with tears.

"Just give it a rest, and whenever you're ready, we can test your vision."

He couldn't rest long. After several seconds I saw him open his eye a crack.

"What do you see?" Cara asked.

He didn't respond. The tension in the room was sharp and breathtaking.

Hesitantly, his sister said, "Can you see anything?"

"Sort of," he said, uncertainly.

The doctor rolled her chair closer. "Can you see how many fingers I have up?"

Matt stared, then squinted, then turned his head to the side. He looked bewildered. "Two," he said, finally.

"Right." She rolled her chair back a short distance. "How about now?"

He strained to see, squinting and moving his head from side to side. "I don't know." His voice was flat.

The three humans and one dog present in the room had been hoping fervently for a different response—Matt more than any of us. He'd wanted so much to gratefully count the fingers in front of him and share the joy of his victory over blindness.

"Okay." Dr. Malhotra kept her calm demeanor and moved her chair closer. "How about now?"

He turned his head from side to side, trying to catch a glimpse. "Maybe three—or four?"

"So you can see to count fingers at about two feet. That's better than what you could do before, right?"

"Right." He seemed far from happy.

The doctor began talking about eye drops and his next visit, but I didn't listen. I was perplexed and troubled.

This is it? More than a year of waiting, the surgery, more waiting, and now all he has is some bizarre vision?

The visit came to an end with Dr. Malhotra saying she'd see us for a follow-up in a week.

"Thanks," was all Matt managed to say, his voice low and heavy. Cara took his arm, he took my leash, and we walked out into the waiting room again. We put on our coats.

"So it's better than it was before?" I knew Cara was trying to find some bright spot, some positive result from this appointment which had turned on us so fast.

"Yeah, a little bit."

"Can you see me right now?"

He peered, as if through a fog, in her direction. "Not really."

"Well, what are you seeing?"

"I don't know. It's weird." He knelt down next to where I stood. Reaching, he felt my head and looked sideways at my face.

I could tell he was seeing something by the way he stared, but I didn't know what.

Can you make out my long snout, my off-white fur, or my dark nose?

"Can you see Guildenstern?" Cara asked for me.

"Yeah, a little bit." He obviously didn't have the words to explain any further.

"So, it's a little better."

"Yeah, it's a little better," he echoed, hollowly.

We rode home in silence. Matt kept his eye closed most of the way and said nothing. I lay in the back seat feeling the dead weight of his depression.

Later that day I heard the rumble of the garage door as Matt's mom pulled in from work. Matt was sitting in the living room chair, listening to a book on tape. I lay nearby, my head on an old pillow. His sister was on the couch watching Oprah. In the corner lay the Nintendo.

"Matthew, how was the appointment?" His mom looked at him from the top of the steps.

"It was all right." He paused his tape player.

"Cara said you can see a little better."

"Yeah, a little."

She went to the kitchen, dropped her things onto the table, then came back into the living room. "Come into my room and talk to me for a second. Do you mind?"

He was reluctant. But, he got up, and I followed behind him, curious to hear his explanation, wanting to be near him.

"Sit down on the bed here with me."

He sat. I made myself comfortable at the foot of the bed.

"So, what's it like?"

"It's blurry."

"Cara said you could count fingers in the doctor's office."

"Yeah—at two feet, with a lucky guess. But I should be grateful, right? Just like the good doctor said, it's more than I could see before."

I hadn't witnessed this much bitterness in a long time. I buried my nose in my paws for relief.

"Honey, I'm not saying you have to be grateful. I just want to understand what you're seeing." She touched his shoulder sympathetically.

He was quiet. I could tell he was fighting to control his emotions.

"It's really frustrating," he said finally, his voice quavering. "I can kind of catch glimpses of things around the edges, but I can't get a good look at anything. And even when I do see something, it's all weird and hard to make out. I'd rather not see anything than see such a freaking mess!"

His mom put her arm around his shoulders and pulled him towards her. "I'm so sorry, Matthew," she said softly. "That sounds so frustrating."

Matt allowed himself to be hugged. I was glad. I knew he needed it.

"It's not your fault."

"I know." She loosened her arms and looked at him. "I just wish there was something I could do."

Of course, there wasn't anything she could do. The same held true for Dr. Malhotra. The next time we saw her, she said the new cornea looked clear, but now it appeared that his retina was damaged—most likely from the ulcer, but no doctor had been able to see through the scarred cornea to detect it.

A visit to a retinal specialist later that month confirmed the explanation. The new doctor ruled out surgery, saying it was too risky. Retinas, he explained, were harder to manipulate than corneas. Trying to remove some of the scar tissue on the retina would almost certainly cause further damage. Matt insisted that it was worth a try, that he had nothing to lose since the vision he had now was worthless. But the doctor was resolute. Even the best-case scenario would be a lot of pain for little gain.

Over the next several weeks, I knew Matt was hurting. I made sure to be there for him. I didn't really do anything special, just offered him my presence. This doesn't count for a lot by human standards, but, as any dog knows, simply being can be the best way to help someone. I knew instinctively that Matt needed time to grieve. He had lost something that was precious to him, and only he could decide when he was ready to accept that loss and move on. In the meantime, I gave him the softness of my fur, the warmth of my body, and the gentle rise and fall of my breath.

Take all the time you want, I told him silently as the days went by. *I'm a dog. I'm in no hurry.*

Chapter 29

Aftermath

I'm not sure exactly what passed through Matt's mind during those weeks. He wasn't one who talked about his thoughts and feelings. I had to infer them, either by smells, his music, or my canine intuition. But in the weeks following the ill-fated surgery, it was obvious that he was withdrawn and despondent.

He spent much of his time downstairs in his room with the door firmly closed. Sometimes he didn't bother to turn on the light, which might not have mattered to him, but it made me feel gloomy. His work on the computer during the day was punctuated by grunts, sighs, and a general listlessness. In the evening, when we walked our neighborhood route, he had no tolerance for error. His commands were curt, and his touch rough. I could feel his anger through the harness, and I sensed that under it was fear. Deeper still, I suspected something uglier—self-loathing. It really worried me.

My human needed a way to express his feelings, but he had barely touched his guitar. Music finally did come to the rescue in the form of an album by a fragile-voiced singer-songwriter named Elliott Smith. Matt took to playing it constantly. I overheard him tell Clay on the phone that Smith had lived in a state of anxiety and depression, been hospitalized for a drug addiction, and recorded the songs just before committing suicide.

"The album's called *From a Basement on a Hill*. You gotta check it out. It's awesome."

I knew he related to the emotions expressed in the music. They were his feelings. Maybe it was comforting to know that someone else felt them and managed to frame them in beautiful music. But I sure hoped Matt would find a better solution to deal with his crisis than Elliot did.

One night, without warning, as he listened to the music, immersed in its melancholy, Matt began to cry. I watched him blink back the tears at first, but as the music swelled, his body shook. Was he crying for the vision he had lost or the end of his hope that it would return? Or was it the helplessness or uncertainty he was feeling? I didn't know. Maybe it was all of these things.

I hadn't seen him cry in a long time, since well before his doctor's visit in January. From my place on the floor at his side, I silently urged him on. I wanted him to empty himself of all his sadness and despair, heartache and loneliness, anger and frustration. I could smell all of it as a toxic odor that filled the bedroom. I could feel it too—a wave of tension finally being let go. It made my body tingle. I went to him and touched my cold, wet nose to his tear-wet face. He reached for me and stroked my fur. He caressed my velvety ears while he finished, emptying the tank of its last noxious contents.

I collapsed onto the carpet with a *humph*. All this emotional discharge was exhausting. The best thing for it, I decided, was a belly rub. I rolled onto my side and pressed my front paws against Matt's legs as he knelt on the carpet. He obliged by rubbing my exposed stomach affectionately. There, that was better.

No need to cry anymore. It's going to be all right. A little more to the left . . . mmm.

I thought Matt's moment of release was a breakthrough. He'd finally let go of so much of the foul emotion that had been brewing inside him. I hoped this meant that now we could get back to living our lives with some measure of peace. But, as the days ahead proved, that moment of catharsis was only the beginning.

After that night with Elliott Smith, Matt took to playing his guitar again, sitting on his bed strumming chords despondently. I imagined he was struggling to sort out the big questions that still remained. Why had this happened to him? How could he find purpose in his life as a blind person? As he played, I heard these questions emerge. Entwined in the music I recognized his self-loathing.

"Look at you. You're weak and dependent. People will pity you, and who can blame them? What good are you now that you're blind? Is there really any value left in your life?"

I wanted to give him answers. I wanted to tell him that every-thing happens for a reason, that it wouldn't be so bad, that his life did have purpose. Most of all, I wanted to tell him that it didn't matter to me if he was blind—I loved him.

But, I couldn't tell him these things, at least not in words. The most I could do was guide him to experiences that spoke the an-swers he needed. The best I could do was to demonstrate to him, over time, my dedication. I could do this, and I would.

In the meantime, Matt was an intellectual. He needed to find answers to his questions in concepts and with words. He needed human support. Knowing his pride and his reluctance to talk to the people close to him, I wondered how this would happen. I decided that my human needed an outsider's perspective, free from the ties of emotion that bound him to his family and friends. But did he realize this?

One evening soon after, while Matt and his mom were eating dinner, I learned, to my satisfaction, that he did.

"I'm thinking about seeing a psychologist." Matt took a large bite of his spaghetti. I watched it, longingly.

"Really?" His mom paused, chewing on this idea. "I'm just curi-ous," she said, finally. "Do you think a psychologist will help you?"

"I don't know exactly," he said. "I just want someone to talk to."

"You know your Aunt MJ is a trained psychologist. She'd be glad to talk to you."

"I know, Mom, but I just—I'd just rather talk to someone else."

That's fine, honey. I guess I think psychologists are for people who have serious issues, but—"

"Well, they're not." Matt's sharp tone cut her off.

"I'm sorry. You're right. Why don't you call your insurance and get a list of people who will be covered?"

"Sure," he muttered into his plate of food.

Both of them were trying so hard, and I knew they were struggling. But for all his curtness and fumbling with words, I think it was one of the most courageous decisions Matt ever made. I was proud of him.

In the entranceway, I lay on the landing. A few steps below, Matt sat in silence. We were waiting, I knew, for the para-transit vehicle that would take us to the psychologist's office.

After several phone calls, Matt had found someone who accepted his insurance, as his mom had suggested. I saw him feel the raised hands on his watch for the third time. Para-transit was no taxi service. We'd taken it several times before, and waiting a half-hour for pick-up was not uncommon. I got bored with waiting, too, but Matt was the one who tended to get upset. Since I knew it did no good to take it personally, I tried to set an example for him and fell into a light nap.

Finally, our ride came. We got in and I looked at the two other passengers riding with us in the large van—an elderly, frail-looking woman and a teenage girl in a wheelchair. The girl was obviously a dog-lover as she immediately gestured for me to sit by her. I gradually wriggled my way over and sniffed the tires of her chair. I met smells of rubber, dirt, and a faint whiff of flowers. Compelling, but not as much as the strong aroma of greasy french fries I picked up from the driver. I gave the girl a polite goodbye look and edged my way toward the front.

The girl and her wheelchair got off first, then the older lady, and finally it was our turn. Matt told the driver the office number, and he pulled up to a large two-story house. Was this the psychologist's home? Maybe he had treats in the kitchen.

No such luck. When we walked through the front door, we were inside a small waiting room with a few chairs scattered around. Several people were reading magazines. There was no receptionist in sight. Without a "find the chair" command in my repertoire, I just stood there, looking adorable. Soon enough, a woman sitting near us came over. It turned out that the room was shared by several medical professionals who used this renovated house for their offices.

"Your doctor will probably be here in a minute," the woman told Matt. "There's a seat here, if you'd like." After showing him the indicated chair, the woman looked at me. "What a beautiful dog!"

Matt smiled politely and nodded. Maybe he had heard this enough times to tune it out, but I knew my beauty counted for more than just good looks.

It had found the chair, hadn't it?

After a few minutes, a door opened and a man emerged.

"Are you Matthew?" His voice was deep and quiet.

When Matt replied that he was, the man introduced himself as Dr. Bob Burma. He was heavy-set, maybe in his forties or fifties, with an old leather smell.

"I see you have a friend here." He looked down at me without smiling. "Would you mind leaving him out here in the waiting room?"

"Oh, don't worry," Matt said. "He's really well behaved. He'll just lay down in your office and go to sleep."

"Yes, but I'm concerned that he might pose a problem for my other patients. Some of them may have dog allergies."

I couldn't believe he was objecting to me going into his office. I was already in the waiting room, wasn't I? What was the big difference? Matt hesitated for several seconds but ultimately gave in. I guess he figured a fight wasn't the best way to begin this visit. So he took the doctor's arm and disappeared inside the inner office, leaving me leashed to the chair.

I lay down for a rest and considered the situation. I hoped this visit would help Matt. If all he got was an empathetic ear and a little encouragement, it was worth the trip. But if he could find satisfactory answers to some of his big questions, answers that would help him gain perspective, well, that would be worth all the kibble in the world. I was dubious, though. How could a man who didn't let a guide dog into his office really guide someone to such wisdom?

I awoke to the sound of the inner office door clicking open. I got up and stretched as Matt and the doctor appeared in the waiting room. Wagging my tail, I sneezed happily and sniffed my human's hand in greeting.

The two said good-bye. I led Matt out the door and down the hall to the building's exit. His step was light and his scent sweet. I was curious to know what had happened, but Matt wasn't providing any explanation. I'd have to figure it out some other way.

Chapter 30

A Course in Miracles

We made our way back via para-transit. Matt seemed in good spirits, buoyed by his appointment. The burly van driver struck up a conversation about the show dogs he raised and then went on about them most of the trip. He obviously knew what he was talking about and took time to compliment me on my good looks.

A few hours later, Matt's mom arrived home from work. "Hi, Matt. How was your appointment?"

Good question, I thought. Maybe now I'd get some of the answers I'd been wanting since we left the office.

"It was fine." Matt didn't look up.

"Was the psychologist nice? What'd you guys talk about?" When he didn't answer right away, she added, "Of course, you don't have to tell me." I think she realized the nerve she'd just touched.

"We just talked." A moment passed. "I told him about losing my vision, the corneal transplant, and all that stuff, and he listened. He thinks I'm doing really well with it."

"Good. So you think it's worth going back?"

"Yeah, I do."

"Well, okay then." And that was that. His mom went into the kitchen to start dinner. If she was as curious as I was to hear more details, she didn't let on.

The dreary weeks of snow and cold confirmed the year's Groundhog Day prediction. Winter wasn't going away without a fight. Still, Matt and I continued our routine, this time with a weekly psychologist's appointment thrown into the mix. After about the third visit, Matt received a package in the mail.

"Here, honey," his mom said. "This came in the mail for you. It's from something called Nightingale-Conant. Do you know what that is?"

"Oh, yeah! That's the CDs I ordered."

"It's awfully big and heavy to be CDs." She placed the box on the kitchen table.

"That's because it's an entire book on CD."

"Oh, what book is it?"

"It's called *A Course in Miracles*. Dr. Bob recommended it. It's like a mind training course."

"Really? Well, if it helps you, then it's worth it."

I could smell the sweetness of her sincerity and knew she only wanted the best for her son. But she was unsure just what that was.

Later, I watched Matt open the box in his room. It was indeed a lot of CDs—a huge binder full of them. He started listening to the book that day. He used the earphones on his portable CD player, so I couldn't hear what the book was saying. But, he seemed totally mesmerized and listened to it every day after that. One by one, the discs went in and out of his CD player. The book had a peaceful effect on him, and I breathed in the heady aroma of his contentment.

Despite his apparent interest, I don't think he heard everything. Sometimes I noticed him nodding off as he listened, his head coming to rest against the back of the chair or his breath growing deep and even as he lay curled up on the couch. I didn't blame him. So many CDs! I found myself napping along with him. Still, he kept going.

I was surprised to notice one day that Matt was nearing the back of the binder. And that was when things changed. Instead of listening nonstop, he began to pause for a minute or two. He'd push "play" for a short interval, then "stop," then sit motionless for a while.

Was he concentrating? Digesting the material? I wasn't sure what to make of this. Was this book really all that complicated? On the other hand, Matt seemed relaxed, almost meditative.

The restful periods became more frequent as the days passed. Often, he didn't even use his CD player. He'd just stop in the middle of whatever he was doing. It was kinda funny. He would be grooming me on the back patio and—midbrush—he'd stop and stare into space. My fur would swirl around us, temporarily unheeded. Or we'd be on our daily walk when Matt would suddenly pause on the side of the street, and I'd sniff his pensive smell. I inhaled it, curiously. Then, I overheard his end of a phone conversation with his brother, Jeff, which shed some light on the matter.

"So, I've been reading this thing called *A Course in Miracles* . . . Yeah, that's what I thought, too, but they're not miracles like turning water into wine or anything. These are moments when you see yourself united with something greater. In that moment you actually become one with everything, and this is when you see things as they really are."

Jeff must have been dubious because Matt went on. "I know it sounds crazy, but I'm hooked! The language is so compelling, so beautiful, I can't stop reading . . . I know. I've finished the whole text, and now I'm doing the workbook exercises. There's one for every day of the year, so I guess I'll be at it for a while . . . Sure, I can send you some of the CDs if you want."

I reached up to scratch under my chin. So, that's what it was all about. I wondered if this was helping him accept his blindness. Maybe he could let go of physical sight more easily with the idea of gaining spiritual sight. I listened as he went on. According to the book, he said, it was possible for a person to learn to see past all fear, blame, and grief. This was done by practicing complete forgiveness.

I blinked in surprise as Matt described this all to his brother. Was it really possible for a human to let go of all fear? A human who was never afraid seemed like a Labrador who was never hungry. Possible or not, I promised myself I would support Matt in any way I could. If he could give up the anxiety he had about living as a blind person, I suspected his life would become happier and healthier. If he could learn complete forgiveness—well, time would tell. I wondered if he'd forgive me for sneaking some extra kibble.

Chapter 31

Amanda

We hadn't been to Oberlin to visit Amanda since early December. I'd noticed that Matt's phone conversations with her had become less frequent. When she called to ask about his eye procedure, he relayed the results in a cool, disconnected tone. Their conversation had been short. "Thanks for calling . . . Okay, bye." No "I love you," no "I miss you," not even a word about us visiting her at school. Matt had been so gloomy and withdrawn in the days following the surgery that it was no wonder the conversation had ended this way. Still, I was curious to know if, now that he had begun to find his strength, he would reach out to bridge the distance that had opened between them. Eventually, I got an answer.

"I was thinking about maybe coming to visit you," he said, the phone to his ear one afternoon. His voice was cheerful, but his nervous smell betrayed uncertainty. "Great! Next weekend's fine." I heard him exhale and sensed a wash of relief pass through him. "I'll check on the buses and call you back. Well, I can't wait to see you!"

The next weekend, we took a very familiar Greyhound. After our arrival in Oberlin, Matt's excitement seemed to grow as we sat inside the busy bus station. I caught a tantalizing whiff of hot dogs and popcorn from the snack shop and looked for any bits on the floor. Then, Amanda was there. The two hugged, I got a pat on the head, and it seemed to me that things had started off well.

We spent that night in her dorm room. I slept on the floor, as usual, trying to ignore the activity coming from her bed. Still, I could feel the release of long-held tension and knew Matt was happy to have his playtime with Amanda again.

In the morning, when he went outside with me so I could do my business, we found a thick blanket of snow. I stuck my snout in it and snorted at the cold wetness. More snow was falling, the tiny flakes whipping against us in the chill wind. The two humans and I spent the rest of the day in Amanda's room, hiding out from the blizzard.

They ate Chinese delivery for lunch, and then Amanda suggested that they watch a movie. Matt agreed, and she selected one she'd watched before but that he had never seen.

"It's called *The Passion of the Christ*. It has Mel Gibson in it and it's kinda graphic. It's about the Crucifixion."

I wasn't much for movies, so while the two watched, I dozed fitfully. In between naps, I woke to hear Amanda describing some of the action.

"He just fell, and now Mary's coming over to wipe his face. It's covered in blood. Now they're nailing his hands and feet to the cross, and his face is all crunched up with pain."

I felt the tension build as Amanda watched and Matt listened. I groaned and turned over, finally falling asleep again. When I awoke, it had ended, and the two were talking.

"The name of it is *A Course in Miracles*," Matt was saying. "It basically says the whole idea of sacrifice is misguided."

"Whadaya mean?"

"Like it says no one has to feel pain or suffer as a sacrifice. And I just can't believe the movie doesn't even show any of the Resurrection! That, for me, is the whole point of the story, and they totally left it out."

"Uh, no offense, but I don't think it's such a big deal. Anyway, I think the movie was well done."

Matt's heart rate was up, but he took a deep breath before answering. "Wouldn't you rather see Jesus as a lesson about love and forgiveness? How can you possibly think that movie was well done?"

"I just do, okay? I'm entitled to my own opinion. Why don't we just drop it?"

But they didn't right away. And when they finally did drop it, things seemed off kilter between them. I was surprised. Matt wasn't usually so adamant about making his point. But the next day was even more surprising.

"Listen, Amanda, I've been thinking," Matt began. "I'm not sure keeping up this long-distance relationship is such a good idea."

"What? Really? Why do you say that?" She seemed as shocked as I was to hear this.

"It's just that, I mean, I feel like we're moving in different directions. Next January I'll be going to Brazil for a year, and, you know, that's a long time."

Amanda, to her credit, recovered quickly. "That's still quite a ways away. Why don't we just wait and see what happens? There's no point in deciding things now."

"Yeah, but I really feel like it's time. I can't explain it. I'm sorry."

The two were silent as we rode to the bus station.

They said good-bye but didn't hug. Amanda gave me a quiet, "Goodbye, Guildenstern." On the bus ride back home, I marveled over this unexpected turn of events. Matt had known about his Rotary scholarship to Brazil for months. And he'd been excited to see Amanda just days ago. I couldn't believe he'd gone to visit her with the intention of breaking up. What had happened? Was it a spontaneous decision he'd made that morning? That was so unlike him. He was such a rational creature. Could their argument about the movie have triggered the break up? It was such a strange thing to end a relationship over—a disagreement about a film.

I repositioned my head against the side of the bus. Matt sat in his seat, his CD player in his lap. From his relaxed breathing, I knew he was listening to his daily exercise from *A Course in Miracles*. The book had become so important to him. Could it be the reason for this unexpected ending to his relationship with Amanda?

Chapter 32

Violet Pound

Back in Pittsburgh, Matt continued his workbook exercises with more and more frequency. One day he paused over and over, in each instance giving off that sweet smell. I'd see him suddenly stop at the computer or just sit there in the middle of playing his guitar. I guess he realized it was a strange sight because when his mom was around, he'd go to another room or wait until her attention was on other things.

The days passed. Winter dragged on with its freezing weather and chilling winds. March, insistent to the end, went out with one last snowstorm. Early in the morning, Matt's mom shoveled a car-width path down the steep driveway, carefully backed down, and left for work. Later that day, Matt and I set out on a walk around the neighborhood. We weren't going to let a few inches of snow stop us from our daily rounds.

We trudged along the usual route. The streets were only partially cleared, and, at times, Matt's feet crunched down on a thick layer of snow. The whitened landscape, while beautiful in an austere way, changed the look of things. It felt different, too. Nothing like cold wet snow half way up your hind legs and salt under your delicate paws to make you appreciate the hot pavement of summer. It must've been disconcerting for Matt, as well. I knew he was used to feeling the slope of the street beneath his feet as a clue to our location. Now he had to estimate. When we stopped periodically to check for the side of the street, it was difficult for him to find. Mounds of plowed snow hid the curb's edge.

Despite the hazards, we made our way down Jefferson Avenue. I stopped to show him the parked cars on the roadside, and he directed me around them. When we got to the less-traveled end, we found it covered by a blanket of unplowed snow. This may have been why Matt didn't notice where the road curved and led us onto an unfamiliar side street. As he urged me forward, I hesitated. I knew this wasn't our normal route. But, I also knew Matt was in charge. My job was to follow his directions and keep him safe while doing so. I continued down the road.

A few minutes later I stopped as we reached a dead end. Matt probed with his foot. Anxiousness rose up in him. Cautiously, he steered me to the right, probably so we could cross the street and backtrack the way we'd come. But the snow made it impossible for either of us to know when we'd reached the other side of the road. Soon we were descending a slope that wasn't the way back.

Matt's pulse quickened, and I heard him mutter "What the . . ." under his breath. He told me to halt and gave me a correction.

"No!"

Of course, I was only following his confused directions and had no idea where we were any more than he did. I stopped and waited. He turned us around again and, in a shaky voice, ordered me up the slope. I led him for a few paces until the path ended; then I took the only obvious opening. It led us down again.

A feeling of helplessness coursed through my human. He obviously had no idea where we were, and I wasn't improving the situation. Nervously, he followed me. The path began leveling off, and I stopped walking when I reached its end. Matt stuck out his foot and found a huge mound of snow in front of us. It seemed we'd strayed onto someone's property. We were two rats in a snowy, backyard maze.

But wandering around through people's yards wasn't considered a life or death struggle. We'd been lost in snow before, and we had survived. I knew we would eventually get ourselves back to a street, even if it took hours. The problem was Matt's feelings of frustration and humiliation. For him, I supposed, getting lost in someone's backyard was like having an accident on the kitchen floor or being caught in the cat's litter box. It was just as embarrassing.

We stood still. A cold wind blew against us as the seconds went by. I was helpless to guide him at this moment, but if we ended up here overnight, I would let him huddle up with me for warmth. However, I knew neither of us wanted things to come to that point. We had to make it home—at least before my dinnertime.

I heard Matt's breathing over the faint noise of cars from some far off highway. Gradually, his breathing slowed. My nose twitched at a faint sweetness, the same smell he gave off when reading *A Course in Miracles*. Was he meditating? Praying? Whatever he was doing, it calmed him down.

"Hello there!" a voice called through the cold. Matt turned his head in the direction of the sound.

"Hello?" he called back. I couldn't believe it. Had he summoned an angel?

"I'm up here in the window," the female voice said.

"Uh, yes?"

"Do you need some help?"

"I guess I do. I'm a little lost."

"You're in my driveway."

"Right. My guide dog and I got turned around, and I'm trying to get back to the street. It's a lot harder to find it in the snow."

"Oh, I see. Well, you can just go to your right up the hill, and you'll be back on Edgewood Avenue. Do you know your way from there?"

"Yeah, I should be fine from there."

"Your dog must be cold."

"Oh, he's okay. He's got a thick coat."

"What's your name?"

"Matt. And this is Guildenstern."

"My name is Violet Pound. That's P-o-u-n-d." Her voice reminded me of Matt's grandmother's, the one who had just moved to Florida a few months earlier.

"Nice to meet you. Thanks for your help."

"Oh, you're very welcome. Maybe someday when it's warmer you can come back and have tea with me."

"Sure."

I didn't know why she was waiting for warmer weather, but I kept quiet.

"Hang on one second. Stay right there." After a minute she came back to the window. "I'm going to throw something down to you. Here." A small object thudded to the ground in front of us. "There's a package of cookies for you. It's right at your feet."

Matt bent down and searched for the gift from above. I marveled at the craziness of the situation. Violet obviously wanted to help him and would have liked his company. And yet, something prevented her from going beyond throwing cookies through her window. I felt for her. In a way, she was as trapped as we had been.

"A little to your right—a little more. There you go!"

Matt picked up the cookies and thanked her with a forced smile.

"Now, let me give you my phone number so you can come back and have tea sometime."

"All right." He got his recorder from his pocket and recorded Violet's number. "Well, take care."

"Bye," she said. "Bye, Guildenstern!"

Following Violet's directions, Matt got us completely up the sloping driveway and back onto the road. From there, we managed to pick up our usual route. At last, we entered the warmth and comfort of the house. We were home.

Later that day, Matt dug the cookie package out of his pocket and threw it away. I watched sadly as the trash can lid closed, trapping the cookies inside. I knew he didn't like store-bought snacks much, but he could've at least left one out for me. But I don't think he'd wanted the cookies in the first place. Just like he hadn't wanted Violet's phone number. And the only reason he'd accepted her directions was because they were our only way out of the backyard maze. It occurred to me that the same person who'd made peace with himself after his shame at getting lost in someone's yard was now suffering another bout of stubborn pride. I suspected he wouldn't be calling the cookie lady anytime soon. It was too bad. She seemed like a person who would offer treats to attractive Labs as well.

And so the days passed. We continued our routine. Matt kept up his workbook exercises. And then, quite unexpectedly, I watched as he dialed a phone number from his voice recorder.

"Hi, Violet? This is Matt. We met in your backyard, remember?"

I listened to him making plans to get together, and I licked my lips contentedly.

Maybe he's progressing faster than I'd thought.

Chapter 33

Getting His Fight Back

Matt slowly began to take an interest in the world again. He had lunch with Violet Pound—several times, in fact. He started volunteering at a crisis center, taking shifts answering their twenty-four hour hotline. He ended his sessions with Dr. Bob and joined a *Course in Miracles* study group that met at the local library. The group's members seemed to appreciate my inclusion, and I wasn't left in the waiting room.

Then there was the Rotary scholarship he'd been granted. In January we'd be heading for a yearlong adventure in Rio de Janeiro. As the trip was still seven months away, Matt had planned one more project for the intervening months. He had registered for two psychology courses at the University of Pittsburgh. As he explained to his mom, they would help him decide if he had a future as a psychologist. Dr. Bob's influence, I was sure.

In May, we went back to school. Matt found a summer sublet on Craigslist and we took a room in a third-floor, two-bedroom apartment a short walk from the Pitt campus. We shared the apartment with James, an affable engineering student on summer break. Luckily for me, he loved animals and didn't bat an eye at the tufts of dog hair I left scattered all over.

James also loved sports. He drove a delivery truck during the day, but he spent most evenings in front of the TV watching ESPN. His favorite feature was ultimate fighting. He explained the concept to Matt one evening shortly after we moved in. They sat on the couch, Matt eating his baked potato without utensils, James staring in rapture at the enormous screen. I stared in rapture at Matt's baked potato.

"Basically, there're no rules. You can use whatever martial arts you want."

"Sounds pretty vicious." Matt finished his last bite. I sighed.

James laughed. "Oh, it is. People get really messed up doing it, but it's a lot of fun. There's an ultimate fighting place near here that I've gone to a couple of times. The guy gives free sessions every Wednesday."

"Really? You just show up and say you wanna fight?"

"Yep. The last time I went, no one else showed up, so I had to fight the instructor. He must weigh over three hundred pounds, and he beat the crap out of me."

"Damn James, you're crazy." But Matt was curious. "Can I tag along next time you go? I think I'll try it."

Just like that, Matt had enlisted in his first ultimate fighting experience. Several nights later, the three of us walked the four blocks over to Ficarra's Fight Club. We were the first ones there, so we waited outside the door at the top of a long flight of steps. Ten minutes later, the instructor arrived.

"Hey, James. You came back for more," he called, climbing up the stairs, one labored step at a time.

"Yeah. I couldn't stay away. This is my friend, Matt. He wants to try."

Matt said hello, reaching out for a handshake. The man's huge hand shook his politely.

"Nice to meet you, Matt. And who's this with you?"

"This is Guildenstern. He'll just be watching tonight."

The instructor let out a big, barreling laugh. "Glad to hear it." He patted my head affectionately. He smelled of cologne and exertion. I liked him.

He introduced himself as Tony Ficarra as he unlocked the door and led us into the studio. We stepped into a large room with a few chairs on one side. Most of it was covered by a well-worn black exercise mat. There were several overhead lights, but the place still seemed dark. The odor was of sweat and dirt mixed with some of Tony's cologne.

While we waited for other students to show up, Tony gave Matt a brief history of the place. "Have you ever seen the movie *Fight Club*?"

"Yeah, great movie."

"Well, it's the inspiration for this studio. It's a place for people to break out of society and just go nuts for a little while. The only rule is no blows to the head or groin. Everything else is fair game." He walked over to a folding chair and sat down. "How do you feel about fighting me tonight?"

"Uh, that sounds all right, I guess."

"Will he be okay with that?" Tony glanced at me.

"Yeah, Gilly's not trained to defend me or anything. He'll probably just go to sleep."

Not likely, I thought. I may not be trained in self-defense, but this was my human we were talking about. He obviously wasn't thinking clearly if he planned on fighting Big Tony.

Meanwhile, James had paired up on the far side of the mat with the one other person who had shown up. Tony helped Matt hitch my leash to a chair then guided him to the side of the mat nearest us.

"Okay," he said. "You're free to tap out whenever you want. Whoever taps out ends the fight, and his opponent gets the victory."

"How do you tap out?" Matt looked a little anxious.

Tony got down and slapped his hand against the mat. Thwop! Thwop! Thwop! "Like that." He got to his feet. "Ready to go?"

Matt laid his glasses aside and said he was.

There was an awkward moment at first. Tony said, "I'm right in front of you." That was his one and only deference to Matt's blindness. They both stood there another several seconds; then Matt made the first move.

He threw his one hundred and thirty pounds into the man's massive bulk, like a peanut diving into a giant marshmallow. Tony took several steps backward but didn't go down. Then Matt got a leg behind him and gave him a hard shove with his shoulder. Tony stumbled. Matt took a step back and rammed into him with all his force. This time Tony went down.

Wow, I thought. *Matt must be way stronger than he looks.*

But Tony had let him play long enough.

His hand reached up and locked around Matt's forearm. In one move he pulled Matt down and started to roll over onto him. Both men were sweating now, and it must have helped Matt, for he wiggled out and slipped free—but not for long. He was pulled to the floor again. I could tell he was getting tired.

From a few feet away, I watched the two struggling against each other. I knew they were just playing, that there was no real danger, but I saw Matt's anxiousness. After another minute I stood up, catching Tony's eye.

Please don't hurt him, I begged, mutely. *He's just a stupid kid who wants to try something new.*

Suddenly, Tony stopped. "Your pooch's standing up, and he looks worried." He chuckled sympathetically. "Let's put him in the next room so he won't see what's going on."

"Okay," Matt said dumbly. He took some deep breaths and wiped sweat from his face. He was too tired to argue.

Tony led me into a small office out of sight of the fighting space. As I found a spot near the door, I realized that I had no choice but to wait for Matt to end what he had started. I could still detect his smell of fatigue and yes, fear, from the next room. It stayed with me as I fell into a fitful sleep.

I'm startled to suddenly find myself standing in the room I had just left. I feel the buoyant surface of the mat under my bare feet. I'm hot and exhausted, though my body is wet. It's the second time I dream that I'm human, the second time I dream that I am Matt.

My limbs feel heavy, leaden, as I hear Tony's voice asking if I'm ready. My head shakes up and down. He grabs my arm, but somehow I slip out of his grip and dance free. My body twitches and wrenches, just barely managing to keep free of the man's grasp. Then my luck runs out as he wraps his arms around me in a hug tighter than the tightest choke chain. He's dragging me down. All I can do is hope that as we collapse to the ground, he might lose his grip. But his hold stays firm.

I am drained, barely managing to wriggle as he begins to steamroll over me, his full weight bearing down on my human body. His amorphous form, which had looked so yielding from a distance, now presses down on me. As he rolls from my chest to my stomach, my breath, which had been coming in shallow gasps, is all but cut off. I'm afraid that I—Matt—we—will suffocate. I try to shout or growl to stop the fight but nothing comes out of my throat. With my last bit of strength, I partially free my chest and belly. I can breathe again. Relief comes in a flood.

But Tony isn't done. While still holding me down, he begins prying my fingers apart. One, two, three, he bends them back as far as they can go. The message is clear: look how easily I can snap them off. Still, I note the control and feel relief. He is showing me he can, and that is the point.

I realize that I am done. A second later I hear hoarse words escape my lips. "I think I'm ready to tap out."

The admission comes with as much dignity as my remaining breath and compromised position will allow. Immediately, the weight of Tony is lifted. I can breathe freely again. I sit up, panting, my face covered with sweat. The room spins around.

"Good match," he says.

I awoke then to Tony's heat and smell, back in the small office. He unfastened my leash and led me into the fighting room. I looked at Matt sitting on the gym floor.

Way to go, Ultimate Fighter. But I was glad to see him unhurt. My body wriggled excitedly as he put a hand on me in greeting.

Then James was by our side. "What'd you think?"

Matt didn't answer, but his stomach churned audibly. "Can you take me to the bathroom?" he finally managed.

"Sure." I followed close behind as they went down a hallway. "Are you all right?" He opened the bathroom door.

"I think I'm gonna be sick."

"The toilet's right in front of you." Matt knelt and emptied his insides in heaves and spits. Oddly, there was no embarrassment in him, only relief and exhaustion.

"Did you have spinach for lunch?" James asked.

"Dinner." Matt's reply came in between bursts of vomit.

"Yeah, I can see the leaves floating around in there."

We made our way back to Tony. "Everything okay?"

"Yeah," Matt said quickly before James could weigh in. I wondered if Tony could detect the spinach on Matt's breath.

But he only said, "You put up a good fight. Come back any time."

Matt beamed, promising that he would. I blinked in disbelief. I didn't see how he could call squirming and writhing on the floor "a good fight." And why anyone would want to come back for more was beyond me.

The two flatmates walked back to the apartment, joined in camaraderie. As I trotted beside them, I considered the evening. I didn't understand the reason for all the brutality. Couldn't they have just gone to the park together? There was more than one way to bond, after all—that didn't involve aggression. I bonded with other male dogs by sniffing their tails, playing chase and tug, and marking their pee spots. We played games of humping and had no qualms about lying down snout to tail. Human males were much more limited. Their interactions had to be competitive and rigorous. The

155

more intense the struggle, the more manly they felt. As I followed the two exhausted fighters home, I decided that dogs were more highly evolved—at least, in this situation.

The following Wednesday when James asked if Matt wanted to go to the fight club with him, Matt replied that we were taking the week off and would go another time. In the end, I'm happy to say, we never did go back. That was our first and last ultimate fight—one too many if you ask me. I was glad to see Matt come to his senses. But, as it would turn out, he was about to get himself into such a lot of trouble that it made ultimate fighting seem like a piece of cake.

Chapter 34

Dr. Matt's Lovely Assistant

It was the end of week one of Clinical Psychology class.

"All right, ladies and gentlemen," announced our professor, "I want you to get into groups to practice these communication techniques."

The ladies and gentlemen began matching themselves with their neighbors. Matt stayed in his seat, looking a little uncomfortable, straining to recognize nearby voices.

"Do you want to be in with us?" It was a pretty, dark-haired girl, sitting behind us. Matt let out a grateful "sure" and turned his chair toward her.

Her name was Sylvia. "And you're Matt," she said.

"Right." He was obviously pleased that she knew his name.

Small wonder. He was the only one in the room who got to bring his handsome dog.

Our group began the activity. In the first round, Matt played the psychologist and Sylvia, the patient. Kelley, the other student in their trio, was the observer.

"So, Sylvia," he began, "how's your summer going?"

"Well, Matt, it's going okay."

"Please, call me Dr. Matt." The girls giggled. I groaned inwardly. "Have you been very busy, or are you taking the summer easy?"

"Oh, it's been pretty low key," Sylvia said. "I've been working in my garden and cooking a couple of new recipes, stuff like that."

"That sounds relaxing. Are you enjoying that?"

"It's been nice. The only problem is that I'm getting married next month, and there's still tons of stuff to do for the wedding."

"You're getting married?" Kelley looked at her in real surprise. "Oops, sorry. But you look so young!"

"Well, I'm twenty-five. To me, it's a strange age. One minute I think it's time to get married, and the next minute I feel like I'm not ready."

"Sounds like you're conflicted about it," Matt said.

"Nice empathizing!" Kelley gave the compliment.

I observed the three switching roles and playing doctor for a while longer. I was pleased to see Matt had found two attractive females to liven up this class. Shortly after, the period came to an end, and I stood up and stretched. Matt retrieved his backpack and reached for my leash.

"Can I help you out?" It was Sylvia, who had come up beside us.

"Sure. Can I take your arm?"

"You might have to bend down a little. I'm kinda short."

He laughed and took her arm just above the elbow. "Oh, that's all right. Short is cute."

I walked beside them, studying Sylvia. She was petite with big, dark eyes. Just then she looked at me.

"He's a beautiful dog. Can I pet him?"

"Well, technically, no." Matt said. "I'm sorry, it's that, you know, he's working right now."

I caught a whiff of her displeasure, but she refrained from touching me, instead guiding us down the hall.

"What's his name?"

"Guildenstern."

"Guildenstern? That's hilarious. He's gotta meet my dog, Kassandra. I bet they'd get along great."

Guildenstern and Kassandra? I thought. We took the steps down to the first floor as I pondered the pretensions of human naming.

"So, Matt, just between you and me, Kelley thinks you're a real cutie."

His face flushed. "Well, uh, tell her thanks. She's nice, too."

"How're you getting home?" Sylvia paused as we reached the front door of the building.

"We're walking. It's just a few blocks away."

"You sure you don't want a ride?"

"Thanks, that's okay. It's an easy walk."

I sighed. Why couldn't he just accept the offer? A few blocks or not, a car was less effort for both of us. He hadn't, though, so we made our way home on foot. As we walked, I recognized a lingering excitement. That "cute" compliment must've gotten to him. Funny, though. I hadn't noticed any attraction to Kelley. If anything, I'd recognized his heart rate quicken at Sylvia's feminine voice. But, she was getting married. Let's see, I mused. Kelley thought Matt was cute, Matt thought Sylvia was cute, and Sylvia thought I was cute. People could be so confusing. Still, I couldn't fault Sylvia's good taste.

She found Matt again after the next class. "Can I walk you out?"

"Sure!" He was obviously pleased at the offer. "How're the wedding plans going?"

"Ugh, don't remind me. Dan thinks he can just sit back and have me plan it all, you know? But I'm not the only one getting married."

Matt had no comment on that, maybe since he had no wedding experience himself. "Where're you having the ceremony?"

"In Hawaii."

"Really? Cool. That's pretty exotic."

"Well, I'm from Hawaii." We passed out of the building and into the cool night. "You sure you don't want a ride home?"

Matt paused.

Come on, I thought. *Don't make us walk again.*

"Why not?" he said, as if he heard my plea.

All right. Now that's more like it.

Sylvia's rides home after class became routine. At her suggestion, she and Matt also began having late dinners together at a Greek restaurant. She made a point of calling her fiancé and inviting him to join us, but he never accepted. Over meals of falafel and lentils, the two got to know each other. Matt talked about Brazil, Amanda, and me. Sylvia talked about her garden, the wedding, and Dan.

One afternoon, a Saturday free from classes, we were at home in the apartment when Sylvia showed up, unannounced.

"Wanna go to the park? Huh? Wanna? Huh?"

Matt laughed, and I wagged my tail vigorously. This boring day had just gotten a whole lot better. We were soon off in the SUV, Sylvia's stereo blaring the song, "Heya," with its syncopated beat and trumpeting chorus. Matt's mood soared. He seemed exhilarated; there was a whole day of possibility ahead.

When we got to the park, Sylvia's dog, Kassie, ran wildly around in circles while I walked beside the two humans. Matt had taken my harness off, but he left the leash attached. The air was warm, and the large grassy expanse inviting.

"Do you ever let Guildenstern off leash?" Sylvia stopped us on the path we'd been following.

"Well, the guide dog school says not to. There's just no guarantee he won't bolt in front of a car or something."

"It's up to you, but just so you know, we're in the middle of Frick Park. It's totally safe; trust me. I'll keep an eye on him if you want."

"Um . . ." Matt wavered, then said, "okay."

Suddenly, I was free! Free to sniff, free to mark new territory. But before I knew it, Kassie was chasing me, growling and nipping at my heels. It turned out she was the craziest dog I'd ever met. An Australian shepherd mix, she evidently thought I was her lost sheep. At first, I was overwhelmed by her assaults. I waited for Matt to step in and save me, but he was too busy chatting with Sylvia. After a few minutes without any peace, I snarled at the little mutt and put my teeth on her neck. I had to show her that I wasn't just some big pushover she could boss around. Still, Kassie was relentless. Finally, I went over to the table where Matt and Sylvia were now sitting and flopped down.

"How about food?" I heard Sylvia ask. "How do you get groceries?"

I thought that was pretty obvious, but Matt answered. "Gilly and I walk to the Giant Eagle down the street from the apartment, and I get a clerk to help me. That, or my mom takes us when she visits."

"Hey, I'm always going to Giant Eagle for something or other. You can totally come with me next time if you want."

"Geez, restaurants, dog parks, shopping, do you ever stop giving?"

Sylvia laughed. "If you weren't so damned charming, I probably would have a long time ago."

"Lucky for me, then, that I am," he said with satisfaction.

A few feet away I snorted. We all knew that I was the reason the two were hanging out in the first place.

On Wednesday evening a few days later, when James was busy fighting, Sylvia came over to review for a test. The two sat in the living room going over the latest clinical psychology study guide. Sylvia had her textbook out, and Matt was on his laptop. Between the two of them, they knew most of the answers, but when stumped, Sylvia leafed through her book and Matt performed a "find" on his computer. After about an hour, they had finished.

"I think it's remarkable," she said, "how you're able to find a lot of the answers faster than me."

"Yeah, that's the nice thing about having my textbook scanned onto my computer." He patted his laptop.

"Technology is so great. Just imagine what it will do for people in the next hundred years."

"Maybe. But I don't think it's as wonderful as everyone makes out."

"What do you mean?"

"Well . . ." He stopped, trying to formulate an explanation. "Take me, for example. Since I lost my vision, I've had to rely more on other people—and Guildenstern. This forces me to be more patient with myself and more accepting of others. If, in ten or twenty years down the road, I get to see again because of some new technology, it'll be great. But, I'll still consider these lessons more valuable than any vision." Sylvia murmured with interest, and he continued. "Technology does incredible things, but it's no substitute for learning forgiveness and patience. I mean, look at us. We have televisions, computers, and the Internet, and our world is still so messed up."

"You're very wise, Dr. Matt." I could see that, despite her teasing, she was impressed.

Matt laughed, flattered. They were both quiet for a minute. Then he went on. "I didn't always feel this way. Actually, I was pretty screwed up after my surgery didn't work last year. But I've been studying this book called *A Course in Miracles*. It's amazing." He went on to describe how his psychologist had recommended this book that taught forgiveness through recognizing the physical world as an illusion.

"Have you ever read any Hindi religious texts? I had to when I was studying to become a yoga instructor. The ideas are really similar."

"You're a yoga instructor? You didn't tell me that." That led to lots of talk about yoga, which led to plans to attend a yoga class together. It turned out that Matt always wanted to try yoga, and Sylvia, of course, was glad to take him. She was offering to show him some of the yoga stances ahead of time when her cell phone rang.

"Oops, that's Dan calling." She pushed a button, and the phone went silent. "He's probably checking to make sure we're not making out."

Matt laughed a little uneasily. "Well, tell him we're only studying. If he wants proof, Guildenstern is our witness." He probed for my body with his foot and found me lying next to him, half-covered by the coffee table.

"I don't know how credible a sleeping Labrador is." Sylvia smiled.

True, my eyes were half-closed, and my breath came deeply and evenly. But I was well aware of what was happening. The tension between them reminded me of facing off with another dog at the dog park. Electricity would crackle as we circled around each other, each one deciding whether or not to make the first move. It seemed Matt and Sylvia were playing this game. I knew better than to get involved. This time it was for humans only.

Chapter 35

Mrs. Sylvia

Yoga became Matt and Sylvia's newest venture together. The sessions were held in the gym of Carnegie Mellon University. The style of yoga was Iyengar, which, Sylvia had explained, included detailed verbal instruction. As promised, she'd guided Matt through a few of the most important positions beforehand.

During the first class, I watched from the back of the room as the humans bent their bodies into strange positions. Matt followed along tentatively. Sylvia would occasionally whisper in his ear and adjust his body for the proper pose.

As we continued with classes, Matt became more adept. Sylvia's interventions became fewer. But even during this first class, I observed his enjoyment. He laughed at his semi-successful attempts at balancing poses, and at the end-of-class meditation, he sprawled on his mat, eyes closed, visibly at peace.

"Yogis teach that the most important part of the class is at the end, with the resting meditation." This particular instructor liked to go beyond the poses and impart bits of yoga wisdom. "They say the movements are only a prelude to resting, and we exhaust our bodies so we can forget about them, if only for a moment."

At the back of the room, I licked my lips in agreement. The resting pose was the most important part of the class for me, too. It was so important that I didn't bother with any of the other positions.

Matt and Sylvia interrupted my light nap at the end of the session. I stood up and stretched the length of my body, leaning forward on my front legs with my hindquarters and tail in the air.

"Nice downward dog, Guildenstern!" Sylvia said.

I looked up at her. *All this time Matt could have been learning yoga from me.*

One evening, at the beginning of June, Sylvia was driving us home, as usual. She and Matt were relaxed and happy from their yoga. I reclined in the back and continued resting.

"Dan's going out of town this weekend."

"Oh, yeah? Where's he going?"

"Wisconsin. It's some research trip for his PhD. So I was thinking you should come over and have dinner."

"Sure." Matt answered readily then caught himself. "You don't think he'll mind?"

"I'm not sure I'll even tell him. He'd be so jealous, it's not worth it."

"Oh."

"I'm inviting other people, too. It won't just be the two of us."

"Well, okay then!" A dinner party sounded more legitimate.

So, we went. Matt and Sylvia were joined by three of her friends. The group talked and ate in the dining room while Kassie led me in a frenetic game of tag that took us bounding up and down the stairs. It was fun until I wanted to stop. But, as usual, Kassie was relentless. She had more energy in her fuzzy bobbed tail than I had in my whole body. I decided that Matt might need my services, so I stayed close to him for the rest of the evening.

When the other guests finally left, Matt followed Sylvia out to the porch where they continued drinking mojitos made with mint from her garden. The subdued sound of soft music drifted through the living room window. Kassie was in her crate, and I lay at Matt's feet, taking in the night air.

"Have you heard this guy before?" Sylvia asked.

Matt bent his head and listened to the singing. "I don't think so. Who is he?"

"Jack Johnson. He's from Hawaii. You can hear it in his songs. Doesn't the beat of his guitar remind you of a beach at sunset?"

Matt nodded and leaned back in his chair. "You're so lucky. You'll be going back to Hawaii next week."

Sylvia sighed. "Yeah, but I don't know how lucky I am."

"Why? Whadaya mean?"

"I'm having doubts."

Matt's head came up. "We-l-l." He stretched the word out. "That's probably normal."

"No, Matt, these aren't normal doubts. These are huge ones. Huge ones. Honestly, part of me would love to call it off."

"Are you serious?"

"Matt, Dan's been so different these last few weeks. Any time I hang out with you, he throws a fit. And when he's not mad, he pleads with me to stop seeing you."

"You know, I can understand. If I were in his position, I'd be jealous. And hearing this makes me feel crappy. I don't wanna cause problems. I mean, it's not fair to you or Dan. Maybe we should stop hanging out, at least until after the wedding." Matt set his drink down, the relaxed after-party ambience gone.

"That's ridiculous! You and I are just friends. It's not fair that just because Dan has jealousy issues, I should have to stop hanging out with someone I care about."

Matt softened at these last few words. "I care about you, too. I think you're an amazing person. My life's been so much better these past couple weeks, and you've done it, like it was the most natural thing in the world. But I don't want to screw up your marriage, you know?"

"You're not screwing up my marriage. My issues with Dan go way beyond jealousy. For one thing, I don't feel, um ... strong passion for him like I used to. We're like friends, I mean, good friends, living together. But I'm not sure that's enough."

"So, then," Matt proceeded carefully, "why are you getting married?"

That question broke a dam of words. "I don't know how to stop it! God, we've been planning this for the whole last year—or at least, I have. All the invitations, all the money. And my mom, she would absolutely flip out if I told her I was calling it off." Sylvia shook her head. "Flip out. Really. I mean, really."

When he was sure she was finished, Matt said, "Okay, I see what you mean, and that would be tough, but are those good enough reasons to go through with it?"

Sylvia had calmed down a little. "I know it sounds dumb, like I'm getting married just 'cause there's a wedding planned, but, you're right. It's more than that. There's Dan."

"Yeah, there's Dan."

"Don't worry. I'll figure this out. And just for the record, I think you're an amazing person, too. I've learned a lot from you, and I feel like I've only scratched the surface."

He brightened. "Thanks."

The two finished their drinks. Sylvia announced that she was tipsy and wasn't up for driving us home, so Matt and I crashed on an improvised bed in the office.

The next morning Matt slept late, but he was still the first one up. He crept quietly into the kitchen with me right behind him. When his search there produced no cereal and, even worse, no kibble, he made his way to the bedroom.

"Sylvia," he called, softly. We heard a rustling of blankets.

"Good morning," she replied, groggily. "You can come in if you want."

We went in and Matt cautiously sat on the edge of the bed. I was staying on the floor.

"Hey, you," she said, reaching out and touching him.

"Hey, you," he answered, taking her hand. He lay down next to her on the bed, his free hand cautiously tracing her figure. "You're so cute all tucked under the covers."

"Why don't you get under here with me, silly?"

He hesitated uncertainly. "Well, okay. I mean, it's nothing I wouldn't do with my own sister, right?" He took off his shoes and climbed under the covers.

"Would you do this with your sister?" She leaned into him, kissing him on the mouth. After a surprised second, he kissed her back.

"No," he said, after they had disengaged. "I definitely wouldn't do that with my sister."

"I would hope not." She playfully gave him a little push.

They both lay there, still. Finally, he asked, "So, where do you keep the cereal?"

"Matt! Stop pretending like you don't know what's going on."

"Yeah, I know." He got out from under the covers and sat up. "I probably shouldn't have come in here. I'm obviously attracted to you, Sylvia, and I love hanging out with you. But I've been trying not to get too close because of the little matter of your fiancé."

"Yeah." She sat up, too. "I can see that. This isn't easy for me, and I just wanna know where we stand."

"Well, now you know. Whadaya say we have some breakfast to celebrate our new understanding?"

My ears perked up at the word "breakfast." I didn't see why he was so hung up on the fact that Sylvia had a fiancé when she obviously liked him better. Still, I had more important things to worry about, like whether she would persuade Matt to let me have some of Kassie's dog food. He was a stickler when it came to making me eat my own food, and if I had to wait, that would bring the count to three unhappy campers.

Chapter 36

The L Word

Sylvia went to Hawaii to get married. Matt's and my lives became quiet again; although, it felt strange. And, I missed playing with Kassie, oddly enough. Yes, she was annoying, but she had grown on me. Matt, meanwhile, distracted himself with school-work, reading, and music. But, he missed Sylvia. As he strummed his guitar, I could feel his emotions bubble to the surface. He wasn't supposed to miss her. How could he miss someone who was getting married? And when she returned, they'd drift apart. Fewer trips to the dog park, fewer yoga classes, fewer dinner parties with mojitos. It was all on its way out and he had no right to object. It was for the best.

Then, she was back. She appeared at our apartment door, doggie in tow. The four of us wasted no time and set off for Frick Park. It had been a long week with no trails to roam, no smells to pursue, no Kassie running around me in crazy circles.

"So you wanna go to yoga tonight?" Sylvia asked after we had finally exhausted ourselves and were heading back to her car.

"Um . . . how about I take a rain check."

"Really? You got plans tonight?" She stopped walking.

"No, it's just . . . " Matt and I stopped, too. "I thought we wouldn't be hanging out as much now that you're married."

"Oh, come on. You don't have to skip yoga just 'cause Dan and I got married."

"Sylvia, you know I don't think it's fair to Dan."

"Fair to Dan? If you were in Hawaii and saw what a jerk he was to me all week, you wouldn't be so concerned about fair." She was getting steamed up, and we finished the walk to the car without Matt commenting. Then she continued. "Look, Matt, I know we did just get married and all, but what he did over the last week really hurt me, and I honestly don't know if I'm gonna stay married for long."

Kassie and I got into the back seat. It was even hotter inside, and my feeling of discomfort increased. Matt and Sylvia joined us in the car.

"Are you serious?" Matt asked.

"Yes, very. I just don't know where to start, you know? I mean, we have a house together, a car together, and then there's Kassie."

"Yeah, it's complicated."

And only getting more so, I thought.

The summer semester ended, and with his mother's blessing, Matt signed up to take two more psychology classes at the University of Pittsburgh during the fall semester. Since his lease had expired, she'd helped him find an efficiency apartment not far from campus, which he rented until Christmas. And she helped us move in and practice the route to the bus stop. Our tiny room had barely enough space for a bed and my dog food bowl, but I didn't mind. I'd been crate trained, after all.

Sylvia began giving us rides to campus on the days she and Matt had morning classes. On Wednesdays, they both were free at noon, and this afforded them a weekly lunch date. One Wednesday, in the middle of October, I lay under the table while the two ate lunch at their favorite Indian cafe, Bagari Hot Breads. The rich aroma of coffee and curry filled my nostrils. The diversity of eating spots in the area was great for them but not for me. I contented myself by looking for stray bits of food under the table.

"I was thinking we should take Guildenstern and Kassie back to Frick Park one of these days," Matt said in between bites of a vegetable panini. "We gotta take advantage of this great weather while we have it, you know?"

"Definitely. I can't believe November's just around the corner. I swear it'll be January soon, and you'll be running off to Brazil. You're such a bastard!"

"Hey, you act like I'm intentionally abandoning you or something. Anyway, a year goes fast. Before you know it, Gilly 'n I'll be right back here knocking at your door."

"Yeah, right. In a few months you'll probably be on some exotic beach with a piña colada, thinking, 'I had a friend once, somewhere really cold. Hmm . . . I can't quite remember her name.'"

Matt laughed. "I wouldn't forget you that easily, Syl."

Sylvia drove us back to the apartment. She didn't have another class until later that day, and Matt's next class wasn't until Thursday. I flopped down on the floor, my head cushioned on a corner of the beanbag chair. I planned to take a nice nap after my busy morning. Matt reclined on the rest of the beanbag while Sylvia sprawled out on the bed, facing him.

"So Dan's mad at me."

"Oh, yeah?"

On the verge of sleep, my ears perked up. It had been awhile since she had complained about Dan, so I was curious to hear their status. I think Matt was even more so.

"I was talking to him last night about trying to tease apart our finances a little. You know, so that if we get divorced, it'll be easier to figure out whose money is whose. He got all sulky and was like, 'You've already given up on the marriage?' But that's not totally true. I just don't wanna have a long drawn out fight in court. If it would come to that, I mean. Don't you think that's reasonable?"

Matt adjusted his position in the chair, and then answered slowly. "I don't know, Syl. I think you guys should try counseling or something before you throw in the towel."

"Yeah! I brought that up again a couple nights ago, and Dan got all defensive. He wants to pretend like we don't have a problem. But we do, and ignoring it won't make it go away."

"I hope you both can work it out."

Sylvia reached down and stroked my ears. Always hoping for more, I turned over and showed her my belly. She laughed, then scooted down on the floor next to me and gave me a slow, luxurious massage. "I don't know what I'm gonna do when you guys leave."

"Whadaya mean?"

"Who will I complain to about Dan? Who will I take to the park for a doggy date? Who will I get to do yoga?"

"I guess you'll have to find a new friend with an adorable dog."

"Ha! Maybe I'll just wait 'til the day before you leave and steal Guildenstern."

"But, I wouldn't go to Brazil without him." Matt patted my head.

"Exactly. You'd be stuck here with me." Leaning over me, Sylvia kissed him on the mouth. It was a deep, passionate kiss. I knew I would soon be forgotten.

When they finally pulled apart, I left my position between them and took up a more secure spot in the corner of the room. A floodgate had opened, and I wasn't going to stick around to get wet. The two were going at it in full force now, and clothing was beginning to come off. I averted my eyes.

Soon they found more pretexts for hanging out in our apartment. Sylvia would drop by unannounced, saying she was passing by and just wanted to say a quick hello. Often, Kassie would come in with her and herd me around the small efficiency while our owners turned a quick hello into a long good-bye. Matt took more initiative at calling Sylvia to arrange doggy dates and evenings of yoga.

After all such outings, they found themselves back at our apartment. There, a light touch became a caress, a caress led to a kiss, and then there was no turning back. After it was over, they would lay in each other's arms, reveling in the freedom their physical closeness now allowed. Pressed against each other, they gave voice to feelings that before had been improper or incredible.

One gray day in early November, in a stroke of boldness, Sylvia declared, "Matthew, I think I'm in love with you."

Matt, swept along, responded simply, "I love you, Syl."

And just like that, it became official. They weren't just friends anymore; they were lovers.

Chapter 37

Oh, Brother

I figured the shift in Matt and Sylvia's relationship would be good for everyone. Since they'd be together even more, I'd reap the reward with more dog park visits. And the loving couple would finally discharge all that pent up emotion they'd been dancing around. Unfortunately, I was wrong on both counts. My park time diminished significantly. The pair was too preoccupied playing together in Matt's bed to bother escorting Kassie and me to the park. I spent many crisp, fall afternoons waiting in vain for them to decide enough was enough.

Meanwhile, their growing emotional attachment brought even more instability. When Dan's name came up, I detected Matt's stabs of jealousy. When a day went by without a call, he fell into his mopey guitar playing. The refrain that cut clearly through his music spoke of his own self-reproach. *I've no right to feel jealous. She's married! She's married!* went the chorus. "I've Gotten Myself Into a Big Ol' Mess" could have been the title.

It wasn't easy for me to hear my human being so hard on himself. Some relief came when he put on his headphones and did his workbook exercises. Only then did peacefulness settle in. I sighed in contentment at these moments, but I wondered, too. Was this *Course* merely a meditation practice, or could it actually help him clean up his mess? I'd realized by then that his affair with Sylvia was a mistake. In my dog world, humping was a great way to relieve stress and elicit good feelings. But I was learning it didn't always work that way for people, especially when more than two were involved.

We arrived at Matt's family home the day before Thanksgiving. Matt's brother, Jeff, and his white boxer, Ghostmut, showed up the next day, earlier than Matt had predicted. This left time for the two brothers to take Ghosty and me to the park up the street. While I roamed around in the grass near them, Jeff offered Matt some weed from a small water pipe. Whether it was the effect of the drug or just being with his older brother, Matt began pouring out the events of the previous weeks. His words stumbled over one another then finally wore out.

"Yeah, boy, you gotta get away from both of them. What if Dan finds out and tries to come after you or something?"

"No, he's not like that. He's actually a good guy, and that's why this is so hard."

Jeff finished off the weed in his water pipe. It made a gurgling sound as he inhaled. "Doesn't that miracles book you're reading say anything about not having affairs? How about 'Thou shalt not commit adultery?'"

"No, it's not a list of do's and don'ts. It's more about freeing yourself from guilt and forgiving the things in life that cause you pain. It's really been helping me through all of this, to be honest."

"So it's okay to have an affair as long as you free yourself from the guilt of it."

"No, Jeff. I'm not saying that."

"Hey, I'm just playing devil's advocate."

"Yeah, well, you have a point. *A Course in Miracles* talks about truth all the time, and I realize this affair isn't exactly honest. And that really bothers me. I'm just saying that rather than torture myself about it, it's better if I accept what I did and move on."

"Okay, sure. And I just think you'd be better off not even hanging out with Sylvia for a while, at least until after she figures out her marriage."

"I know, Jeff, I know. That would be ideal. But it's not that simple. It's like me telling you you'd be better off not smoking pot and then expecting you to stop cold turkey."

"Hey, speaking of turkey, it's almost time for dinner," Jeff said. "Man, is it gonna be good!" He rubbed his hands together in anticipation.

Jeff whistled for Ghostmut, and Matt called for me to come. I had been listening to them, but I had also found an interesting bush to smell, so I pretended I didn't hear. Unfortunately, Jeff spied me, and the game was over.

"For a guide dog, he's not very obedient," Matt's older brother observed.

Nobody's perfect, I thought.

Thanksgiving became a memory, and Matt turned his attention to his final course requirements. He passed his days by slavishly pecking at his keyboard, trying to squeeze out twenty-five pages on the topic of schizophrenia, something that interested him little. In fact, he'd squirmed his way through most of the semester, enduring classes that didn't hold his attention, classes that emphasized the medical model of psychology, the diagnosis of illness, the scientific method. But Matt, I'd heard him tell Sylvia, wanted to study what was right with people, not what was wrong with them. I think he envisioned himself helping people the way Dr. Bob had helped him. But these classes in psychology had missed the mark.

He finally completed his paper and took his last test in mid-December. The semester was over. I knew it would be good for both of us to go home for Christmas to see Matt's family, to relax in that familiar, comfortable environment. We would be staying until we left the country on the first of January.

There were important things to get done before then. I needed a final vet check-up, my shots updated, and special papers to travel overseas. Matt had to put new information on my dog tags and get a fresh supply of vitamins, dog toys, and Nyla bones. Of highest priority, of course, was packing an ample supply of kibble to tide me over for our first days there. I wasn't leaving home without my kibble.

"Thanks for dinner, Mom," Matt said after finishing his last bite of stir-fry. "Would you mind if Sylvia dropped by tomorrow?"

It was the day after Christmas, and Sylvia had already called a number of times since we'd been home.

His mom looked up from the newspaper. "Sure."

"Did I tell you that she and Dan are separated now?"

"They are?" His mom was as surprised as I was.

"Yeah, as of a week or so ago."

"Where is she living?"

"Well, she's still at the house with Dan, but she's moved into the office."

"I see. Well, you realize no matter what room of the house she's sleeping in, they're still married."

"Yeah, Mom, I know," Matt said, annoyed.

Sylvia came over that evening. This time Kassie didn't come with her. Matt led her to the living room and showed her the squeaky mouse I'd gotten for Christmas. She cooed over it, then over me. I wagged my tail amiably and rolled onto my back for a belly rub.

Jeff was in the living room, too, his nose in the paper.

"So what're you up to tonight, Jeff?" Sylvia asked.

"Don't know yet. I'm trying to find a show to go to."

"Well, if nothing turns up, you can watch *Les is More* with us. Dan gave me the first season for Christmas. It has a lot of lesbians in it."

Jeff looked up. "Did you say lesbians?"

Sylvia laughed. "I thought that might get your attention. Here, take a look." She handed him the box, and he read the back. "Looks like a flesh-fest," he observed, handing it back. "I'll let you two kids go ahead."

"All right. We'll be downstairs if you change your mind." She and Matt headed to the downstairs bedroom, and I followed behind, leaving the squeaky mouse upstairs. There was no DVD player in the room, so Matt set up his laptop to watch the show.

The theme music began, an up-beat pop song with soft female vocals and a lot of bass. Sylvia sat close to Matt, her voice low in his ear as she described the characters on screen.

"That's Jennifer talking. She's the one Kim's going to have an affair with. She's got a mini-skirt on that's just like the one I'm wearing. Here, feel." She placed his hand on her leg. I saw his hand touch the hem of her short skirt. He withdrew it quickly.

"Nice."

"Yeah, I'm wearing fishnet stockings to go with it. I'll show you." She led Matt's hand back to her leg. He traced the criss-cross pattern up over her knee, where the stocking ended. His hand lingered on her exposed flesh.

Don't do it, I warned him, silently. *You're just gonna regret it.* But Matt wasn't listening.

"You don't have to stop," Sylvia said. "I'm not wearing any underwear."

He moved his fingers further up her leg, then under her skirt. I knew where this was going, and I let out a disgruntled groan.

"Do you have a condom?" she asked.

"Uh, no. Do you?"

She did, as it turned out, have one in her purse. After making sure the door was locked, she reached for him, and it was business as usual.

I buried my head in my paws and politely ignored the goings on. It occurred to me that the television program they'd been watching was not unlike his current situation. With seduction and an affair, the only thing missing was lesbians.

Chapter 38

Judgement Day

The next day Matt got up and fed me my breakfast. As I devoured my morning kibble, he moved to the kitchen and fixed himself some cereal. His mom was reading the newspaper at the kitchen table.

"Good morning," he said groggily.

"Good morning." I heard her turn a page. A minute later she folded up the paper, rinsed her dishes, and put them in the dishwasher. "Matthew, when you're done eating, I'd like to talk to you in my room."

"Uh, sure." Something was wrong, and we both knew it.

"What's up, Mom?" As requested, Matt and I had joined her in her bedroom.

She closed the door with a click before responding. "Jeff found a used condom on the floor of the downstairs bedroom last night. Do you know anything about it?" A horrible awkwardness followed. "Yeah," Matt said after a long pause, "that was mine."

"So I take it you and Sylvia had sex there last night."

I closed my eyes, embarrassed, as if I had been the culprit.

"Yeah, we did," Matt said.

Nothing like stating the obvious, I thought.

"Well, I have to say, I'm really disappointed in you."

Matt's head hung down. "I'm really sorry, Mom. It was a stupid thing to do. I just . . ." He struggled for an explanation. "It was . . . I mean, I didn't plan it. You know how you do things without think-ing, and then you're really sorry after?"

"Well, it was an awful lapse of good judgment." She paused, and then added, "By both of you."

"Mom, I know." Annoyance came through in his voice. "So Jeff found the condom and then ran to you?"

"No, actually he told Cara."

"And then Cara told you."

"Yes, and I'm glad she did. Matt, I don't approve of what you're doing. I know you say Sylvia is separated, but for better or worse, she's still married, and you and she need to respect that."

He nodded his head.

"But what really upsets me," she continued, her voice rising, "is that you violated my trust in you when I let Sylvia come over here."

"Mom," he said, getting off the bed and kneeling on the carpet. "I'm really, really, sorry, okay? I hope you can forgive me."

"Okay, Matthew, stand up. Just don't bring Sylvia over here anymore. I can't control what you two do outside this house, but I really hope you start making better choices."

"All right, Mom."

His mom moved to the door and opened it, signaling that the conversation was over. I followed him out of the room and back down the hallway, shaking myself midway to dispel some of the tension.

He called Sylvia later that morning and told her that they needed to talk. They agreed to meet that evening at Town Tavern, on the main street, a few blocks from his house. That night, we made our way through the familiar residential neighborhood, climbing the hill that led to the highway. It was cold but not snowing. The route we took was easy, and there were no mistakes. As we reached the vicinity of the bar, Matt called Sylvia's cell phone. She was there already and walked out to meet us.

180

"So, what's up?" she asked when they were seated and had gotten their drinks.

Over the blare of the jukebox, Matt explained about the condom and his talk with his mom. "The thing is, I'm done with deceiving people. I mean, obviously it really sucks that my whole family now knows that we had sex in the downstairs bedroom, but in a way, I feel relieved. And, I think I'd feel even better if you told Dan what's going on between us. I'm sick of feeling guilty about this, and I'm sick of trying to stop it and failing."

Sylvia listened. She fidgeted, obviously uncomfortable. "Matt, I know, it's been hard for both of us. But I am getting a divorce. And, anyway, how do you just tell your husband you've been cheating on him?"

"How about something like, 'Dan, I've been sleeping with Matt?' or 'Dan, Matt and I have been having an affair.' The word choice really isn't important."

She laughed, but he didn't. "Look, I'm going home unless you call Dan right now and tell him."

"Matt, please don't be mad."

"Are you calling him or not?" His voice was harsh.

"All right, I will." The jukebox was quiet now, and the beeps could be heard as she punched in the numbers on her cell phone. She switched the setting to speaker, and we heard it ring. My ears perked up to catch the words.

"Hello." It was Dan's voice.

"Dan, hey, it's me."

"Sylvia, where are you?"

"Listen, I have to tell you something." She took a deep breath, then plunged right in. "I've been sleeping with Matt."

An awful silence followed. Finally, Dan said, "Yeah, I kind of figured that."

"It's been going on for months."

"Sylvia, come home." She said nothing. Across from her, Matt said nothing. "Sylvia, where are you?" Dan asked. "Are you with Matt?"

"I'm at a bar."

"Come home, and we'll talk about it."

"I'll be there in a little while. Bye." She hung up. "Well, there you go. Happy now?"

"Let's get the check." Of all of the emotions I sensed in Matt at that moment, happiness was not one of them.

Matt and Sylvia met one last time, right before we left on our Rotary trip. His mom had agreed that they could talk in the living room to say good-bye.

"Here's a CD I made for you. It's a mix of stuff I think you'll like," Sylvia said.

Matt took the CD and gave her a hug. "Thanks, Syl."

"I'm gonna miss Guildenstern's ears most of all. They're like velvet. Do you think he would mind if I cut them off and kept them here 'til he comes back?"

"Well, I think he might. Wouldn't you, Guildenstern?"

I didn't respond. Sylvia was rubbing my belly, and I was in heaven.

A few minutes later, we walked her to her car.

"Good luck with Dan."

"Thanks. He says he's moving out as soon as he can find a place."

Sylvia and Matt said one last good-bye. Then, she drove off.

As I watched her car disappear from sight, I mused over all that the two humans had been through: the dog parks, the yoga classes, the playtime, the affection, and the guilt. I was glad that Matt had finally put his love of truthfulness ahead of everything else. It had taken strong encouragement from his mom, yes, but he had done it.

Suddenly a flash of memory brought me back to my potty-training days, back to Erin telling me "No!" for peeing in the house.

It'd happened a lot before I'd learned to hold it until I got outside. She never called me a bad dog, though. I guess she knew that no matter how many mistakes I made, I was still basically good.

I knew that was true about Matt, too. He had made his share of mistakes and would probably make many more. *A Course in Miracles* might help him forgive, but no book in the world could teach him how to be perfect. His life experience was his best guide, and I was just an adorable companion along for the adventure.

Wow, I thought, taking a long leak in the yard. *We've been through so much already, and we haven't even gotten to Brazil.*

Chapter 39

Rio, Two Kisses

Our flight departed from Pittsburgh, went on to Washington DC, made a layover in Sao Paulo, and finally brought us into Rio de Janeiro, Brazil. It was about ten hours of airplane time and twice that counting layovers and airport waiting.

For me the trip was an incredibly long and boring affair. My only entertainment consisted of listening to the exclamations of surprised passengers as they caught sight of me sprawled around Matt's ankles. Sleep was my best ally in these hours. Not only did it offer escape from the boredom of flying, but, it gave me refuge from my empty stomach. Matt, following guide dog school recommendations, hadn't fed me before our trip in order to avoid accidents during the long journey. I would have happily suffered a full bladder over an empty stomach, but the choice had been made, and there was nothing I could do but wait.

Matt, with a substantial breakfast under his belt, enjoyed the flights. His sweet smells shifted from patient relaxation to downright exhilaration. On one leg of the trip, we sat next to an elegantly dressed, perfumed woman who ordered her food in accented English.

"Are you Brazilian?" Matt asked.

"Yes, but I think of myself as part American, too. I've lived in the United States for almost twenty years."

"Oh, I see. Do you miss Brazil?"

"Yes, a lot, actually. Except for my husband, all my family still lives there, and it's really nice when I can go back." She stared out of the window for a few moments as if considering her bicultural life; she then took up the conversation. "Have you been to Brazil before?"

Matt explained about his month-long visit to Salvador, adding that he was excited to be going back.

"And you're doing this alone? You are so brave!"

"Oh, thanks, I don't know about that. I just love to travel, really. It's so fascinating to be in another country and to see all the differences. It forces me to learn new ways of doing things, and I love that. New experiences are what make life worth living, don't you think?"

The woman nodded thoughtfully. "That's true. Traveling does expand your horizons. But isn't it hard for you, I mean, because of your sight? How will you find your way on your own?"

Matt paused as if thinking how to answer. "I don't know. I guess I'll just follow Guildenstern here." He chuckled as he nudged me with his foot. The woman laughed, and the two got to talking about me—my handsomeness, of course.

I wondered about Matt's comments. He knew as well as I did that following me wouldn't get him anywhere, at least not as long as neither of us knew where the heck we were going. And yet he played it off like it was no big deal. Maybe that was easier for him than admitting the truth. He had no idea how we would do it on our own any more than the woman did! And maybe, I pondered, some part of him needed to prove that we could.

We were greeted in Rio's airport by a representative of Pontificia Universidade Catolica do Rio de Janeiro, the college where Matt would be studying for the next year. Five other international students had already arrived, and we hung out with them for another half an hour while waiting for the last few travelers.

A young man from Mexico, upon seeing Matt's two enormous suitcases, backpack, and guitar, teased him that he had packed like a girl. Matt said nothing in his own defense; though, I saw his embarrassment. He and I both knew that his mom had done most of the packing.

After all the new students had appeared, we boarded a small van headed for the city of Rio. From the floor where I lay, I wasn't able to see out the bus. But even through the closed windows, I couldn't miss the pungent odors of some of the areas we passed through. I found the smells intriguing but noticed that Matt and many of the others covered their noses.

The Columbian girl sitting next to Matt described the impoverished areas we passed. We were going to the southern zone, Zona Sul, she explained. It was the touristy area, containing the famous beaches of Ipanema and Copacabana as well as the university's campus.

We finally reached the upscale neighborhoods of the Zona Sul, and the exodus began. One by one the students were deposited at host family apartments. Tired and hungry, we waited our turn. As luck had it, ours was the last stop. Finally, the coordinator parked in front of a tall old building and got out to help Matt with his bags. The older gentleman guided us to the gate, pushed the buzzer, and conversed with the unseen doorman through the intercom. After some discussion he turned to Matt and spoke to him in slow, patient Portuguese. Matt's face lit up with comprehension and a smile. Apparently he had retained some basic language skills from his short visit to Brazil two years earlier.

Meanwhile, I furrowed my brow in consternation. I hadn't caught a single word of the strange language, and Matt was making no attempt to translate for me. I realized then that if I wanted to understand Matt when he was talking to Brazilians, I was going to have to learn Portuguese.

Looking back it seems obvious, I suppose, but at the time this realization came as a shock to me. I guess I'd just assumed I would arrive in Brazil understanding everything. And why not? Matt didn't think I comprehended his conversations in English, but I did. So, why shouldn't I be able to follow his conversations in other languages, too?

We were buzzed in through the gate but didn't go far. Matt and the coordinator sat down on the building's steps. They were waiting for something—what, I didn't know. I lay down on the pavement at Matt's feet with a heavy sigh. The tropical sun beat down around us. We were in the shade of a palm tree, but the humid climate was still oppressive.

What was really weighing on me was the thought of having to learn a whole other language. I wasn't sure I was up to it. Maybe, I thought, I could just learn important words like "dog," "dinner," and "belly rubs." That would probably be enough to get by. Matt's guide work commands would still be in English, after all.

One hour and several frustrated phone calls later, we were left in the hands of a motherly middle-aged woman who lived in the apartment building. Fortunately, she spoke English. Her Brazilian-accented Scottish brogue made her sound both foreign and familiar. As she guided us upstairs, she explained to Matt that Maria, her cousin whom we would live with, was on her way home from her weekend cottage in the country.

"She should be along shortly, dear," she said after showing him our bedroom in the apartment. "If you need anything, just pick up this phone on the wall here and ask for my apartment, two-zero-three."

Matt thanked her, and she was gone. He sat down on the bed. I could smell his exhaustion, so I had to act fast. I touched his knee ever so gently with my nose and felt his attention on me. He said nothing, but the way he got up from the bed, I knew he'd gotten the message.

A minute later he'd managed to locate a bathroom where he mixed water with my dog food. Back in the bedroom, I scarfed down my breakfast, or dinner, or whatever it was to be considered at that point in the day. My sense of time had been hopelessly skewed by the twenty hours of travel. I made my familiar *lap, lap, slurp, crunch* as I devoured the delicious meal. This little bit of normality seemed to comfort Matt, and it certainly comforted me. When I had finished, he lay on the bed and was asleep in seconds. My belly was full. I soon made myself comfortable at the foot of the bed and followed his lead.

I awoke some time later. It was incredibly hot. The air was thick and heavy with moisture. I stretched, remembering where I was. Matt was still in bed, but he lay awake and relaxed, listening to his CD player. I guessed he was doing an exercise from *A Course in Miracles*.

My ears perked at the sound of a noise from inside the apartment. A woman's voice called a loud *"Oi!"* in greeting. Matt got up and headed down the hall, and I followed.

A large, pale-skinned woman was dropping her bags in the living room. She must have weighed twice as much as Matt. Her face was red, and she was breathing heavily.

"Hola!" Matt extended his hand.

The woman laughed uproariously. *"Hola, não!* Rio—two kisses!" She came close and planted a kiss on Matt's left cheek, then his right. Her round face glistened with sweat in the tropical summer's heat, and she left two red lipstick smooches. Then she caught sight of me and gasped. *"Que fofo!"* There followed a whole string of undecipherable Portuguese words. I understood none but felt sure they were all commenting on my canine beauty. So when our new landlady knelt down in front of me, I understood what she wanted. I wagged my tail graciously in greeting and gave her my most winsome look as she began stroking my fur. I was Matt's best ambassador, and I knew how to play my role well.

Maria turned to my human. *"Qual é o nome dele?"*

Slowly, Matt said my name.

"Gueeld-stan?" she repeated.

He quickly corrected himself, giving her the shortened form.

"Gilly," she repeated after him, her Brazilian accent making my name rhyme with wheelie.

After the excitement concerning me had passed, Maria led Matt to a stool at the kitchen bar. She busied herself with the task of cooking and began clattering an assortment of pots and pans. For the next half an hour or so, Matt sat and chatted as amiably as he could with the chef-at-work. I felt his effort and subsequent strain and realized he was pushing the limits of his basic vocabulary.

Our new landlady did most of the talking. Her Portuguese was carefully enunciated for his benefit and also incredibly loud. At first I thought her voice boomed to compensate for Matt's poor language skills or perhaps his lack of vision, but I eventually came to realize that this exaggerated way of speaking was just part of her personality. Exaggerated or not, she was feeding him, and for that I was glad. He hadn't eaten all day and devoured the omelette she had made. I was sure his *"Obrigado!"* was a grateful thank you.

Maria went on feeding Matt for the next week. There were many lopsided conversations during the food preparation—she mostly talking, and, he mostly listening. I lay on the kitchen floor, inhaling the tantalizing aromas and trying desperately to understand some of the strange words leaving their lips. It was difficult, frustrating work. I didn't have a translation dictionary, and even if I had, I wouldn't have been able to read it. I was a dog. I gave up focusing on the words and let my awareness drift. I sensed Matt's confusion in his new surroundings, his discomfort with Maria's loud and unrestrained ways. The food smelled so good. I was hungry. Matt was hungry, too, I knew. I drooled a little.

"I have one brother and one sister," Matt told Maria. I blinked in surprise. Had that been English or Portuguese? With a sigh I relaxed again. I felt Matt's hunger, stronger now. The food smelled so good.

"I don't have any sisters, but I have one brother, too," Maria said. "He's a lawyer. He's married with two children. They live in Sao Paulo. Do you know where that is?"

My head shot up; my ears pricked. I had understood, just for an instant, but I had understood. I focused harder on the words, cocking my head in concentration. Gobbledygook. Rats! I'd lost it. I tried again, but it was no use. My attention wandered again to the smell of the food, then to Matt at the counter. He couldn't wait to eat.

" . . . the most populated city in Brazil. But it's not as good as Rio. There's no beach!"

"Do you like the beach?" Matt asked.

"Well, no, I never go. But Rio is much better. Sao Paulo is too big. Too much traffic! Too expensive! And they don't have Carnival! Do you know Carnival?" Maria launched into an explanation of Carnival in Rio.

I understood what she said! Not everything. But, when Matt managed to get a word or question in edgewise, I understood what he said. Only when I focused on the words did I get lost. The words, I realized, were still cryptic. Matt was the linguist here, not me. I was a dog. My specialty was in understanding him.

Over the next few days, I became better at following Portuguese conversations. How it happened, I didn't know. I just knew I could understand—not all of them, just the simple parts that Matt seemed to get. When his attention faltered or exhaustion overtook his ability to listen, I, too, got lost.

I see now that my comprehension came through him. Matt was my window into the world of Portuguese. I think it was an intuitive canine understanding coming into its own, much like with the dreams I'd had, the vivid dreams in which I became my human. I still remembered them clearly. And it was happening again, only this time I wasn't asleep.

Matt and I learned more about Maria as the days passed. She lived in the apartment with Ignacia, an older woman who was unrelated but who she treated like a mother. The apartment, she told Matt proudly, she had inherited after her father had died.

She talked about some of the other students she had hosted. Her favorite had been a German boy who spoke nearly perfect Portuguese and had taken care of her for several weeks when she had fallen ill. Her least favorite had been a student from Puerto Rico. He was filthy. He had raised his voice at her—here she screamed at the top of her lungs to demonstrate. Once, she said in a voice shaking with righteous condemnation, she had smelled the scent of drugs coming from inside his room. She'd confronted him, and they'd had a huge argument.

Maria began to fear him. She became so terrified that he would do her bodily harm that she had locked the doors one day and hadn't let him back in the apartment until he had promised not to do drugs there anymore. Shortly after that he moved out.

"And thank God," she concluded. "He was a terrible person—a terrible, terrible person. I hope things will be better between us."

Matt assured her that they would be, that she had nothing to worry about, that he wasn't going to do drugs in his room. I realized, however, that drugs or not, he would have to be careful to keep on Maria's good side. She saw the world in black and white, and he didn't want to get put into the wrong category.

Chapter 40

An Education in Determination

Matt wasn't the only student staying with Maria. Philip, a Spanish-speaking, first-generation Cuban from Miami, occupied the room next door to ours. He was rarely ever home, however. He had come to Rio with two other friends from Miami on his school's study abroad program, and he spent almost all of his time with them. While the three young men were there for a semester of studying, their real goal was to party.

During that first week, Matt accepted their invitations to join in on their nightly excursions. I went along too, of course. Although I sensed that my human appreciated their efforts to include us, he established no strong connection with them. Each evening they ventured out to a neighborhood bar or dance club. There were dozens to pick from. But they were smoky, noisy places, and Matt's confusion and discomfort was evident. Verbal communication was reduced to the occasional shout. I could see his isolation and feel his vulnerability. It was no surprise when he started passing on Philip's nightlife invitations.

One morning Matt woke up much earlier than usual. Philip was up, too—I could smell his cologne from the bathroom. I sensed we were going somewhere.

"You looking forward to classes, Matt?" Philip's question came around the mouthful of food he was chewing.

I realized then that this must be the first day of their intensive language classes I had heard them talking about. Across from him at the breakfast table, Matt was smearing jam onto his bread. I watched as the excess fell to the tablecloth. I rooted for some to reach the floor.

"Definitely!" Matt's enthusiasm was genuine, I could tell.

"You need me to go with you, or are you cool?" Philip downed the last of his coffee.

"Uh . . ." Matt stiffened. "Well, what time are you leaving?"

"Just gonna brush my teeth, and then I'm outta here. I'll wait for you if you want, though."

"Okay, yeah, I'm just finishing up here."

Outside in the street, I sniffed for the right spot to make my morning mark on the world. Philip shifted from one foot to the other.

"Come on, Gilly, do your business!" Matt tugged on my leash, and then turned his head toward Philip. "You can go ahead if you want."

"No, it's fine. Anyway, I think he's done."

No, I'm not, I thought, but we went anyway, half walking, half jogging down the streets, finally stopping at a bus stop.

Philip looked at a wrinkled pamphlet in his hand. "The packet from school says any bus marked PUC will take us to campus. Sweet! Here comes one right now. Get ready."

The huge vehicle skidded to a stop, and we rushed to board. Philip went up the steps first, Matt behind him, and I brought up the rear.

The driver caught sight of me and began shouting. *"Não pode ter cachorro no ônibus!"*

Philip stammered something in response, and the driver only shouted louder as he motioned us away. The bus took off in a cloud of exhaust, leaving the three of us standing on the sidewalk.

"Dude, your dog's not allowed on the bus."

"That's not true!" Matt's body was tense and his face flushed. "There's a law here, a federal law. The school told me about it. I don't know what that guy was thinking."

We stood in awkward silence.

"Shit, what time is it?" Philip checked his watch, answering his own question. "Maybe we should take a taxi or something."

"No, man, that's not fair! Let me just—"

"Wait, here comes another bus. It says PUC."

We boarded the new bus successfully; the driver offered only a casual glance in my direction. I lay down at Matt's feet with a *humph.*

Maybe this guy has a Lab, I thought.

Once he'd calmed down, Matt explained to Philip that Brazil had passed a federal law just a few years earlier. It granted guide dogs access to all transportation for collective use, both public and private. This was a fancy way of saying that I was allowed on the bus, the same as anyone else.

"Yeah, then someone needs to tell that other bus driver," Philip said.

But, as we discovered in the following days, that other bus driver wasn't the only one who didn't know about the law. Again and again, we were told to get off the bus.

"Não posso levar nenhum animal!" The driver was emphatic. This was our second rebuff of the morning a few days later, and we were going to be late for our classes. Philip, one foot into the bus stairwell, sputtered out an angry string of protests in a mix of Spanish and Portuguese, and then he backed off.

"Let me get on the bus first," Matt said in a calming voice. "Maybe if they see me with Gilly, they'll understand."

The next bus came, and Philip guided us to the steps. I followed Matt on, and Philip stood in the doorway behind us.

"Cachorro no pode entrar." The bus driver only glanced at Matt. I was his target.

"Yes, he can get on," Matt said in his clearest Portuguese. "He's a guide dog."

"Sorry," the man said. "I think there's a special bus that can take you."

Matt didn't move. Philip had joined us on the platform next to the driver and spoke up in a firm voice, "He's a guide dog."

An old woman sitting in a front seat took up the cause. "It's true. Guide dogs can go anywhere!"

As if she had broken the ice, other passengers began chiming in, calling loudly to be heard over the buzz we were creating.

"It's a guide dog!"

"It's the law!"

With that, the driver waved us on. Matt and Philip sat down, and I sat in front of them on the floor. Matt reached down and gave me a victory squeeze. I licked my lips contentedly as the bus lurched on towards the campus. Personally, I couldn't understand why these drivers were so slow in recognizing my Labrador appeal.

This breakthrough became a strategy that the two humans used. When boarding a bus from then on, Matt and I went first. The driver didn't have time to react before we were standing right next to him. If he protested, he usually directed it at Philip, who followed us. By then, however, the three of us were already on board. He could only shut the door behind us, not in our faces. And if he persisted, even after Matt explained our rights, the other passengers came to our aid. Their support would crescendo in a volley of protests and exclamations. I felt like a rock star! I wondered how many bus rides we would need to take before all the drivers had completed our little training program.

As happy as I was to be successfully boarding buses with Matt, I really didn't like the rides. They were rough and bumpy. The city's rush hour was intense and stressful, and the drivers alternated between slamming on their brakes and jerking into full gear. Over and over, I found myself propelled across the floor. I clawed in vain at slick surfaces, my toenails clicking as I frantically scrambled to gain traction.

One day, the bus stopped so suddenly that I skidded away from Matt and fell halfway down the steps leading out the back door.

"God, Gilly, are you okay? I'm so sorry, boy! Come on up here," he said, patting the seat next to him.

It's about time you got the message, I thought. Not needing a second invitation, I was up in a flash. Now I was riding high!

Matt began regularly inviting me up onto the seat next to him where I would lay sprawled across his lap—and one or two other seats. He did this cautiously at first. I think he was wary of being reprimanded. But, no complaints came. The buses were hardly ever full, so I wasn't taking anyone's space. I only attracted more coos and gushes than ever. The only thing cuter than a dog on the bus, it turned out, was a dog on the bus flopped over his human's lap and the adjacent seats. With some smugness, I remembered guide dog training. All that sitting up straight at Matt's feet was proving to be an obsolete skill, just as I'd suspected all along.

Because of Matt's Spanish background, he placed into level three of the five levels of Portuguese language classes at the university. He was always in a good mood at school. I observed his constant expression of interest and concentration during class and knew he was totally engaged. He hung on the teacher's every word, even though he may not have always understood it.

I was glad to see him so stimulated. I knew that decoding the cryptic language, which he described to one of his classmates as "Spanish on crack," would ultimately make or break his experience in Brazil. He spent long stretches in his room studying. His computer read the Portuguese in a tinny, electronic voice. He scrolled through the text word by word, sometimes letter by letter, to decipher the meaning. It was a time-consuming process. An hour would crawl by as he labored through a few paragraphs, pausing periodically to use online translating sites.

I had to bear the boredom of these study sessions. Sometimes I escaped into sleep with dreams that were much more appealing, but sometimes I found my ears absorbing the words spewing from the computer. In spite of myself, I learned more Portuguese. My vocabulary went beyond my personal favorites of "breakfast" and "dog food" into other, more human realms. I was becoming semi-bilingual.

On his first Portuguese exam, Matt received a 3.8 out of 10. I saw his teacher shake her head as she told him the results. She was obviously worried that he wouldn't pass the class. But, by the end of a month of intensive study, he had proven her misgivings to be unfounded. He passed with a 6.6 out of 10. It was hardly a stellar mark, but on his last essay, he received a 9.1. His writing and reading had improved dramatically. I was proud of his progress and knew first hand that it was the fruit of his hard work rather than any innate talent he had for languages.

School had become Matt's main focus as well as his only social outlet. When the month of intensive Portuguese classes ended, he faced a problem. Six weeks of vacation time now stood between him and the start of the regular semester in March. Philip had his crew of friends from Miami, and Matt had only the company of his landlady and her mother.

Maria continued to cook for him in exchange for double rent payments. While he enjoyed her food, her company began to weigh on him. I saw this first hand. On a good day, he would listen patiently and laugh at her ability to string stories together without so much as a breath in between. But there were bad days when he became impatient and irritated. He still couldn't understand everything she said, and it took great effort to follow her monologues. Finally, he would retreat to the safety of our bedroom.

The two of us spent more and more time alone. He gave me belly rubs and scratched my ears, and I gave him the solace of my companionship. He also found relief in *A Course in Miracles* as he faithfully continued the exercises. And it was during this time that he discovered another source of stability. He began practicing yoga again. Without an instructor or classmates, without even a yoga mat, he went through the movements on the floor near his bed. I recognized the well-learned positions from the classes with Sylvia. Apparently, he'd remembered them, too.

I felt his tension melt during the slow, methodical acrobatics. Afterward, he would play guitar, composing happy, hopeful music. He even wrote a song of gratitude about Maria. In such lucid moments, he saw clearly that she wasn't the cause of his suffering. She was just a fellow traveler.

I was impressed with my human. I saw him using all the tools he had available to keep himself in good spirits during tough times. He was proving to himself that we really could make it on our own in a foreign country. And yet, I saw it was a lonely life we were leading and that no matter how much study or music or yoga he did, connection with others would make our trip more rich and alive. I wondered how we were going to find it.

Chapter 41

Carnival

C arnival week, the last week in February, arrived. I listened as
Philip talked excitedly about it to Matt.

"The whole city like stops working, dude. There's these huge
competitions between samba schools to see who can put on the best
desfiles. They're like parades with dancers and shit. But, you gotta
buy tickets to get in and see them, and they're expensive. I'm going
to the *blocos* instead. That's basically the same thing except the
parades are in the streets. There's no tickets or nothing."

Matt listened with interest. I could smell his curiosity and knew
he wanted to experience one of these blocos for himself. But he said
nothing to Philip. Maybe he was self-conscious about inviting
himself along. Or maybe he was wary of hitching a ride on a run-
away train. I'd already seen that the Miami student's penchant for
partying far outlasted my human's. True to form, once Carnival
started, Philip disappeared for twenty-four hour segments at a time.
At one point, he arrived back at the apartment and reported he'd
gotten so drunk and exhausted that he'd passed out on the sidewalk
only to wake up the next day in time for another block party.

Meanwhile, Maria's sixteen-year-old niece, Tatiana, was visiting
from the countryside, and Maria, drawn by the reckless excitement,
decided that they would go to a block party on one of the last days of
Carnival. As Matt and I lounged in the living room, I could hear the
two females in the bedroom, laughing and exclaiming over the
effects of their costumes and outlandish make-up.

"Does Matt want to go?" Tatiana asked.

"I don't know," Maria replied.

After some discussion, Tatiana came into the living room. She really did look different, wearing a fancy dress and headpiece covered in sparkles with lots of unusual colors on her eyes and mouth. "Hey, Maria and I are going to a block party. Wanna come?" Without hesitation Matt said, "Well, sure."

Maria came into the room then. "You're going to have to stay with me," she bellowed. "Carnival is very dangerous."

Matt winced and then forced a smile and an assent.

"And where's your costume?" she asked in shock, as if he were sitting naked in front of her. "You can't go to a block party without a costume!" She marched over and took Matt's hand and placed it on her head. Sure enough, I saw him feel the thick curls of her wig and the bandana wrapped around her forehead. "Matt, I have something for you to wear!" Before Matt knew it, Tatiana had looped three large, gaudy necklaces around his neck. "There, now you're ready." Giggling, she added, "What about a costume for Gilly?"

I shuddered at this idea.

"We can say he's really a person wearing a dog costume," Matt said.

I appreciated his effort to spare me humiliation; however, I wasn't even sure I wanted to go at all. Why stress in the crowds when I could enjoy a peaceful nap at home. Of course, no one asked my opinion, and Matt took me along. I consoled myself by observing that I was the only one *not* looking ridiculous. At the bus stop, Maria signaled the first bus she saw. The huge exhaust-spewing vehicle careened to a stop and opened the door.

"Wait!" The driver hollered as Maria led Matt up the steps. "Dogs aren't allowed on here."

There was the usual commotion as Maria and other passengers protested that I was a guide dog. Finally getting the picture, the driver relented. Pointing at Matt, he said, "I thought he was dressed up like Jatoba."

After a hearty chortle, Maria explained that Jatoba was a character in a Brazilian soap opera that had aired the year before. He was blind, had a guide dog, and even looked a little like Matt. I remembered, then, hearing the name shouted out as we'd walked the city streets. Apparently, this wasn't the first time we'd been mistaken for the TV stars.

Fitting, I thought.

Some thirty minutes later, we arrived at the block party where the action was well underway. Partygoers were packed on the sidewalks and overflowed into the street. They wore exotic outfits, like nothing I'd ever seen before. A makeshift band of drummers pounded out a marching beat, and a chorus of voices belted out a song that I only partly understood. It seemed to be about a young man who fell in love at a block party only to find out that the girl of his fancy was really a guy.

Tatiana soon left us in search of a particular young man who she had arranged to meet. I busied myself with trying to get my mouth on some delicious-smelling Carnival trash. With a quick jerk, I managed to snatch a chicken bone from the sidewalk, but then Maria caught on and told Matt. Without her niece to supervise, her attentions had focused in our direction.

"Everyone's wearing costumes," she said to Matt. "There's a pretty girl dressed like a fairy right in front of you. I think she likes Gilly. Talk to her!"

Matt seemed to have no idea what to say to the fairy. As it turned out, he didn't have to say anything. The girl was evidently entranced with me, in spite of my lack of finery.

But Maria had decided that Matt needed to be involved. "Feel her costume." She grabbed his hand and put it on the girl's waist.

Matt trailed his fingers down several inches and made a polite comment about how pretty it was. He was obviously embarrassed.

Maria wasn't satisfied yet. "Feel the skirt," she told Matt.

He did. It was made of some stiff, puffy fabric. Suddenly, Maria began laughing uproariously. I saw that Matt had his hand on the girl's thigh, just where the tiny skirt ended. He pulled away as if burned, his face flushing red while Maria laughed with the fairy.

I seized the moment of distraction to snag a half-eaten cheese stick from the ground. This time Maria didn't notice.

Why not? I thought, savoring the smokey flavor. Even if Matt wasn't enjoying himself, that didn't mean I couldn't have a little fun.

Later, Matt and I wound up back in our bedroom. He lay on the bed, exhausted. I lay on the floor, wishing that he'd make room for me on the bed. It was small, yes, but he'd been known to make exceptions.

No such luck. After a while, Matt roused himself, picked up his guitar, and began to play. Through the music I felt his fatigue and, beneath that, a growing frustration. He didn't like life as a border under our current roof. He wanted his own place or, even better, an apartment with friends. He wanted independence.

At the same time, he was scared to go exploring on his own. He cursed himself for not going to Carnival alone. He hated having to rely on people like Maria for help. And the worst thing was that, when he finally did get to talk to someone, the noise and confusion, Maria's interference, and that stupid fairy skirt had made it impossible to form any real connection. He felt trapped. Isolated.

I saw then that I wasn't alone in wanting something more for Matt's and my life here in Brazil. Matt felt something was missing, too. He was starved for connection. Like me, he was a social animal, and he needed the sustenance of meaningful social interactions. But, he wanted to eat on his own terms, not at the obnoxious urging of his landlady.

I sighed. I understood my human's predicament and empathized with his feelings of isolation. On the other hand, I just knew better times lay ahead for us during our stay in Brazil. How did I know? Maybe it was canine intuition. Or, maybe it was simple trust in Matt's capacity to thrive. Whatever it was, I felt sure we were on our way to more satisfying experiences.

In the meantime, I thought, he could improve the current situation by letting me up on the bed. *Don't I count for meaningful social interaction?*

Chapter 42

Go with God

Matt was up early. I smelled excitement on him and decided it was a good sign. A morning walk? A special breakfast? Then, I watched him put his laptop in his backpack, and I remembered. Today we started classes.

In the dining room, Matt fixed his cereal and juice and I ate my breakfast—a regular one. Philip was absent, but I noticed a banana peel and empty coffee cup at his place. He must have eaten and left before us. That meant we were going to school by ourselves.

The late summer sun blazed down as we set out for the university. It would be another hot and sultry day. I smelled Matt's nervousness and knew that walking this route without Philip was intimidating. All our first independent forays were. But, I counted on Matt's fierce desire for this next step in our Brazil adventure to spur him on.

We completed the first two blocks downhill without any problems; although, Matt was already beginning to sweat, and I was panting heavily in the tropical heat. I stopped at the edge of the highway, cars whizzing and buses rumbling in front of us. Matt waited for a break in the traffic for what seemed like forever, but no luck. When the highway traffic did ease up, the cars from the street to our right cut in front of us, turning left. I envisioned us standing there until dark, after everyone had finally gone home. Then, a stocky middle-aged man was next to us, his hand on Matt's shoulder.

"Hey, you can't cross here," he said in loud Portuguese. Matt was startled by the stranger's touch.

"You can't?" he asked, collecting himself.

"No, you have to go over there."

"Over where?"

"Come with me. I'll take you."

Matt reached out gratefully for the man's elbow, but the man grabbed his hand and placed it firmly atop his shoulder.

"I know how you guys do it. Just like Jatoba." So with Matt's arm on his shoulder, he led us across the side street. When we reached the other side, I expected the man to go on his way, leaving us to cross the busy thoroughfare by ourselves. Instead, he said, "Come on with me. This highway's really dangerous."

"Thanks." Matt sounded as surprised as I was at the stranger's helpfulness.

After he had escorted us across the two lanes, our good samaritan turned to face Matt. "Are you okay from here?"

"Sure, thanks so much." Matt sounded confident, but I knew it was a front. He had only a vague idea where the bus stop was, but he was embarrassed to accept more help. The two said goodbye, and we turned right, in the direction of the stop.

From that chance meeting, Matt had learned two things. First, the best place to cross the highway was on the right side of the intersecting street. And second, unlike in the United States, blind people in Brazil held their guides on their shoulders rather than their elbows. I had noticed already that in Brazil the bubble of personal space was much smaller and more permeable than what we were used to. The man who had just helped us had grabbed Matt's shoulder before even saying hello. All this was valuable information for Matt, but it didn't tell him where the bus stop was. So after walking several blocks, he told me to halt.

"Excuse me," he called out to the footsteps passing by.

Immediately, a female voice responded. "Yes?" When Matt asked about the bus stop, she answered readily. "It's further up ahead. Do you want me to take you there?"

"Uh, yes, please." He reached out tentatively and found the woman's shoulder, which he gingerly held as we walked the next block and a half. Apparently, my human liked the new holding technique. Following behind him, I could see how it was different from holding someone's elbow. It allowed him to get closer to his guide, to get a better sense of the person's center of gravity.

"Which bus are you catching?" she asked when we had arrived.

Matt told her the four-three-five.

The woman checked with several others who were waiting to confirm that our bus stopped there. "I'll wait and tell you when your bus comes."

Matt looked confused. He turned his head in the direction of the chattering people and I knew what he was wondering. Wouldn't it be easier for her to leave us with one of the others so that she could be on her way?

"Don't worry," she said, seeing his face. *"Não custa nada."* It costs nothing.

I caught the sweet wash of appreciation that flowed through Matt as he thanked her. Não custa nada. We would hear this repeated countless more times from helpful strangers while we lived in Brazil.

Our bus came, and the woman guided Matt to the door. *"Vai com Deus,"* she said as we climbed through the back door.

Go with God? I thought, curiously, climbing up onto the seat next to Matt. Only later did I realize that this was a common way to say good-bye. I mulled over our experiences as the bus lurched away. I had a warm sensation in my stomach, almost as satisfying as a belly rub.

Finding our way around the university campus proved even easier than finding the bus stop. Students were everywhere, and many of them were curious about the gringo with the cute dog. All Matt had to do when we got lost was stop and look confused for about five seconds. It took only that long for someone to come to our rescue.

Our visibility only increased. One day a student named Gustavo introduced himself to Matt while we were waiting in the photocopy center. He said he worked for the campus radio station and wanted to interview Matt for one of the broadcasts. When Matt agreed, Gustavo pulled out a recorder and microphone right then and there. After the formality of asking Matt where he was from and why he had come to Brazil, the interviewer cut to the chase.

"What's your dog's name? . . . How old is he? . . . What's his breed? . . . Does he like Brazil?" And so it went for the next fifteen minutes until Gustavo finished the interview, thanked Matt, and went on his way. At that point, I don't think Matt minded yielding me the limelight. He understood that I was the charismatic member of our duo.

The campus newspaper soon tracked us down in a similar fashion. This time the questions were more obviously weighted towards me. After eating lunch with the newspaper reporter, Matt was asked about my favorite food, what I liked to do for fun, and whether or not I had developed any canine relationships, platonic or romantic, during our stay in Brazil.

This time Matt answered a bit less enthusiastically. I'm guessing he would have rather talked with the young female reporter about human platonic or romantic connections, with her as a candidate. Instead, he forced a smile and explained that my favorite food was whatever remotely edible substance I managed to get into my mouth and that I liked playing with the soft, squeaky dog toys that were frowned upon and deemed unsafe by the guide dog school. As for my canine relationships, he said that I had met many four-legged Brazilians in the streets of Rio.

"But I don't think he has a girlfriend. He's a dog. He just likes to sniff butts."

This wasn't exactly true. Some butts I liked to sniff more than others, but I didn't protest. I knew Matt was just jealous that I had the spotlight.

A media blitz was fast snowballing around the irresistible image of my gently swaying, slightly overweight form as I half-led, half-followed Matt to and from his classes. The campus radio and campus newspaper were succeeded logically enough by the campus television station. By then I had realized that Matt was getting tired of all the exposure and was just a little jealous that all the attention focused on me.

Come on! It's television! So what if the channel is only campus-wide?

How could Matt, in good conscience, deny the collegiate crowds my adorable face? To my satisfaction, he accepted, though I suspected it was more to practice his Portuguese with a wider audience.

The interview began smoothly enough. They shot some video of Matt sitting on a bench in a scenic area, answering some now very familiar questions. But then the director, a film student in her last year, decided to get some action footage. We were in an unfamiliar area, on an unfamiliar path, and when we attempted to show off my guiding skills, Matt and I were hopelessly out of sync.

"I think he's confused because we don't normally go this way," Matt explained to the director, but I knew this wasn't the image of competence he'd wanted to display.

When the cameraman commented, "He seems to like flowers," he unwittingly made things worse. I had found some exotic sprouts in the grass, and while they tasted slightly bitter, they still made a nice snack.

"Gilly, no!"

"Okay, guys. I think we got enough."

The director thanked us. Neither Matt nor I ever saw the results of that interview. But, maybe it was just as well. I sensed Matt's displeasure with the whole celebrity thing. He wanted more than a five-minute interview or a ten-minute video shoot. He wanted to connect with people in ways that went beyond talking about me.

Then, a week or so after our video, an unfamiliar student stopped us on campus. He introduced himself as Eduardo and asked all the usual questions about me. He explained that he was working on a sociology assignment at Benjamin Constant Institute, the school for the blind in Rio. Was Matt interested in joining him there for a visit?

Matt, probably curious, was interested. A few days later, we took a bus with Eduardo. On the way, I listened as he filled in Matt on what he knew about the school. There were programs for children, as to be expected. But there were also classes for adults that focused on practical skills. Eduardo said those included basket-making, pottery, and braille literacy. Matt didn't seem impressed with the class options for adults.

"Since when is basket-weaving a practical skill? Just because people are blind, they wanna weave baskets? Personally, I hate arts and crafts."

Eduardo laughed. "Okay, I see your point, but the braille classes are practical, right?"

"I guess so."

Lying on the seat next to him, I couldn't help but smile to myself. I knew my human had no interest in improving his meager braille skills. But he might have enjoyed a pottery class. I could use a couple new dog dishes.

When we arrived at the huge, impressive-looking building that was Benjamin Constant, Eduardo showed us around and introduced Matt to Ms. Ferreira, the teacher he worked with. I was delighted to see the little kids in her classroom, and they were fascinated by me, of course. But I could tell Matt didn't think there was anything here for him—until we were about to leave. It was then that I heard it. A guitar. I was an expert at recognizing this particular instrument. But it was producing music that was more intricate and quite different from what Matt played. And he heard it, too, because he stopped in his tracks and asked Eduardo to follow the sound.

We made our way to a closed classroom door where Matt stood for a few moments, clearly mesmerized. When the music stopped, he knocked on the door. I couldn't believe how forward he was being, with no misgivings about interrupting a lesson. It seemed he was possessed by the music.

Inside, a teacher was giving a guitar lesson to several young children. Matt apologized for interrupting and introduced himself as a student from the United States. He said he loved Brazilian music and, since arriving, had been looking for someone who could teach him bossa nova and other popular styles. The teacher good-naturedly gave him his phone number and instructions for contacting him at home.

That evening Matt spoke to Ronaldo, the guitar teacher. They arranged for Matt and me to meet him at his house the following Tuesday night. He lived not far from the school, a half-hour bus ride.

Exactly one week later, we arrived at Ronaldo's, having been guided by the kindness of strangers, smoothly and safely.

"You made it!" Our new friend ushered us into his apartment. "And you brought your guitar all the way here! You're really a warrior."

He introduced us to his wife, who was about to give their infant daughter a bath. She said hello and then excused herself. Ronaldo led us to a back bedroom, where he sat down across from Matt with his guitar. Thus began the first of the most challenging but satisfying music lessons I ever saw Matt take. In addition to learning the complex chords and distinctive rhythms of Brazilian popular music, he learned to sing in Portuguese. Ronaldo was a patient, supportive teacher who took to driving us home in his car.

During that first meeting, Matt asked the cost of the lessons. I think he was prepared to pay any price.

"Nothing," Ronaldo said.

"No, really. Do you want to charge by class or by month?"

"I'm not going to charge you. I'll consider these classes as part of my volunteer work at Benjamin Constant."

Matt was speechless for a minute. He then explained that he would take the money from his scholarship funds.

"Well, we can put a price on the lessons if you want. But for me this won't be a job. It's a favor I can do for someone else."

At that, Matt was silent for a minute. "Thank you," he finally managed.

Under Ronaldo's tutoring, Matt's first endeavor, naturally enough, was "The Girl from Ipanema." Learning this iconic song marked the beginning of their many hours spent playing music, many hours of shared enjoyment.

In time, the two began composing together. Ronaldo played chord progressions and melodies he had written, and Matt added the lyrics in English. They recorded in the teacher's studio, and a handful of strikingly beautiful songs, the fruits of their rich relationship, resulted. The trip to the school for the blind had proven more rewarding than Matt had ever imagined, I decided.

No basket weaving needed.

Chapter 43

A New Home

At the beginning of the new school semester, Matt had signed up at the foreign students' office to be notified of available housing. He soon began receiving e-mails, and I smelled his excitement as he listened to the messages on his computer. The places to rent tended to be rooms in large apartments shared by students, and they were all in nice neighborhoods, relatively close to campus.

One afternoon, after checking the newest listings, he called and set up a visit. The apartment was in Ipanema, on Barao da Torre, a street we'd never been to before. I knew it would be a challenge for us to find this place, but Matt was ecstatic. The possibility of a new home with other students was a godsend, and he was just too excited to stress over the details.

That Thursday we walked the usual route to the highway. A man smelling strongly of poodle helped us onto a bus heading for Ipanema. Once on board, we sat near a woman who was even more awash in the scent of dogs. She chatted happily, telling us all about her five German shepherds. To Matt's great relief, she also told us when to get off the bus.

As the bus pulled away, we found ourselves on the sidewalk near a large plaza. My nose twitched with the smell of fresh fruit and fish, and I heard the competing cries of vendors. Matt continued to stand in his original spot, taking in the sounds. I think he was listening for someone whom he could ask for directions, but no one came. Finally, he urged me across the street in the direction of the voices.

As we entered the large open area of the plaza, I began sniffing the ground ravenously. It was a clear violation of guide dog protocol, but I just couldn't help myself. Delicious-looking tidbits of food littered the ground—remnants of ripe mangos, papaya, and even some fruits I'd never seen before.

"Your dog has a banana in his mouth."

I eyed the man who had just blown the whistle on me. Matt, after correcting me, seized the chance to ask about Barao da Torre. With Brazilian courtesy, the stranger offered to take us the last several blocks.

Soon we were in the lobby of a large building. A porter came up to us and Matt explained that we had come to see Gabriel in Penthouse 2. The man called upstairs, and in a minute a curly-haired young man with olive skin was shaking Matt's hand.

"You came here alone?" he asked in Portuguese, guiding us up the steps to the penthouse.

"Yeah. Well, sort of."

"*Caramba,* man!"

Once inside the apartment, Matt took off my harness and leash. While Gabriel showed him the small living room and modest kitchen, I did my own exploring, looking for edibles. The previous treats had been scrumptious, but they were already a distant memory at this point. I made my way out an open door onto an enormous patio lined with plants. The sun shone dowwn warmly as I sniffed happily around the perimeter. It was without question the largest open area in an apartment I'd ever seen. There was even a grill. Judging by its smell, it hadn't been cleaned in a long time.

Gabriel and Matt soon joined me. "The inside rooms aren't very big, but the veranda is what really sells this place."

"Cool!"

Gabriel continued like a proud parent. "Yeah, wait'll you see how big it is. Here, here's one end of it." He led Matt to the half-wall, half-fence that surrounded the porch. "Go ahead and walk to the other end. There's nothing in your way."

Matt began walking. He took five, then ten, then twenty paces and kept going. Finally, after forty paces he had found the plants on the far side.

"You weren't kidding. This is huge!" he hollered to Gabriel down the length of the enormous porch.

"So what do you think?" Gabriel had walked down to stand next to Matt.

"It's awesome! You could play sports out here."

"We do." Gabriel laughed. "But it's good for parties, too."

The two students discovered they both had eleven o'clock classes, so Matt cut my sunbathing short, and the three of us caught a bus near the plaza. On the way to the university, they discussed getting Internet access and a cleaning person for the apartment. Gabriel admitted that the current roommates, all guys, weren't much for cleaning, but they had talked about it. It wasn't very expensive to pay for this kind of service in Brazil, he explained.

We reached the school, and Gabriel walked with us to our building. As the two parted, they agreed to talk again on Saturday.

"Hey man, even if you don't move in, you're still welcome to come over for a barbecue."

Matt thanked him gratefully. He was practically floating as we climbed the steps and went inside.

We did move in, of course. The next day after classes, I watched Matt stuff everything he owned into his two suitcases. I positioned myself in between them and his guitar, my head resting on one of the case straps. I had no intention of being left behind. On the way out of the apartment, Matt paused, and then turned back. He slowly moved to the divider which separated Maria's section of the apartment from his and pushed it open a crack. The room was dark, lit only by the flickering light of the TV. Along with the sounds from the set, I heard Maria's even snores.

"Tchau," Matt said softly. As we left for the last time, I felt strange and a little sad that we weren't giving Maria a real good-bye.

And so began a new chapter in our life in Brazil. Overnight, we went from unwelcome borders to fun-loving bachelors in a penthouse about four blocks from one of Ipanema's famous beaches. It was a dramatic improvement for both Matt and me. Gabriel helped us learn our new neighborhood. He showed Matt how to get to the beach, the bus stops, and, best of all, a sandwich and juice bar called Big Nectar. It was just a block from the apartment and became a source of cheap and easy meals for my human in the months ahead. It was also a great place for me to lick the floor, which I did any chance I could get. It wasn't long before I was veering there of my own accord. Matt sometimes got mad when he unexpectedly found himself at the outdoor cafe, but it was just so hard for me to resist.

At the apartment, Matt's Danish roommate, August, helped him get his computer connected to the network. Matt was thrilled since this Internet connection was much faster than the one at Maria's, and now he could talk to his family over Skype.

I was thrilled with August, too, but for other reasons. He cooked meat on the grill almost every night and had no qualms about sharing. But he was careful not to get either of us in trouble. When bits of steak fell from the grill, rather frequently, I gobbled up the tasty morsels. I loved Matt's generous friends.

August was a character in every sense of the word. His unabashed goal was to get laid in Brazil by as many women as possible. He went out to a different bar or club almost every night in search of new conquests. He wasn't always successful, but he was persistent. On the nights his outings proved unfruitful, he called one of the backups he referred to as his "pretend girlfriends."

Matt struck up conversations with these ladies when they came over to visit. I think he initially felt sorry for them, seeing them as victims of his flatmate's voracious appetite. But after a while he probably realized that they were only getting what they were willing to put up with: a "pretend boyfriend."

Nor was August always on the giving end of the promiscuous stick. One afternoon he told Matt gleefully that he had lined up three dates in a row for the coming evening. He would see Cristina at four for an early movie; Erin was on for dinner at seven; and to finish the night, Sandra had promised to come by for a visit around ten or so. In Brazilian time, that meant she might drop in sometime before midnight.

As the hours ticked by, Matt and I watched August's first date and then his second, turn to no-shows. One sent a last-minute text message offering an excuse. The other didn't bother to explain. By then our ladies' man was so frustrated that he decided to go out to the bar rather than wait around for date number three.

"If Sandra comes by, tell her I'm at Shannigans." But she never did.

Gabriel was a fun-loving soul, too, and took on the job of organizing parties at our apartment almost every weekend. He manned the grill on those occasions and cooked up food for the dozens of international students who flooded the enormous patio. Matt and the other housemates had fun drinking fruity-smelling cocktails from the blender and flirting with the female students.

I loved the parties. Drunk people, I discovered, were much more likely to drop food, either by accident or in response to a little soulful eye contact on my part. Over the months, the parties grew in size and intensity. Finally, at the end of the semester, Gabriel decided to throw himself the biggest send-off the apartment had ever seen.

The ideal number of students that could fit on the patio was somewhere between forty and sixty, depending on who you asked. However, word of mouth and mass texting meant that party attendance had a way of mushrooming out of control. Attendance at the previous two parties had topped a hundred people before Gabriel, whose name was on the lease, had finally called down to the porter and begged him to halt the stream of newcomers.

But on that last night, the Mexican student abdicated any shred of responsibility for the place he would soon be leaving. No one called down to the porter. Instead, everyone drank. Matt watched in a mixture of amusement, and then, horror, as the apartment became first cramped, then packed, and finally suffocatingly stuffed with Brazilians and gringos in various stages of intoxication. Undeterred by the mayhem, I dodged around legs and crawled over feet to scarf as much food as I could manage.

Eventually, Matt did the only sensible thing. He located me amidst the confusion, and we abandoned the chaos for refuge at Big Nectar. Matt ordered his usual: a banana and cheese sandwich with a cup of *acai*.

At some point after we left, the police were called to put an end to the penthouse Armageddon. By four in the morning, the guests had evacuated the premises, and Matt and I made our way back. As we gingerly walked down the hall to our bedroom, Matt's feet struck empty beer cans, and the sticky floor pulled at the bottoms of my paws. Our bedroom, at least, had remained locked and out of harm's way.

The next morning I woke up early. The smells of the party left overs from the night before were too alluring to ignore. I slipped silently out to the patio where spilled beer, food scraps, and other tasty substances were waiting. I went to work, nosing happily through the refuse, licking, tasting, and devouring whatever I could find.

"Gil-ly!" Matt called an hour or so later. I didn't respond. I was preoccupied.

"Gilly!" he called again, this time with a note of urgency and worry. I didn't like to hear him upset so I finally went to him, sniffing his hand in greeting.

"Good morning, dog!"

I panted a silent good morning in reply.

"Ew, Gilly, what've you been . . ." He sniffed my breath and recoiled in horror.

Of the many delicious things I had eaten that morning, probably the strongest and most offensive smelling for him was vomit. He had cleaned up my own vomit on enough occasions to know the difference between the dog and human varieties, and this was unmistakably the human kind. I had been turning the chunky remnants of last night into a pre-breakfast snack, washing it down with laps of spilled beer. I considered it a delicious way to start the day, though Matt obviously didn't share my opinion. He rushed me to the bathroom, washed my muzzle, and brushed my teeth as thoroughly as he could manage. It was a while before he had breakfast.

Chapter 44

The Complexity of Human Love

Matt had gotten everything he'd wanted: a great apartment, friendly housemates, and a vibrant social life. As the semester drew to a close, however, I saw his enthusiasm for his situation fading. The parties had been fun at first but were losing their appeal. And it wasn't just the disgust of cleaning up afterwards. It was more than that.

On off-party nights, Matt took to practicing his yoga routine on the large outdoor patio. I watched his graceful movements and felt the inner stillness that they reflected. He continued his study of *A Course in Miracles* and was now incorporating many of the ideas it contained into his music. As he played, I heard with increasing clarity through melodies and lyrics his connection to something deep and beautiful. The songs filled me with warmth and happiness. They reminded me of the love and affection that I'd felt when I was held as a tiny puppy.

Erin, I haven't forgotten you.

The old guard in the penthouse departed, and, through word of mouth and the Internet, Matt found three new people to take up the empty rooms. They were more subdued, sensible companions, and the decadent parties of the previous semester became history.

We began spending most of our time with Rafael, a Brazilian student we'd met at the university. Rafael's best friend, Adriana, lived in our apartment building, and he was always in the area visiting her. He developed the habit of climbing two more flights of steps to visit with us in the penthouse, too.

Every time Rafael came to see us, he'd ask if I'd been on a walk yet. Regardless of the answer, he persuaded Matt that the three of us needed a jaunt around the neighborhood. We became a common sight in the plazas near our apartment. In these large open areas, Rafael talked Matt into letting me out of my harness and leash.

It was wonderful!

Not since my days in Frick Park with crazy Cassie had I been so carefree. I investigated to my heart's content. As Rafael chatted with Matt, he was careful to keep an eye on me. He was the perfect companion. When we were together, he was constantly cracking jokes, telling stories, and good-naturedly correcting Matt's Portuguese. His comments could be witty and his laugh, infectious.

I appreciated that one upshot to his companionship was a significantly reduced workload. When he was with us, Matt held his shoulder, which left me to heel at my human's side. I took advantage of this by sniffing and tasting as we walked. Rafael became as adept as Matt at removing slobbery refuse from my mouth.

The two friends began going to the beach together. They would sit on the sand and talk while they soaked up the sun. Matt loved swimming. He always came out of the surf, hair slicked down, water dripping onto his face, smiling triumphantly. Meanwhile, I spent hours dozing peacefully under a large umbrella. I was allowed on the beach because of my guide dog status and the novelty of a dog on the beach got me lots of attention from the bathers walking past. They would see me and come over to talk. Some even bought me water or coconuts from the vendors. A few especially thoughtful visitors rubbed my belly while I blissfully lay on my back.

Matt's relationship with Rafael deepened over time. Rafael helped him with his grocery shopping, accompanied him to doctor visits, and had him over for lunch several times a week. He called Matt frequently to suggest an outing or to just check on him. He had a knack for being there without becoming overbearing. Rafael became a cross between a twin brother and a favorite uncle. Rarely did I see Matt feeling smothered by his friend's good intentions or at odds with his suggestions. One particular day proved to be the exception.

Rafael found us after class and informed Matt that free malaria vaccinations were being offered on campus.

Matt shuddered. He told Rafael about his many eye surgeries and how he now hated shots. Rafael listened without comment. A minute later, Matt asked, "Why are we stopped?"

"We're in line to get vaccinated."

"What! Are you crazy?"

"Mathews, calm down. We're almost to the front."

Matt became even more agitated. "Weren't you listening to me? I just told you how much I hate shots! Why did you bring me here? I'm not getting vaccinated."

"All right, all right, relax. If you don't want one, I'll just get mine, and then we can go."

Just then we reached the front of the line. "What an adorable dog!" The woman in charge of the immunizations smiled at me.

I blinked at her in agreement.

Then she looked at Matt and Rafael. "So, who's going first?"

"I am," Rafael said.

"Actually, I'm not getting vaccinated," Matt said, quickly.

"Oh, you already got your shot?" My human just forced a smile and shook his head.

"He doesn't like needles," Rafael said.

"Oh, don't worry. It'll just take a second."

"No thanks. I really don't need one."

"How could you do that?" Matt's voice was both accusing and angry as the two left the vaccination area.

"What? I told you I was gonna get vaccinated," Rafael said.

"Yeah, but you didn't say you were doing it right then and that you were taking me along."

"I never imagined you were so against it. Sorry."

"You thought you could just get me there and I'd change my mind."

An awkward couple of minutes followed this exchange, a rarity for the two friends. Then, out of the blue, Rafael commented, "I guess it's good you didn't get near the needle. I might've gotten a stab in the heart instead of the arm."

Matt laughed, and the tension was behind them.

What Rafael really had in his heart was my human's best interest. And he didn't try to hide this fact. One day as we were leaving the dog park, I listened as the two got caught up in a conversation about how long they would live. Matt speculated that he would last well into his nineties, citing his long-living relatives. Rafael said that he wanted to be the first of the two to go.

"Why?" Matt asked.

"If I die first, I'll be able to look out for you from heaven."

Matt stopped walking and took in the full effect of his friend's very sincere comment. He was taken aback, I sensed, by the amount of affection it conveyed.

But I wasn't surprised. Rafael had only put into words the way he treated Matt in their daily interactions.

"Thanks." Matt was clearly touched.

Our Brazilian friend remained an almost angelic presence in our lives. He helped Matt to experience Rio de Janeiro in a way that I, alone, could not. With me, Matt gained a measure of independence. With Rafael he had gained interdependence.

I loved Rafael. He was always suggesting we stop at a park or plaza to allow me some time out of harness. He gave me big, adoring hugs, and played with me like I was his own dog. I know Matt loved Rafael, too; although, he didn't use that particular word with him. At the time I didn't understand why. It seemed to me that they had become as close as brothers, as close as lovers, even. Granted, they didn't play with each other like Matt had with Sylvia, but my human seemed as happy in Rafael's company as I'd ever seen him with anyone. Why not call it love?

His reluctance puzzled me. He talked to Rafael about love, especially when his friend got upset at someone—a bus driver who wouldn't let us board or a store owner who refused to let us enter.

"It's not their fault," he'd say to Rafael. "They don't know any better. We just need to show them love, and trust that they'll change their minds."

"You want me to love someone even when you show him a copy of the law and he refuses to read it?"

"Well, yeah. I mean, we should stand up for Gilly's rights as a guide dog, for sure. But we also need to love the people who are ignorant of them."

"It's one thing to be ignorant; it's another thing to refuse to hear the truth."

Matt would insist that getting upset just made it worse. "They still deserve our love."

"You love them, then. I'll call the police."

One day, Matt and Rafael were sitting at a picnic table on campus. While Rafael read one of his textbooks, Matt listened through the headphones attached to his computer. I was lying at his feet, almost asleep, when an aroma of peace and contentment roused me.

"I just finished *A Course in Miracles.*"

"Great," Rafael said. "Just in time to make it to class."

"No, I don't think I'm going to class right now. I'm just too . . . I don't know."

"Really? Well, I have to go to mine."

"That's okay. We'll be fine here."

After some convincing, Rafael went off to his class. Matt continued to give off an air of well-being. Next to him, in the warm sun of the spring afternoon, I wondered if this was it. Had he reached some kind of enlightened state? What would happen next?

But nothing happened. Matt just sat there, and, after a while, the aroma seemed to fade. He got up, and we made our way to the bus stop. I was sorry to see his elevated senses slip away, but he didn't seem to mind. We caught a bus and rode toward home.

As I lay across the bus seats with my head in Matt's lap, I did some reflecting of my own. Since Matt had first begun *A Course in Miracles,* he had used the program as a spiritual guide. Although his work with it had been steady, his life had wound on with mistakes, frustrations, and successes, like all the other people I'd observed. Had his efforts been worthwhile?

I decided I couldn't be the judge of that. I did know that my respect and admiration for him had increased over time. I had watched him express himself through his music, find release in yoga, and seek wisdom in his studies. As with Rafael, my love for him had grown.

But we had a bond even stronger than the one I shared with Rafael. We had been through the ups and downs of the last several years together, and we both had learned from them. I was no longer a young, inexperienced guide dog, and while I didn't have the benefit of Matt's beloved spiritual text, I didn't need it to know that Matt and I shared something special. Our bond went beyond our physical closeness, beyond our emotional connection, beyond our mental understanding. I was a part of my human, and he was a part of me.

Chapter 45

How to Say "I'll Miss You"

As part of Matt's scholarship in Brazil, he was expected to give ten talks to local Rotary clubs. He was asked to speak about his experiences in the USA and Brazil—in Portuguese.

His initial presentations, given after only a few months in Rio, were rough. Each time, I knew he was in trouble even before his first word. I would watch him fidget in his seat, looking uncomfortable and unhappy. I would feel his heart pound and smell his sweaty palms. When he'd finally make his way to the microphone and deliver the lines he'd memorized, it was painful to watch. He'd speak about his home in the United States and his developing appreciation of Brazil, but the effect was far from captivating. Sometimes I intentionally fell asleep just to avoid watching him flounder.

Gradually, over the next months, his Portuguese and his poise improved. More importantly, Matt realized he had two huge assets in grabbing and keeping the audience's attention.

The first was being blind. He discovered that by addressing this subject with straightforwardness and humor, he could tap into people's natural curiosity without it seeming awkward. He could even dispel some of its myths.

I, however, was his best asset. In any country, I was a magnet for attention, but in Brazil, where guide dogs and guide dog schools were still a rarity, my novelty nearly approached movie-star status. Most people had no clue how dogs like me worked with people, and Matt had the perfect chance to tell them. It didn't hurt, either, that most Brazilians held animals in high regard. They rarely refrained from gushing over my adorable face. Knowing this, Matt got better and better at engaging his audience. And I sensed that the more he succeeded, the more he enjoyed it.

Before long, the hardest part was not giving a talk but scheduling it. The clubs themselves didn't come knocking on scholars' doors asking for presentations. Rather, scheduling involved contacting key figures in the various groups to set up speaking dates. Luckily we had been paired with a Rotary counselor who did all this networking for us.

Her name was Marlene. In her mid-seventies, she was articulate in both English and Portuguese. Marlene drove us to the Rotary meetings and punctuated Matt's talks with her own keen observations. And she did so much more. With Marlene as our hostess, we went to restaurants, to the theater, and to lots of other fun and cultural places in Rio. What a life!

After several months of this, Matt joked that our Rotary companion was really his Brazilian grandmother—in my mind, a sweet sentiment but a little misleading. Marlene's high spirits and devilish sense of humor defied that stereotype. I'd have to say she was more like a college buddy—an older one, yet one eager to keep up-to-date with her younger friends.

Once, when the three of us were at a restaurant, the humans' conversation was put on hold when Matt answered his cell phone.

"Hey, Chris! . . . Not much, man. You? . . . Oh, that's cool . . . . Shit, man! That sounds amazing! . . . Listen, dude, call me later, will ya?"

After he said goodbye, Matt looked up, sheepishly. "Sorry. That was just a friend telling me about a party he went to."

"Did something happen there?" Marlene asked.

"No, I don't think so. It was just really big with a band and stuff."

"Well, forgive me for asking, but why did you say shit?"

Matt winced and looked embarrassed. "Oh, I was just commenting about how cool it sounded."

"I see. So in English, shit can be something good as well as something bad."

"I guess that's right." Matt laughed. "I never thought of it that way."

"You know, in Portuguese, shit is never a good thing." Marlene had a little smile on her face. "We say *merda* when all hell breaks loose. Maybe for shit in this case, we would say *porra*. The word means sperm, but people use it to show they're angry or surprised."

Matt nodded. Right then he was probably thinking shit—in a good way.

The tenth and last Rotary talk which Matt gave that year was hosted by the Rotary club in Jardim Botanico, a really upscale neighborhood in Rio. By then, Matt and Marlene had gotten their act down pat. He would talk about himself for the first five minutes, me for the next ten, and then give Marlene the floor so she could wrap up with a few stories about the three of us.

That night, Matt stood at the microphone in front of about fifty people who were eating and drinking. I rested in my usual spot on the floor near his feet, looking cute. I had my part down as well, but I hadn't needed to practice. I snoozed as Matt said all the usual things about himself, but my ears perked up when he got to the good stuff about me. Then, he added some comments about our experiences in Brazil.

"What I love most about this place is the generous spirit of the people. When we need assistance, they don't just get us across the street. They walk with us to our destination, even when it's out of their way. And when we take a bus . . . well, Gilly's great, but he can't read bus numbers any more than I can. So strangers will help. Sometimes they wait with us for fifteen or twenty minutes, just to make sure we get on the right bus. It's not that people aren't helpful in the United States; it's just that in our country, each person is expected to be as self-sufficient as possible. And sometimes people are afraid to offer help in case it's not wanted. So let me tell you, I didn't always appreciate the Brazilian approach. The first time someone grabbed my arm to take me across the street without my asking, I almost bit his head off."

The audience laughed.

"Anyway, I've learned to accept the help I'm given even if it's not in the exact form I'm expecting. It's only in rare cases that I tell people, politely, to please back off." The listeners laughed again.

Then it was Marlene's turn. She told the story of the three of us trying to catch a cab outside a restaurant one afternoon.

"Several taxi drivers slowed, then sped away when they saw Gilly. When I finally got a driver to stop and told him my friend's guide dog would be traveling with us, he flat out refused. People leaving the restaurant stopped to help us, and pretty soon we had a crowd. I think some just wanted to see what was going on, but several of them began arguing with the driver, saying he was breaking the law. He kept insisting that he didn't let animals in his cab. Finally, someone shouted, 'Then what're *you* doing in the taxi?'"

When Marlene delivered the punch line, she got the biggest laugh of all.

Matt ended by playing a song on his guitar. It was a classic bossa nova called *"Chega de Saudade."* I'd heard him sing it before and knew the Portuguese word *saudade* meant you were longing for something you lost. So I wasn't surprised that before he started singing, Matt told everyone that we'd be going home in two weeks and he was already feeling saudade.

December 23 marked the first day of summer in Brazil. It was also our departure date back to Pittsburgh. In the last days of our stay, Rafael helped Matt organize a good-bye party in the penthouse. It was nothing like Gabriel's had been. People of all ages were present, everyone brought a dish to share, and Matt played a handful of songs for the indulgent crowd.

The day before leaving, Rafael came over to help pack. I think Matt would have been content to shove all of his stuff in his suitcases and sit on the lids to get them closed, but Rafael insisted on arranging everything neatly. Just as he had done with his mom a year earlier, Matt now stepped back and let his friend organize away. It was amusing to me that Rafael paid so much more attention to this than Matt did. I realized it was just one more way Rafael showed how much he cared.

He and Adriana went with us to the airport. Marlene, too, met us there for one last good-bye. Tears were shed, perhaps more over me than Matt.

"I don't know why we're all so upset," Rafael said. "You'll be back within a year."

Matt agreed, laughing, though I sensed he wasn't so sure. He wanted to come back, of course, but he just didn't know if it would really happen.

After the last hugs, we headed towards the gate, accompanied by an airport employee. I caught one last look at Rafael as we headed to security. I was going to miss him.

The trip home proved to be more pleasurable than expected. Matt and I were moved from a crowded row in coach up to first class.

"We just want your companion here to be as comfortable as possible."

The head flight attendant gave me a big smile. Another attendant got me a pillow and blanket while Matt sipped a mimosa. Passengers seated near us seemed fascinated. Several nudged their companions when they spotted my long snout and brown liquid eyes peering out at them.

Now this is how to treat a guide dog, I thought, snuggling down into my blanket.

It was jarring to arrive in Pittsburgh in the dead of winter. I couldn't believe how cold it was, especially after the extreme heat of Rio. Matt took to wearing his coat even when inside the house during our first few weeks back.

After the initial excitement of reuniting with his mom, catching up with his sister, and hanging out with his brother, I saw Matt begin to pine for the life he had left in Brazil. He seemed sad and listless. Our daily walks in the snow did little to boost his spirits. He composed songs on his guitar about the saudade he felt for his old life in Brazil. His music spoke of his longing for the sun, the beach, the penthouse, and, most of all, his best friend.

Matt talked with Rafael on Skype almost every day. His friend's jokes and wandering anecdotes helped keep him from sliding into depression. Rafael also served as a sounding board for his frustrations.

"I need to do something. I don't have a job, and anyway I'm not happy here."

"Whadaya wanna do?" Rafael asked one afternoon.

"I don't know!" His voice changed from frustrated to wistful. "But I do know how happy I was in Rio, going to the beach and hanging out with you."

"So why not come back then?"

Matt laughed in disbelief. "I don't have a scholarship anymore. How would I get the money?"

"You could teach English." Rafael said this like it was the most natural thing in the world. "People here are always looking to improve their English skills. And you're a native speaker. That should get you a lot of students."

Matt considered the idea then conceded its possibility.

One evening over dinner he broached the subject with his mom. "So, I found a school in Rio where I can get a TEFL certificate to teach English there. Whadaya think?"

I felt his intensity as he waited for her answer. I knew her support was important to him.

"Do you really think you can make enough money to live on by teaching English there?"

"Yeah! My good friend Monica, this girl I met in Rio, has been doing it for a while now. I talked to her over Skype just yesterday. If she can do it, why not me?"

"Well, I know you miss Brazil and want to go back." She sounded thoughtful, serious, and a little sad.

I could sense that her motherly instinct was to persuade him to stay. She didn't, though. Instead, she gave him her blessing and said she'd help him pay for his TEFL course. She had seen how difficult the last several months had been for him, and, first and foremost, I knew she wanted her son to be happy.

Also left unspoken between them was something they both knew: in the worst case scenario, his plan wouldn't work; his few thousand dollars of savings would dry up, and he would be forced to come home, regroup, and try something else. Matt seemed determined, however, not to let that happen. I, too, wanted to see him succeed. I missed Rafael, the beach, and the delicious smells and tastes on the streets of Rio. The streets of our suburban neighborhood in Pittsburgh were entirely too free of chicken bones.

Viva, Brazil!

Chapter 46

Going Downtown

Our plane landed in the early morning at the Tom Jobim international Airport in Rio. Rafael was there to meet us. He had gotten up at four a.m. and taken the bus from the city. Upon seeing him again after more than two months, I leaped several feet into the air. I couldn't believe we were back together again. When I came down, my tail was wagging like a window wiper on high speed. Harness or not, I couldn't hold back my excitement, and Matt didn't try to stop me.

"See, Gilly, I knew you'd be back before the year was out," Rafael told me, glowing with pleasure at my greeting.

Rafael, I thought, *you are one wise dude.*

After he helped us move into the apartment he'd found for us, the next step was figuring out our commute. The school we'd be going to was in downtown Rio, and getting there alone was something we'd never done before. Matt and I were used to navigating the nearby beach neighborhoods, where the streets followed a fairly predictable grid pattern and the people were assertively helpful. But it wasn't clear if Brazilians in the more stressful city center would be the same.

As Matt discussed this with Rafael, I heard worry and doubt in his voice. I think Rafael heard it, too, because he offered to make a dry run with us the Friday before classes were to start. Matt accepted gratefully.

They found the school's address online, and we caught a bus that dropped us off along a highway within walking distance. Traffic roared by, and there wasn't a tree in sight for me to pee on. But Matt wasn't even thinking about a pit stop. He was paying close attention to where we got off, which direction we turned, and how many streets we crossed, making notes on his voice recorder. Soon, I began paying attention to the food vendors that lined the smaller streets we walked down.

Finally, we reached the street we were looking for, Rua da Quitanda.

"What's the number again?"

"Ninety-five," Matt said.

Rafael paused, and then led us back a few paces. "There doesn't seem to be a ninety-five on this street. Are you sure this school is real?"

"It better be real. I paid real tuition."

If Rafael was joking, it hadn't seemed so funny to my human. We approached a street vendor selling some sort of sweet-smelling Brazilian dessert. I looked at it longingly.

"Is this Rua da Quitanda?" Rafael asked.

"Sure is," the vendor replied in a gravely voice. My mouth watered at the smell of cooked coconut.

"Do you know where number ninety-five is?"

"Ninety-five . . ." The man looked around.

"It's a language school," Matt added.

"Ah, I know! It used to be right over there." He pointed to a building that was undergoing some sort of renovation. "Lots of gringos came to study there, but I think it closed."

I saw Matt's nervousness. At Rafael's suggestion, we crossed the street so he could get a closer look at the now unnumbered building. Some construction workers were out in front, and Rafael approached one.

"Excuse me. We're looking for a language school that used to be here."

"Yeah, it moved. I think it's just a few blocks down that way."

Matt exhaled audibly. It still existed. He hadn't been suckered after all.

Two blocks down the road, Rafael spotted the school's new site. We went inside and confirmed that Matt and I were indeed starting class at nine a.m. on Monday morning.

On the bus back home, the two laughed about the confusion.

"What kind of a school moves their headquarters two blocks down the same street?"

"It must be run by the Brazilian government!" Matt seemed giddy with relief.

As they laughed and joked on the way home, I reflected that Matt had stopped taking notes on his recorder when we got to the first address. It was only a few blocks difference, but our walking route would change completely. Hopefully we would be able to rely on help from others.

If not, he won't be laughing then.

Early Monday morning we caught our bus and exited into the noisy, chaotic center of the city. Not a minute after getting off in the middle of downtown Rio, a man approached us.

"What are you looking for?"

Matt told him the address, which thanks to Rafael, was now correct. The man checked the street numbers around us to determine which way to go.

"I'll take you there," he said, and with an "obrigado," Matt took his shoulder.

Our helper was short and on the heavy side, with the air of a street vendor, but I couldn't be sure. He walked us to the address while making chitchat about the weather. Matt thanked him again and said good-bye. I sensed his overwhelming gratitude mixed with disbelief.

It had been so easy!

The commute continued going smoothly over the next few weeks and it was even more enjoyable when Tim began traveling with us. Tim was from England, a fellow student in our TEFL class. The three of us got in the habit of taking the same bus home together after school.

One day during the second half of the course, Matt called out his stop to the bus driver after Tim had gotten off. "Let me off at Rainha Elizabet, please." This was our standard request.

"This bus doesn't go up that far," the driver said.

"No?" There was surprise in Matt's voice.

"No, we turn right and go towards the lake."

Apparently, Tim had gotten us on a bus that diverged from our normal route. There had been no way for the novice gringo to know. He had probably just looked for the word Copacabana printed on the side.

"I can get you pretty close though."

This seemed reasonable enough. Matt would have to ask directions, but I was sure someone could help us. Rio's inhabitants hadn't failed us yet.

A few minutes later, we got off. Matt obviously had no idea where we had landed, only that it was "pretty close." No one was around to help, so we began walking straight ahead. I realized it was an arbitrary choice. It seemed Matt preferred walking to standing still.

I could see that we were on the right side of a busy highway. Vehicles flew by; the roar of traffic was a dull ache on my ears. We crossed one street, then another, then the next—each time with Matt paying close attention to be sure cars weren't turning in front of us at the intersection. Soon the level street began to slope upwards. I remembered that the bus home usually passed through a tunnel a few blocks before our street. Maybe we were walking up over the tunnel, and our street lay on the other side of the hill. There was no way to be sure.

The hill continued up, and the walking was stressful. The flow of vehicles was relentless, and the threat of a car turning in front of us was a constant worry. I began to wonder if this was really the right way. Then a young man walked by. Matt stopped and called out, but he was already gone. After another few blocks, Matt finally caught the attention of a woman coming up behind us.

"Excuse me!"

"Yes?"

"I'm looking for Rainha Elizabet. Is it this way?" I saw Matt point in front of us.

"Rainha Elizabet?" The woman seemed surprised. "You're really far from there!"

Matt winced at the news but, still pointing, asked again. "Is it this way?"

"No, you have to go back to the bottom of the hill and turn right."

I wanted her to help us. I know Matt did, too. But, she was going in the opposite direction, and he didn't seem to have the nerve.

"Okay, thanks," he said, forcing a smile. We turned around to begin the trek back down.

We crossed the streets again, one by one. As we backtracked, Matt's right ear, the one with no hearing, was towards the highway. It was probably a welcome reprieve from traffic noise, but, by his hesitation before crossing each street, I could tell he was having a harder time reading traffic flow. I was having trouble, too. The street crossings weren't straight shots; rather, they involved veering left as the highway curved.

We arrived at the next corner. It wasn't a right angle, and, without meaning to, I placed Matt at the curb facing the highway. Not realizing this, he motioned me forward, out onto the busy street. I hesitated.

"Hop up!" Matt impatiently gave me a nudge with the leash. I obeyed, stepping out onto the highway. The near lane was momentarily free, and we began crossing. We made it to the middle of the two lanes, and I stopped. Cars whizzed by right in front of us. Matt realized something was wrong. He turned us around to backtrack, but cars were now speeding by in the lane we had just crossed.

He froze.

I felt a sickening jolt of fear slam through him. I could feel the air from the vehicles just in front and behind us moving at alarming speeds. Horns honked. Cars swerved to avoid us. We were cornered inside a pack of raging beasts.

Then, through the din of traffic, I heard a male voice holler out. "Don't move!"

This seemed like excellent advice, which was why we were frozen to the spot. Then I saw the voice's owner. He was running toward us, between the on-coming cars. He grabbed Matt's arm.

"You're in the middle of the highway!" he screamed, sounding as terrified as Matt smelled. We stood motionless for a few more seconds. Then, at a break in the speeding traffic, he led us back across the street.

"You need to be careful!" He was panting and a little wild-eyed.

"Sorry, thanks," Matt stammered. It seemed he was in mild shock. I could almost feel his stunned numbness.

"Vai com Deus," our rescuer said, and he was gone.

Matt finally pulled himself together enough to urge me on down the hill. At the next sound of someone passing, he stopped to call out for help. He wasn't taking any more chances.

This time an older man stopped. Matt asked if he could accompany us down the hill, and he agreed without hesitation. As we started out, Matt holding his shoulder, the man asked where we were going.

"Rainha Elizabet," Matt said, stupidly. It seemed he was in no condition for further social pleasantries.

"That's far!"

Had we been going in circles? It seemed we were still not any closer to our destination. But, thankfully, our helper walked us to the bottom of the hill, and, without being asked, turned right and guided us through a maze of streets towards our home.

"Thank you so much," Matt told him when we arrived at our block.

"Não custa nada."

The two shook hands, and Matt and I went inside our building.

"So, when Gilly and I finally got back here, man, I was wiped out! I mean, I was shaking. My next nightmare's gonna be me, standing in the middle of a friggin' freeway with traffic screaming on all sides." Matt took a big swallow of his beer as he finished his story.

His flatmates listened sympathetically, though I knew they couldn't really imagine what it had been like. I spent the night recovering, too. I had felt every drop of Matt's tension in addition to the whoosh of the cars screaming by which had caused it. I didn't want to be in a situation like that ever again.

I wondered how many more scares it would take before Matt learned to request help when he really needed it. There was only so much I could do for him. It was clear to me that the more readily he got assistance when necessary, the more effective we would become.

In my mind, his fierce determination to step blindly forward wasn't all bad. There was a lot of courage in it. It carried him through college and on to Brazil. But, that determination needed to be coupled with an equally strong humility. At that moment in his life, he was still learning how to balance the two.

Chapter 47

English Classes with My Owner

M att graduated from the TEFL course with a respectable high B. Now that he had his diploma, he was ready to start his pseudo-career as an English teacher. The graduating students had been provided with the names and telephone numbers of four English schools that would hire them under the table. Matt called the first school, English Plus, and set up an interview. I wasn't allowed into the interview room with him and was forced to sit in the reception area and wait.

Shades of Dr. Bob, I thought.

"The woman interviewing me was polite, but I could tell something was bothering her," Matt told Rafael later. "I thought it was my being blind. And so, you know, I explained about my computer talking and how it has my English books on it and I can get on the Internet and make my own lessons. So, she didn't say anything about that. Instead, she asked about Gilly. I told her that he was really friendly and well trained. But she just kind of sucked in her breath and said he couldn't be with me during lessons."

"Why not?" Rafael was obviously indignant. I was, too.

"Yeah, that's what I wanted to know. At first I was really calm. I told her he was a guide dog, and that a federal law protects his rights, and so on and so on. She said she knew all that, but some people are allergic to dogs. I was like, 'Yeah, maybe one in a hundred, but I don't have to teach them. I can work with the other ninety-nine.'"

"Obviously! So what'd she say?"

"Well, she didn't say anything. She just sat there. Then, all of the sudden I had this flash of insight. I said, 'You're allergic to dogs, aren't you?' She didn't answer right away, but finally she admitted it. Then I just started laughing. The whole thing seemed so absurd."

"So is she gonna hire you?"

"I don't know. She said she'd call."

She never did, of course. Nor did any of the other schools. If Matt was miffed, he didn't show it. He told Rafael that if they didn't want him, it was their loss.

In the absence of a job, we filled our time by going to the beach with his flatmates, hanging out with Rafael, and getting together with old friends from the year before. It wasn't a bad way to spend our sunny, unemployed days. Still, when he played guitar in his room, I could hear restlessness coming through. He was going through his meager savings and had no English students to show for it. It wasn't that he minded not teaching, but he needed to make some money to support himself. Otherwise, we'd be going home in a few months.

One of the friends we visited during these uncertain days was Adam, an American from California. He had lived in an apartment under the penthouse and frequented many of the wild parties thrown during the time of Gabriel and August. He was tattooed, muscular, and pursued girls with a ferocity and determination that made old August's antics with women seem quaint.

"Hey, man, what's up?" Adam opened the door to his apartment and greeted us enthusiastically. "I didn't even know you were back in Brazil!"

"Yeah, I couldn't stay away."

"Come on in, man."

Matt and I moved through the doorway and into the apartment.

"There's a couch like two feet in front of you if you wanna sit down."

Matt made himself comfortable on the sofa. "Mind if I let Gilly off the leash?" My ears perked up.

"Nah, go ahead. This place is trashed. Gilly roaming around can only make it cleaner."

Matt unfastened my leash, and I immediately began to fulfill Adam's request by searching the large living-kitchen area for anything edible I could clean up.

"So what're you doing back here?"

Matt explained that after two and a half months at home, he had decided to return to teach English.

"That's what I've been doing for almost a year now." Adam had dumped a pile of clothes onto the floor and was now sitting on a chair across from Matt.

"Seriously? Where at?"

"Well, first I taught for a school in Botafogo. But the pay was shit, and I had to get up really early for most of the classes. I had business people who wanted to get in an hour and a half of English conversation before they went to work. It really sucked."

"Wow."

"Yeah, but then I got some private students and was finally able to quit."

Over near the refrigerator, I paused to hear Adam's answer. This might be important, even more than the sliver of cheese I had found in the corner.

Sure enough, Matt was interested too. "Really? How'd you get private students?"

"Just through contacts at the school. People knew people who wanted a private English teacher. The pay is a lot better, and the hours are decent."

"That is so cool." Matt then told Adam about the TEFL course and the interviews that hadn't panned out. "I guess what I really need are some private students."

"Aw, man, I'll totally give you a student of mine. I was gonna leave them all for my friend, Jack, but I can let you have one to get you started."

"Dude, are you kidding?" Matt reacted as if he'd won some big prize. "That'd be great! But don't you need them yourself?"

"Nah, I'm leaving in like two weeks—going back to California."

"You're not serious! Why?"

"I'm ready to move on, you know? I'm gonna go back home, make some money with my brother's company, and then I'm planning to do some traveling in Southeast Asia."

"Wow, cool. Way to go, man. Keep on exploring."

"Yeah, I hear the women in Thailand are really hot."

Now that sounds like the Adam I remember from the old days, I thought.

After a conversation weighing the comparative sex appeal of various nationalities, the two exchanged cell numbers, and Adam promised to get in touch a few days before he left.

I could hear Matt get up. "Come on, Gilly!"

I pretended not to hear. I had found a dirty plate under the kitchen table.

The talk with Adam visibly boosted Matt's spirits. Not only would he shortly be receiving his first private student, but he was reassured that private students were out there. It was just a question of finding them. He didn't have the advantage of getting leads from an English school, but surely there were other ways to get some of these all-important English-language lovers.

He asked Rafael for help posting ads on the Internet. They made sure to include the phrase "Native English Teacher" at the top. This was his biggest selling point, the two decided. Rafael also came up with the idea of listing his ad in the university's newspaper. It came out once a week and was widely read on campus. The ad was free to post, and Rafael assured him it would generate interest from the students and faculty at this elite private school. And they were likely to have some discretionary funds.

Matt was beginning to get a taste for marketing. He told Rafael he wanted to post flyers around the university to get more publicity. Since neither Matt nor I were much for flyer posting, he asked his friend for help.

"I put up the flyers," Rafael reported a few days later.

"Awesome, thanks!"

"Yeah, and look what I found on one of the bulletin boards."

His friend proceeded to read him an ad for English classes with an American native speaker that featured the use of music, films, and multi-media activities to stimulate learning.

Matt was chagrined. Why hadn't he thought of saying something about multi-media, he lamented to Rafael. So what if he, himself, wouldn't be seeing the film clips? He would be hearing the English, and that was all that mattered. The two discussed how they could separate him from the pack of other English teachers out there.

Of course, I was the obvious solution.

"Gilly's the key!" Matt said, excitedly. "He gets tons of attention from everyone who passes him on the street. He's the perfect billboard! I just need to put a sign on him about the classes."

I had mixed feelings about becoming a walking ad campaign. I enjoyed getting stared at by the masses and leaving a warm, fuzzy feeling in the hearts of all who saw me. But, it seemed a little sinister to turn my attention-getting power into a shameless ploy to drum up business. But, as usual, my human didn't ask my opinion on the matter. He was too enthralled by his own genius.

They used pieces of a cardboard box as backing. On them they glued two identical computer printouts with the words "English Classes With My Owner." The next line listed Matt's cell phone number.

"Maybe if we get some string, we can tie the sign to his harness," Matt said.

Rafael, as it happened, had string at his house. He spent an afternoon with Matt cutting tiny holes in the cardboard signs, looping the string through, and tying it tightly around the sides of my harness. It took several tries, but he finally managed to get the signs tied so they were visible to people with a side view of me. One sign hung on the left of my harness, the other on the right, and they were short enough so that I could lie down without them touching the ground. The only problem, they discovered, was when I wanted to lie on my side. One of the signs would inevitably get squashed.

"Well, you won't want to use them all the time," Rafael said, "just when you're going for a walk and you want to advertise."

The project completed, Matt insisted that we try them out right away. The three of us went for a stroll along the wide sidewalk that lined the urban beaches of Rio. It was a sunny, late autumn day. Warm, but not too hot. Perfect for walking and advertising, Matt told Rafael.

"Are people looking?" he asked, as we made our way through Ipanema.

"Oh, yeah. Lots of them."

As if to confirm this, a fruit vendor hollered as we passed. "Look at that! English classes! Look at that!"

Matt was clearly thrilled. It was only a matter of time, he told Rafael, before his days would be filled with eager students and the money would be rolling in.

Chapter 48

Students

As it turned out, the signs I was forced to tote around never worked their magic. Occasionally, we would hear people comment on them, and one of the porters from a neighboring building showed some interest. But no students resulted. Luckily, the following week, Adam came to the rescue.

"So, I'm gonna be able to give you two students."

"Fantastic!"

"Yeah, I was gonna give you all three, but the one lady has a problem with dogs. I think she's afraid of 'em or something."

"Oh, that's okay."

I bet I could have won her over, but I wasn't making the decisions.

"I was thinking I'd take you with me for my last classes. You know, let you guys get to know each other. That way you can see where they live, too," Adam said.

"Yeah, that would be perfect." Matt sounded excited and relieved at the same time. Up 'til then, I don't think he'd even thought about the challenge of finding the students' homes. The first few times, before we both learned the routines, it would be difficult. Adam's help would be a huge boost.

He dropped by our apartment the next day and the three of us walked to see the first student. Her apartment was, by a remarkable coincidence, only two blocks down the street from ours. Still, Matt was leaving nothing to chance. Using his voice recorder, he took careful note of the turns taken and streets crossed.

The student was a woman in her sixties named Carla. She greeted Adam in loud, thickly accented English. He introduced Matt, presenting his strengths—guitar playing, languages, and me. While I clearly impressed her, she was thrilled to hear about Matt's musical abilities.

"Oh! I have a guitar! Maybe you can help me learn to play it."

When Matt agreed, Carla turned to Adam. "I just hope he doesn't charge me more for the classes," she said as if Matt couldn't hear.

Matt pretended he couldn't. "What kind of music do you like?"

When she mentioned the Beatles, Matt smiled, pleased. He and Carla talked about the Fab Four for a few minutes, and then Adam's class began. He had her read from a travel guide written in English, stopping her occasionally to correct her pronunciation.

"That's plenty," she said after a while, closing the book. Then she and Adam chatted for the rest of the class. Compared to what Matt had been prepared for through his TEFL course, this would be a breeze.

"She pays twenty-five *reais* an hour," Adam said after we'd left her apartment. "It's a little less than the going rate, but they're easy sessions. And, she does four hours a week. It adds up."

Matt, I could see, was thrilled with the arrangement. I knew that twenty-five reais was about twelve dollars. For this, he would talk in English and play Beatles songs on the guitar for an hour. It was ideal.

The second student lived in Flamengo, about thirty minutes away. We walked three blocks down to the street bordering Copacabana beach where Adam normally caught the bus. It had been a gray, overcast day and was now almost dark. We walked along the beach street toward the bus stop, the wind pushing against us.

Suddenly, Adam stopped. I watched as three hooded men on bicycles began to circle us strangely. I recognized Adam's fear and had the sense that these guys were trouble. I stared at them as they rode around us, wondering what would happen next. I wasn't trained to defend my human.

"Is this the stop?" Matt was oblivious to what was happening.

"Hang on," Adam said in a low voice. Another minute went by. I watched the men continuing to circle us as in a children's game gone sinister. Then, miraculously, they slowly rode away.

"Damn." Adam looked pretty shaken.

Matt, for better or worse, was still clueless. "What?"

"There were these guys on bikes, but they just left. I think they were going to rob us."

"Oh, wow," Matt said, soberly.

"I'm not sure, but your dog might've scared 'em off."

Matt laughed. "Gilly? Really?"

We started walking again. "This is a beautiful city, but some nasty shit goes on here. I didn't tell you about my friend, Jack. Remember the guy I said I was giving one of my students to?"

"Yeah, I was wondering about him."

"Well, he was killed last week in Lapa."

Matt stopped. He looked stunned. Adam and I stopped, too.

Lapa, I knew, was the neighborhood near the city's center where hundreds of people congregated on weekend nights, filling the bars and dance clubs, providing customers to the street-vendors who blanketed the area. We'd gone there with his friends a number of times. We knew first-hand that muggings were common there. In fact, Matt had once had his wallet lifted right out of his pocket. When he had turned around to confront the thief, he had bumped into a huge, unyielding hulk of a man who was obviously there to protect his partner.

Matt eventually got over his anger as he found that many of his friends who'd spent time in Rio had had similar experiences. But, getting killed . . .

"Yeah, it was opening night at the bar he had just bought," Adam said. "Jack had spent all this time getting a loan from the bank. So when one of the bartenders told him a customer had left without paying for his drinks, Jack chased the guy down the street. When he caught up to him the guy pulled out a gun and shot him twice in the chest."

"Aw, man," breathed Matt.

"They sent his remains back to the United States for burial."

Matt was silent.

"Don't get me wrong," Adam said. "I love Rio. But it's got the seediest underbelly of any city I've ever been in."

We caught the bus to Flamengo. It was rush hour, and for everyone just getting on, it was standing room only. Matt and Adam held onto the overhead bar, and I lay at Matt's feet. Then a young woman stood up and indicated for Matt to take her seat. He protested, but she was adamant.

"I'm getting off soon."

Matt thanked her and sat down. He was getting better at accepting such kindness and swallowing his pride.

A half an hour later we got off the bus.

"Man, that girl who gave you her seat was totally checking me out!" Adam said as the bus roared away. "That's one thing I'll miss about this country. When girls like you here, they let you know it. They don't pretend not to care like American girls. They just stare you down."

He said the last three words with relish. Matt laughed, though I sensed a twinge of regret that this exciting world of eye contact was closed to him. I sympathized. I liked noticing when people stared at me in admiration, and I knew Matt would have, too, especially if they were good-looking women. If only I had been trained to guide him to sexy, attractive female humans. But, sadly, they all looked about the same to me—except the ones who were eating, of course.

It was three or four blocks from the bus stop to the student's apartment. Matt recorded the directions, but by the end, I could see his confusion. I had a feeling he would be asking for a lot of help on these streets in the weeks to come.

"His name's Chico," Adam said as we rode the elevator to the twenty-fourth floor of an enormous apartment building. "His dad's name is Paulo, and his mom's, uh, I forget his mom's name. It's something Japanese. The whole family is Japanese, but I think Paulo and Chico were both born in Brazil. Oh, and they have a housekeeper named Ana. I'm pretty sure she has the hots for me."

Matt met the housekeeper, the mom, and finally Chico, who shook his hand loosely and mumbled a greeting. Formalities dispensed with, the twelve-year-old overcame his shyness and asked about me.

"This is Gilly. He's working right now, but I'll take off his harness so you can pet him, okay?"

"Okay."

I wagged my tail and sneezed happily as Matt pulled the leather strap over my head.

"Hi, Gilly." Chico patted my side shyly.

I stared into his eyes imploringly. *Chico, you could make a key ally in my fight against hunger.*

"What does he eat?" Chico's English had only the slightest accent.

"Just dog food."

"He looks hungry. Can I give him a banana?"

Matt hesitated. He never let other people feed me. He'd been programmed since guide dog school to guard the bond that food established between human and dog. But, I think he recognized, that bonding with his new student was just as important.

"Okay," he said, "but just one."

I watched in rapture as Chico reached to the center of the table, took a banana, and peeled it. The strands of skin unfolded, one by one, revealing the deliciously ripe snack.

"Here, Gilly."

I took it politely from his hand and then lay down to enjoy my prize.

Chico's mother was off to the side watching the performance. "Matt," she said, speaking in Portuguese. "One thing that is very important is helping Chico with his homework. He has English exercises from school, and his science is in English, too. Will you be able to help with this?"

"Oh, sure. Chico can read aloud from the books and handouts he gets. If we have questions, I can find answers on the Internet." He explained about his talking laptop computer.

"Oh, you have a computer!" This seemed to satisfy her concerns over a blind English tutor.

Adam began the class, and Chico's mother faded into the next room. They went over an English grammar exercise from school. Then they took a break to allow Chico to show off his skills on a small golfing green in the living room.

"Chico's an awesome golfer," Adam said. "He wins tournaments all the time."

Matt listened to the two putting and offered his enthusiasm when a shot was made. I was distracted by the wonderful smells coming from the kitchen.

Finally, the lesson was over. Adam, Matt, and I walked to the bus stop.

"They pay really well. Fifty reais an hour, and Chico has 2 two-hour classes a week."

Matt's excitement was obvious.

"So you'll be making twelve hundred a month just with these two students. It's not a bad deal, really. I'm just sorry my other lady is too scared of dogs. I had to give her to someone else."

Matt was clearly in no mood for regret. Thanks to Adam's help, he now had students and income. With any luck, he'd find other classes to teach. He thanked Adam profusely on the way home. He was an English teacher. His plan was working out, and he could stay in Rio.

I was equally happy. I had a hunch that the loophole Chico had opened up with his banana could be exploited during future classes.

Teaching for Matt and snacks for me: an equal opportunity arrangement.

Matt went on to find other English students. Some of them he enjoyed working with; some of them were a challenge requiring patience and discretion. Some of them even gave me snacks. But, Chico and Carla were special. Matt's relationship with these two humans grew far beyond teacher and student. Chico's mom began inviting him to eat dinner with the family after the lessons. Carla served him lunch before they started each class. This generosity and willingness to treat him like family deepened his connection with both the young boy and the older woman.

I was glad that he had found this support. The easier things were for Matt, the easier they were for me. Even if the benefits didn't always translate directly into food for me, they were important to our mutual well-being. Fortunately, they often did.

Chapter 49

A New Challenge

As the weeks stretched into months, Matt became comfortable in his routine of teaching English and going to the beach. We spent lots of time with Rafael, who still insisted that I get plenty of off-leash time at the dog parks. It was everything Matt had come back to Rio to do, and yet, there was something missing.

He was restless. I could feel it. And I heard it, too, in the lyrics and melodies of the songs he composed. He wanted a new adventure, a new challenge. He missed the old days when learning Portuguese was so stimulating, when exploring the novelties of Rio seemed to offer endless possibilities. Most of all, he wanted to find an audience for his music, an audience that didn't fall asleep the way I usually did. He'd learned so much from Ronaldo: new chords and song structures, new rhythms and approaches to lyric writing. Now he wanted to get other people excited about his songs.

Humans, I knew by then, were funny creatures. They could be happy when times were tough and dissatisfied when times were easy. Matt had gotten everything he'd wanted in Rio. He had good friends, a paying job that he enjoyed, and the beach. Now he wanted more. I didn't know if this ambition was driven by a desire to use his talents effectively or if his success in Brazil was going to his head. *Only time will tell,* I thought.

France. That was the new object of his intrigue. Looking back, I can see why it attracted him. The country held, particularly in the eyes of Brazilians, the mystique of an artistic and cultural mecca. It appeared in all the novellas. It was the fashionable destination for the *haves* of Rio. Matt had soaked up his share of this fascination and now was determined to make his way there and experience it for himself. It was the perfect place, he told Rafael, to find an audience for his music.

"French people know how to appreciate art. And they love bossa nova over there. I'm telling you, Rafael, Gilly and I are gonna be a hit!"

I'd seen the way the French exchange students in Rio gushed over me and knew he was at least half right. Whether or not they were going to like Matt's music? That was another story.

Before going to France, Matt had to learn some French. He discovered, through a friend, a French native who had married a Brazilian girl and was teaching private English lessons in Rio. So, with the small surplus he had from his English teaching, Matt arranged to hire him. For two ninety-minute classes a week, he studied the basics of French with his gringo counterpart.

They started with the most essential things he'd need: ordering from a menu, talking about himself, and, most importantly, asking for help and directions. As the weeks passed, they began to examine the basics of sentence structure, past and future tenses, and the subjunctive.

Matt wasn't a linguistic savant by any means. Even with his fluency in Spanish and Portuguese, he struggled with the pronunciations, the strange grammar, and the overwhelming difficulty of training his ear to a foreign tongue. But, he loved the challenge. The language was like a new world, and he was dedicated to exploring it.

As he began finding his footing with French, I could sense his desire to travel to the mother country grow. He talked with his teacher, Ronan, about a plan. Class by class, he began piecing it together. He would fly back home to spend Christmas with his family, and then continue on to France. He had at least two friends he had met in Rio who were now living in Paris. They could help him there. He could make money, he said, teaching private English lessons, just like he was doing in Rio.

"I don't know," Ronan said, hesitantly. "It's not like here in Rio. People in Paris don't really have a habit of hiring private English teachers. They learn English in school. They don't always learn it well," he added with a smile, "but if they want to improve, they enroll in a course."

Matt was undeterred. I realized that his whimsical musings had already hardened into a fixed idea. And anyway, the point for him was going to France, not making money by teaching English.

"Well, what about playing guitar in the metro?"

Ronan laughed. "Yeah, you can try. But first, you need to get a permit. Then you have to audition for the city. Only the artists it picks get to perform in the metro."

It wouldn't be easy; that was clear. But, Matt seemed to relish the challenge. And the trip was still some months away. It was now the beginning of September, which gave him a few more months of French classes to hone his speaking skills and find a place to live.

Then, something happened that wasn't in Matt's plans. It was a Friday night, the point in the week when many in Rio cast off workweek burdens and headed to Lapa. His flatmates had invited him to come with them, and he had accepted. I was a little surprised. He and I had gone to Lapa only a few times since he'd been mugged there. I knew he didn't much like the chaotic streets and jostling crowds, but who was I to object? There would be plenty of delicious garbage strewn about the streets.

I was daydreaming about the trash and salivating slightly when, without warning, Matt led me into our bedroom, gave me a good-bye pat, and shut the door. He wasn't taking me? I was stunned! I spent every waking moment with him, and now he was leaving me at home, just like that. Was he afraid I'd steal his limelight? Eat too many goodies? I didn't know the answer. After sniffing around the bedroom and finding nothing edible, I lay down with a *humph* and went to sleep. I dreamed, of course, of Lapa.

I am at my human's side, no leash and no harness, free to watch over him and lick up tasty food scraps. I observe silently as Matt and his roommates meet up with some Brazilian friends, and the group of seven catches a bus to Lapa.

They buy alcoholic drinks from a street vendor and drink, standing on the crowded sidewalk. I scour the ground, delighting in bits of salty melted cheese and droplets of beer from crushed cans. Lots and lots of beer cans . . . While I scavenge, the people shout at each other over the noise. The buzz of the crowd and the blaring music from nearby nightclubs create a chaotic mix of sound.

I can smell the sour fragrance of Matt's caipirinha—a concoction of sugar, lime juice, and ice mixed with a heavy dose of cachasa, a Brazilian alcohol. Its potency makes it a convenient way to imbibe a large quantity of alcohol in a short period of time. Matt needs to deaden his senses, I know, for any chance of enjoying the night ahead.

Around midnight, the group of friends splits up. Some are calling it a night, while the remaining energetic souls are going into a nightclub. I see Matt's tired face and feel sure he's going home. I can't blame him, really. Even I have begun to get bored with Lapa's smelly streets. Then, suddenly, I have one of those strange feelings that come in dreams. It's an urge to get Matt into the club. The sounds, the smells, the spectacles of Lapa all blur as I become completely fixated on this one goal.

"So are you coming in with us?" *One of Matt's housemates asks the question.* "If not, you could probably split a cab with Daniel and the others."

I catch a whiff of interest from Matt at the mention of a cab. No, I think. I go to him and sit down pleadingly in front of him. He can't see me, of course, but my desperate gaze bores into him with the force of a full-body lunge. "Go inside! Come on, just do it! It'll be fun! The night is young!"

"Uh, how much is it to get in?" *Matt looks doubtful.*

255

My tail wags furiously. I turn to look in the direction of the club, then back at Matt. "Go! What's a trip to Lapa without the nightclub experience? Come on, think of it as a study of Brazilian nightlife!"

"Well, I guess I'll go in with you guys," he says.

I sneeze ecstatically. He's doing it!

Inside the club, the music blares. The songs are a hodgepodge of styles ranging from samba to doo wop. People are crammed into the club's small interior, and the heat of so much humanity raises the temperature from warm to balmy. Matt stands with his friends for a few moments but is soon swept away by the movement of the crowd. One of his housemates puts a hand on his shoulder, guiding him back. Then, he is unwittingly carried again by the shifting current of bodies.

One by one, the members of Matt's group find dance partners. And, in keeping with Rio's nightclub etiquette, one by one these dance partners become make-out partners. It normally happens in a matter of minutes.

"Can I kiss you?" is the standard line— direct and to the point. Sometimes the even more direct use of body language is all it takes to bring two sets of lips together.

The night wears on. Song after song plays. It feels late, maybe three in the morning. The club is beginning to thin out. Hopefully, my human and his group will be leaving soon. Why did I want him to come here anyway?

"I think we're the only two people not making out right now." Roberto, from Matt's original group, hollers to him over the music.

Matt laughs at his friend's quip, but I sense that he is wondering why he's bothered coming to Lapa in the first place. Then, a female maneuvers toward him through the crowd.

"Hi. Do you speak Portuguese?"

"Yeah," he says, a little taken aback.

"Okay, well, my friend wants to make out with you."

He is clearly stunned by this bold assertion. After a moment's hesitation, he asks, "Can I talk to her first?"

"Do you wanna make out or not?"

Matt seems sufficiently cowed and says, "All right." The next minute he is embracing a shapely girl with long, curly hair.

"I'm really drunk," she informs him before beginning a deep, passionate kiss. There's a moment of awkwardness before he begins to relax and kiss her back.

The two spend time leaning against the wall, continuing what the inebriated young woman had so aggressively started. Finally, she breaks away.

"I think I need to sit down."

It then becomes apparent just how unsteady she is. I see Matt's desire to kiss her quickly fade—replaced by a desire to make her drink water and send her to bed. He sits down next to her. She introduces him to a few friends she has come with. Then, Roberto is tapping him on the shoulder, saying that the group is ready to go.

"Well, it was nice to meet you," he says to the girl, whose name is Rita. As they're saying a final goodbye, he hands her a business card he's made for his English teaching.

"Maybe we can do something sometime," he says vaguely. She thanks him.

It's more likely, I think as we board the van heading back to Copacabana, that she will wake up the next morning with a splitting hangover and no memory of the business card's owner. What was that all about anyway? I muse. Matt should have just gone home early. The whole thing had been so silly. Dreams are like that.

I woke up then, alone in the bedroom. I was feeling bored and alone. I didn't like being cooped up. It was late. Where was my human? He had some nerve going off and leaving me like this. I gave the bedroom another once over just in case I'd missed something edible the first time, and it was then I discovered that the bedroom

257

door hadn't been completely closed. I went out into the apartment to explore.

Another hour or so later, the housemates returned home. My anger dissolved upon seeing Matt, and I greeted him with enthusiastic jumps and a shower of happy sneezes. I smelled Lapa on him—litter, sweat, and cigarette smoke. Matt rubbed me all over, happy to be reunited.

"Uh, I think Gilly got upset at you for being left at home."

"Oh, no. Why?"

"He found the watermelon I left on the kitchen counter and there're pieces of the rind in front of your bedroom door. Looks like he was giving you a message."

The truth was, I hadn't planned on leaving the rinds in that particular place just to spite Matt; that's just the way it happened. The watermelon had distracted me from my boredom and slightly diminished my ravenous hunger. I knew it had been rash behavior driven by animal instinct. But then, if my dream had been accurate, I wasn't the only one who had satisfied an animal instinct that early morning.

Chapter 50

Rapid Romance

B y the middle of the next week Matt hadn't heard anything from his kissing partner and had apparently written the whole thing off. Then, checking his e-mail several days later, he found a message from an address he didn't recognize. I listened to the computer voice read the Portuguese text with its thick English accent.

"My friend, Rita, really liked getting to know you last Friday. She tried to call your cell phone, but it was turned off. Her Internet is down but if you e-mail her, she'll be able to read it when she goes to the Internet cafe. I hope you write to her. She's a very nice person."

Matt smiled as his computer finished reading, and I could tell he was pleased.

I wondered why this Rita hadn't e-mailed him herself. If she could get e-mail, obviously she could send it. Why go through a friend? It was a strange game they were playing.

Matt wrote back to Rita's friend thanking her, and then sent a few lines to Rita. He said he had enjoyed getting to know her and that it would be fun to hang out. He wasn't really a fan of Lapa, but maybe they could go to the beach or take his dog for a walk in the park. He signed the letter with a kiss, a standard good-bye for Brazilians.

The next day he received a reply. "Hi, kitten," was the opening line. This, I knew by now, was the Brazilian way of calling someone cute. She said she was happy to hear from him. She was very busy with her studies at the university, but she would like to get together, maybe the following weekend. She, too, closed with a kiss. And so they began a correspondence that continued through the next few weeks. Each weekend they talked about getting together, and each weekend something came up—the rain, a family function, illness.

Finally, one sunny Saturday, they managed to set a date. It wasn't the beach as Matt had hoped. It was a club in Ipanema where Rita and her friends liked to go. It wasn't a bad place; we had been there many times before. Matt managed to persuade his housemates to go with him. But, as he led me into the bedroom, I realized he didn't intend to take me along.

I couldn't believe it! Two times in less than a month! This Rita character had better be worth it.

A minute or two after Matt shut the door, I got up to investigate. Rats! He'd closed the door tight this time. There was no garbage can to overturn, no food to devour. I was stuck. With nothing left to do, I got up on the bed and went to sleep.

I awoke as Matt pushed the bedroom door open. I ran to greet him. He smelled of caipirinha, smoke, and disgust.

"Hi, Gilly!" He seemed to brighten as I pushed my wet snout against his hand. "Don't worry, you didn't miss anything—just another make-out session. I invited her back here to meet you, but she said no."

I lay down on the floor near the bed. *Better luck next time.*

"Brazilians are so weird," Matt muttered to himself. "They make out with you in public, but they won't visit your apartment."

It's okay, I told him, silently. *You can sleep with me tonight.* I wasn't sure how much consolation this was, but it was all I could offer.

The next day, as I listened to Matt play his guitar, I saw his confusion resurface. The music was charged and unsettled. What was he doing with this girl? Why had he kissed her again? What did he want from her, anyway? Self-reproach filled the room as he played on. Finally, the music subsided, and I sensed a calm decisiveness come over him. Placing the guitar on his bed, he opened his laptop and began to write.

A song, I thought.

And an important one judging by his focused attention. But, as my ears pricked to make out his computer's voice, I heard not English lyrics, but a short message, in Portuguese.

"Dear Rita,

How are you? I'm thinking about how we got together the first time in Lapa and again in Ipanema. In the little time that we've talked, you seem like a really cool person—intelligent, kind, and fun-loving. But, I think that I made a mistake, twice, in kissing you without appreciating these qualities. I hope that we can find a reason to get together beyond just making out. Maybe we can start over and get to know each other as friends."

An interesting approach, I thought as I watched Matt finish the e-mail. *He really seems to want clarity. Well, I hope it works out for him.*

Rita wrote back the next day. She said she found his idea of starting over as friends appealing and that she'd like to go to the beach with him and meet his dog.

Well, I wanted to meet her, too. She was going to fall in love with me; I just knew it. Maybe then Matt would have a girlfriend, and I'd be back on easy street.

On a sunny Saturday, Matt led a pretty, red-haired girl into the apartment. He introduced her as Rita. I greeted her warmly, sneezing once and wagging my tail.

"He really likes you."

My human was just being hospitable, trying to make her feel comfortable, but actually, I did like Rita. I could smell other dogs on her, and a cat, too. She had a kind radiance about her, though I could tell she was nervous. Matt could tell, too, and soon suggested that we head for the beach.

Walking on the sand a few blocks from the apartment, the two began to relax in each other's company. Matt talked about his English classes and the trip he was planning to Paris.

Rita was enthusiastic. She had studied some French and said she hoped to go to Europe someday. She loved art and culture. She had been in an acting company with friends and had put on plays in other cities. But, she explained, sadly, the group had broken up. Now that she was at a university, she didn't have time for it, anyway.

She talked about her friends and their various interests. She talked about her animals. She talked and talked and talked. It was as if a cork had been popped, and all the conversation they never had was spilling out of her. Matt smelled glad, and he listened attentively. Maybe he appreciated doing something other than kissing. Finally, they tired of walking, and we sat down in the sand.

"Do you always keep Gilly on a leash?"

"Well, no. But, if I let him off, you'll have to keep an eye on him. He tends to wander away." Rita agreed.

Suddenly, I was liberated! While the two sat talking and laughing, I traipsed across the beach, following the smells that promised something edible. I made my way up onto a rocky incline nearby. This place was called Arpoador, I knew. It divided Copacabana from Ipanema. But, I didn't care about any of that. What I cared about was eating, and this huge rock offered delicious rotting things in many of its nooks and crannies. After a while, I heard Matt and Rita coming up behind me.

"Gilly!"

I looked up from the gooey substance I was licking. The jig was up.

"Oh, I'm so sorry!" Rita said.

"Don't worry. He gets into things all the time." Matt pulled me away from my find and put the leash back on.

I was liking Rita more than ever now. She had a hands-off approach to dog handling and was easily engrossed in her own storytelling. As far as I was concerned, she and Matt had a real future together.

Rita, it turned out, loved the beach as much as Matt, but she went to ones closer to her home. She was from Niteroi, the smaller city just across the bay from Rio. She invited him to come visit her the next weekend so she could show him her favorite beach.

The next Saturday, Matt and I caught a van. It passed through Copacabana, took us to the center of Rio, and crossed the bridge to Niteroi. Rita met us as we exited, and we caught a bus to the beach. The whole trip took Matt and me almost two hours. I was dubious that any beach could be worth so much travel. There were perfectly fine ones just minutes from our apartment, after all.

Only after we had spent the afternoon with Rita did I begin to appreciate the magic of this new place. She explained that it was part of a nature preserve protected by the Brazilian government. Different from the urban beaches of Rio, it was bordered by natural forests and a small mountain that hikers could climb. When the ocean currents made swimming along the main shoreline impossible, a small inlet provided access to calm seas. The closest inhabitants to the area lived in a secluded neighborhood of quaint houses. Many of them were built into the natural surroundings.

Whether or not it had something to do with the lovely young woman at his side, I saw that Matt was captivated by the area. In the following weeks the pair returned again and again to this slice of paradise. They walked on the beach, swam in the ocean, and hiked the trails through the forest. They stopped often to kiss, which was a good thing because I needed to catch my breath. I wasn't used to getting so much exercise.

It didn't take too many days before the two humans began abandoning the trails and me altogether to disappear into the underbrush. They emerged minutes later more out of breath than I was.

The three of us even hiked to the top of the nearby mountain. It was more effort than I usually expended, but all the fascinating smells I inhaled hinted at edible treasures under every root and stone. Dogs weren't normally allowed on the trails, but once again, my guide status gained me access.

At the top of the mountain, I would collapse. But I enjoyed the fresh, clean air bursting with oxygen and the fact that we'd finally reached the top. Luckily, going back down took a lot less energy.

On the beach, I didn't stay nearly so close. Sometimes the two left me in the sand with their things so they could go swimming, and I'd seize the moment to strike out on my own. I'd wander along the beach, sniffing for remains of sandwiches or salty snacks. When I didn't find discarded food, I often found affectionate people more than willing to share. Matt and Rita would eventually come rushing up, apologizing to my new friends.

"He looked so hungry. I gave him a hamburger," explained one woman I had won over.

When the water was calm and Matt and Rita were particularly distracted by swimming, I had time to make my way up onto the nearby rocks in my never-ending quest for food. The first time I did this, I stumbled upon not just scraps but full course meals of rice, shrimp, chicken, and other delicacies. Finding this was the surprise of my life!

That day, Rita and Matt caught me in mid-feast. After Matt put me back on the leash with a stern reprimand, Rita explained that the meals were left by Brazilians who practiced an African religion called *Macumba*. The foods were offerings to the spirits. Whatever spirits appreciated this bounty, I'm certain they couldn't have enjoyed it any more than I did. The buffets on the rocks were the seventh layer of heaven for my taste buds, and I sought to reach that gourmet pinnacle every chance I got.

In early December, Rita invited Matt and me to her house. I loved it there. It had a shady front yard with large trees that dropped their ripe fruits right onto the ground. There I could graze until I got a stomachache or until Matt realized what I was doing and called me back to the porch. Rita's mom kept chickens on one side of the house along with a funny bird I'd never seen before. She called it a cordorna. Matt later found out it was what Americans would call a quail.

And I wasn't the only canine at Rita's family home. Several dogs lived on the premises, but I wasn't quite sure which ones were family members and which were frequent visitors, like me. Two dogs were tied up in the yard most of the time, and two others came and went, jumping over the low wall around the property to roam the neighborhood at will. One of these, a black dog, named Madruga, snapped at me the first time I got close to her. She'd become tough and feisty from her time on the streets, and I quickly learned to stay out of her way.

The household's animal population was rounded out by a pet cat, caged birds, a band of tiny monkeys who lived in the fruit trees, and Rita's pet rabbit, whose wire cage swung from a pulley system of ropes. Rita said she was keeping him safe from hungry dogs. It seems a former pet rabbit had been done in by one of the dogs and ended up in the family's soup pot. I, for one, would never think of bothering her rabbit, and I didn't care for soup.

Matt met Arminda, Rita's mom, who was a housewife and spent her free time volunteering at her church and singing in the parish choir. They had exchanged only a few words during their first meeting before she turned to Rita and instructed her to make Matt lunch.

I could tell Matt was very pleased with this arrangement!

On our third visit to Rita's house we met her dad, Joao, as it was his day off from his job as a butcher. In the small living room, Joao shook Matt's hand, offered him a beer, and then asked him about his favorite Brazilian soccer team. This was, I'd seen, a loaded question in Brazil. It was like identifying one's political party. Matt knew as much about soccer as I knew about flying airplanes, but he did remember the name of the team his old friend, Philip, had rooted for back in Maria's house.

"Botafogo. That's my team."

Joao grunted in acknowledgement. "I'm Flamengo." An awkward silence followed until Joao offered, "Botafogo is okay."

Rita's dad was turning back to the soccer match on TV when Arminda spoke up from the kitchen.

"Joao loves soccer so much because he was a great player when he was younger, right Joao?"

"I knew how to play," he said, his eyes still on the TV.

Arminda came into the living room and sat down on the couch next to her husband. "He was good enough to be a professional, but then the accident happened, and his knee got messed up. We were all devastated, but life went on, right Joao?"

"Yeah, you gotta take life as it comes."

"That's a great way to look at it." Matt seemed happy to agree.

"Well, we think it's wonderful that you're as active as you are," Rita's mom said. "You travel to other countries and teach English classes."

"Oh, thanks. I guess I'm just living my life like anybody else."

"Well, you're a very blessed person," Arminda said. "Rita has three cousins who are blind, all sisters. And they're so afraid to go out alone that they hardly ever leave the house. They use canes. They don't have a dog like you do."

"I'm lucky to have Gilly."

Lying near the entrance to the kitchen, I blinked in agreement.

"Gilly," Joao called. "We're gonna take you and Matt hunting! We're gonna catch us some 'possom, Gilly."

"Dad, he's not a hunting dog!" Rita said. "You're not taking him anywhere."

By mid-December, Matt had met the rest of Rita's family and remaining friends. The two had gotten to know each other better than seemed possible in the span of two months. They both knew he was leaving, but it was a reality they had simply ignored, growing more and more attached as the days went by. Now, reality was becoming unavoidable. Our departure was imminent, and Matt, though saddened to leave Rita, took on the excited scent of an adventurer.

It had been exactly one year since we'd flown out of Rio at the end of Matt's Rotary scholarship. This time, our trip to the airport included not only Rafael and Adriana but also Rita. Nobody knew how long we would be gone, and I think this uncertainty added to the melodrama. Rafael and Adriana gave Matt fierce hugs, and Rita gave him enough good-bye kisses to last for years. She told him if he didn't come back, she would come to Paris to find him. After one last kiss, Matt took a flight attendant's shoulder, and we boarded the airplane.

I saw clearly that Matt was leaving an even richer life behind than he had the year before—his English students, the beach, his friends, and above all, Rita. As much as I hated to go, I sensed it was important for him to follow his dream of finding success in France. Better to act now than to have regrets. If this new experience proved even half as enriching as Brazil, it would be well worth the effort. And, if it turned out to be a mistake, well, we could always come back to Brazil. Couldn't we?

Chapter 51

Not in Kansas Anymore

Once again, we arrived in a new country, this time at the Charles de Gaulle Airport in Paris, France. It was early February. We'd spent Christmas and the month of January in Pittsburgh with Matt's mom while he made arrangements to rent a room just outside Paris.

On the plane, Matt reviewed the last two tapes of the French language program he'd gotten for Christmas. I slept for most of the five hours we were in the air. Unfortunately, this time it hadn't occurred to anyone to put us in first class. But the flight was uneventful, and, while I missed the luxurious pillow and blanket treatment, I had no complaints.

We were escorted to the baggage claim by a French airport employee who spoke to Matt politely in English. I could tell he was disappointed that he couldn't practice any of the conversational French he'd been studying so hard. I was just glad to be off the airplane and stretching my legs. I hoped that wherever we were going was close and that my breakfast would be served soon.

Our new landlady greeted us at the door to the apartment building. Her name was Alison, and she was a tall, sturdy woman, not young, not old. She asked politely about our flight in fluent, mildly-accented English as she showed us to our room. I could smell her cat lurking somewhere nearby. I licked my lips hungrily. Where there was a cat, there was cat litter. This place definitely had potential.

The room was just large enough to fit a couch that pulled out into a bed.

"You can feed your dog out on the porch here." She showed Matt how to open the sliding glass door leading outside. A blast of winter cold flooded the small space.

"Usually I just feed him indoors."

"Yes, the problem is that it will be difficult to clean the carpet."

Matt looked like he wanted to argue but stopped himself. It was her home.

I finally got my breakfast. Thank goodness Matt had not forgotten to bring kibble. He hadn't packed his own breakfast, but luckily, Alison offered him some bread from her bread machine. He accepted without hesitation. By the speed with which he devoured slice after slice, I realized he was as hungry as I'd been. I guess the food on the plane hadn't been very filling.

"My son, Orson, is with his father today. He will come home tonight," Alison told Matt. In between mouthfuls of bread, Matt asked about her son. He was four, she said, and loved Star Wars.

"He would be pleased to practice English with you."

"I would be pleased to practice French with him. He could probably teach me a lot."

After the bread, Alison took us outside and explained that the river, Marne, flowed some fifty feet behind the apartment complex. Dog smells were everywhere, and I kept my nose low to the ground to grab quick sniffs as we walked on the wide path by the water.

"I will give you a key so that you can come and go as you please. I will be busy during the day; I teach physical education at a school near here. At night, I take care of my son. If you want to go to Paris, the train station is just three blocks away. There is a small market in town where you can buy food."

"All right, thanks." Matt and she were speaking in English. "Maybe you could walk into town with me the first time so Gilly and I can learn the route."

"Yes, maybe."

Back inside the house, Matt collapsed onto the foldout couch that was now his bed. I heard his stomach churning. The bread

269

hadn't filled him up, but I had the sense that more than his remaining hunger made him uneasy in these unfamiliar surroundings. There were still so many new routines we would have to establish, and I imagined it was all weighing on him. He hadn't even figured out how to take me outside the apartment yet. The walk with our new landlady had gone by in a blur, too fast for him to get his bearings.

And then there was Alison. It wasn't that she was unkind. She had been civil. But it was a far cry from the warm reception and overflowing hospitality we had gotten used to in Brazil. Well, Matt had wanted a change of culture, and he'd gotten it. Hopefully, she would offer some help as we got used to this new environment. At least she had a cat.

By mid-afternoon, Matt had learned his way from his bedroom to the bathroom and kitchen, but there had been no sign of lunch for him. I guess he wasn't comfortable asking Alison for more food, and she had offered none. Later that day, however, there was a bright spot.

"Marc!" I pressed my muzzle against our old French friend in greeting as he entered the apartment. His scent brought back the happy times we'd spent together in Rio.

The three humans sat down in the living room to watch the soccer game. Matt and Marc reminisced about old times in Rio. Alison served more of the same bread from that morning but this time offered jams and Nutella to accompany it. Matt devoured piece after piece with even more gusto than he had that morning.

After the game, Marc suggested that Matt play some guitar. He agreed and proceeded to play two Beatles songs, a bossa nova, and a Cuban folk song for the pair of onlookers. They listened politely, applauding after each number.

"That was great," Marc said. "Why don't you play one of your own songs?"

Dutifully, Matt picked up the guitar again and began playing a song I recognized from years before. He'd written it for Amanda. It was about longing, nostalgia, and confusion. Its chorus asked the question, *Are we in love?*

He was playing now for himself as much as for the small audience. I knew he was suffering from the strangeness and uncertainty of our arrival in Paris. Had he made the right choice in coming here? It was cold, unfamiliar, and unfriendly. He felt more vulnerable than he had in a long time.

Then the music was over, and the two listeners applauded. "Whoa, good show," Marc said.

"You're very talented," Alison said. "It's too bad I can't sell tickets for people to come listen to you."

Matt smiled, glowing from the compliments. "I came to Paris to get better in French, but I'd really like to share my music with people here."

"Well, maybe you will," Marc said. "People here really value artists."

We'll see, I thought.

Chapter 52

City of Lights

Matt filled the passing days with French TV and grammar lessons on the Internet. He was learning French, yes, but I knew this wasn't enough. As always, I could tell with his music. His discontent was coming through clearly. Matt was eager to make our maiden voyage into Paris. He hadn't come all this way just to stay stuck in an apartment learning the language. He needed to get out and experience it. Equally important, he needed English students to help pay his rent.

Orson, Allison's young son, was cute but too young to teach him French, and Allison didn't have the time or desire. It was all Matt could do to persuade her to let him go to the grocery store with her. Finally, a break came. I heard him arrange over Skype to meet with Luciana, a friend from Rio, to get a French lesson at her apartment. She gave him the name of the metro stop near her building and told him to call when he got outside the station. She would come get us and walk us to her apartment. They set the class for that Wednesday.

Wednesday arrived, and Matt was ready to go. Ready, but far from prepared. He had no idea how to get from Alison's house to the train station or how to navigate through the metro system. And, of course, neither did I.

As it happened, French schools were off on Wednesday, which meant Alison and Orson were home. Matt told Alison that he planned to go to Paris and asked if she could help him. He needed to know how to get to the train station and then what transfer to make onto the metro to get to Luciana's. Alison found a metro map and gave him some directions, which he saved on his recorder.

"Would you walk the three blocks with me?"

"That's difficult because I have to stay here and watch Orson."

"Oh." I caught a whiff of his displeasure, though Matt said nothing. "Well, could you just describe the route?"

"Yes, I can do that for you. First, you must walk right along the river. Do you remember us walking that way on Sunday?"

"Uh, yeah."

"Well, then you will come to some steps that lead up to the street. You must take these steps and then go left for three blocks."

"Okay. And the train station is right there?"

"You must cross the street and turn left, and the entrance is there, yes."

"Thanks."

He went to his room and got his backpack and wallet and my harness. I followed close at his heel. I could smell his misgivings about how this was going, but he was clearly going to try. He knew France wasn't going to be easy.

"Mathieu," Alison said, as we stood at the front door, Matt fiddling with the latch. "I can take you in the car if you prefer."

"Really?" He turned around.

"Yes, Orson can come with us. But, you really must learn to go to the station yourself. I will not be able to take you in the future."

I felt Matt burn at these words. What he'd really wanted, I knew, was for her to walk the route with him so he could learn it for himself. But, that was more than she was willing to do. So he pushed down his pride and accepted her offer.

Alison let us off at the entrance of the train station, and Matt said a cheerful *au revoir* to Orson. We went inside. He had no idea where to go, so obviously, neither did I. We wandered through the station, stopping first at a wall, then at a large sign, then at some turnstiles. Finally, I took a minute to collect myself. It was tough guiding like this.

Did he need to buy a ticket? I didn't know. When we'd taken the metro in Rio, the guards had let him through for free as a person with a disability. They had even accompanied us down below to the tracks where they had waited with us and gotten us on the right train. Was there a similar sort of system here? The turnstiles opened and closed as people passed through on either side of us.

"Excusez-moi," he said, but no one stopped. Finally, someone approached us.

"Oui, monsieur?"

"I'd like to go to Chetley Station, please." I'd been listening to his French since we'd arrived, and just like in Brazil, I had started to understand much of what Matt said in this new language.

"Very good. Do you have a ticket?" I saw by his authoritative manner and uniform that the man was a station employee.

"No."

"Come with me."

Matt motioned me forward towards the voice. I took a few steps and then stopped.

"Can I have your . . . your hand?" My human was flustered. I don't think he knew how to say elbow or shoulder in French.

"Pardon, monsieur?"

Matt extended his hand towards the man. He took it and led us to a line of people. He spoke something in rapid-fire French. Then, he was gone.

Matt cautiously inched his way forward in the line. At last, he found the ticket window and purchased a one-way ticket to Chetley. As he received his change, he said, "I would like some help getting to the train, please."

The woman asked him something in her quick French. Matt didn't understand it, so I didn't either. After an awkward moment, he repeated his request. "I would like some help to go to the train, please."

"D'accord, monsieur. Une minute."

Matt stepped to the side and waited. Soon, another woman arrived and led us onto an elevator to the train platform; then she stayed to help us board our train. When we sat down, I gave a sigh of relief.

About twenty minutes later, we heard a voice announce our station. Matt and I found our way to the door and exited onto a train platform. Two other people got off, but before Matt could ask for assistance, they were gone. He swiveled his head around, listening in all directions. The station was quiet. A minute went by, then another. We would have to do this on our own.

Matt urged me forward. The train tracks were on our left. Every few steps he stopped and asked me to turn right. I guess he was looking for a corridor leading into the station. Naturally, what he didn't know was that the only thing on the right was a long graffiti-covered wall.

At the end of the platform, I stopped. There was nowhere to go. A rustle coming from the corner attracted Matt's attention. It was a man, very shabbily dressed and strong smelling. He had his back to us. Maybe he could help, I thought. Then I heard the sound of liquid on concrete and smelled the urine. Matt did an about face and urged me in the opposite direction.

"Welcome to Paris," I heard him mutter.

Backtracking, we finally found a place to turn off of the platform and made our way down this new path.

"Find the steps," Matt told me as we moved. I, personally, was hoping for an elevator, but none was in sight. Neither were any steps. I continued forward, and then stopped. Another set of train tracks was just in front of us.

Matt stuck out his foot.

No! These aren't steps! Matt, stop!

Of course, he didn't know it was the train tracks. His foot hung over the edge now, probing for the next imagined step. I stood, watching in silent horror, unable to help.

Someone was approaching us, calling out in rapid French.

"Pardon?" Matt turned around.

The man took his shoulder saying something about the train. Matt finally understood what was happening, and I breathed a deep sigh of relief.

"Where are you going?" the man, large and dark-skinned, continued in French. Matt told him he was looking for Chetley Station.

"Where are you from?" the man asked, switching to English. With what I could see was a mixture of disappointment and relief, Matt answered in the same language.

As our savior guided us through the massive station, he explained that he was originally from Nigeria but had been living in France for twenty years. He led us up steps, down corridors, and then waited with us at the metro line until our car came. Our destination was seven stops away, he explained. Matt thanked him again and again. Then we were on the metro car, rumbling through the bowels of Paris. I lay down at Matt's feet with a sigh. I missed Brazil.

Once we finally made it to the apartment, Luciana proved a very willing and able teacher. She patiently answered Matt's questions about French slang and verbal shortcuts. Then she read slowly from a simple textbook. After a while, she turned the class over to Matt so he could help her with English. It was already very good. She just wanted to practice the subtle nuances that set foreigners apart from native speakers. They focused on phrasal verbs and pronunciation. I focused on getting some much-deserved beauty rest.

Matt, I knew, was grateful for the lessons, but he wanted more than the one class a week that Luciana could give him. He set up weekly sessions with a French teacher in Paris. We settled into the routine of making two trips there each week.

The commute was difficult for both of us. The path winding from Alison's apartment along the Marne River was covered with the scents of other dogs, and they drove me crazy. I constantly wanted to stop and sniff, but Matt would have none of it. I learned to pause and squat for a few seconds so that Matt would stop and remove my harness. The only problem was that if I didn't actually do any business, he would get furious. He felt taken advantage of, I knew. I didn't like to see him like this, but I just couldn't help myself. Guide dog or not, it was my nature to sniff after my own kind.

Matt finally got the bright idea of carrying some of my new French dog food in his pocket. When I broke away from a sniff, he would reward me with praise and a croquette. The food reward significantly speeded up our progress. I learned much later that Matt had anticipated a paradigm shift. In later years, the strategy of using food rewards to motivate guide dogs was taught in guide dog schools. My human was a groundbreaker!

In spite of fewer pit stops, the trip was a struggle. Particularly in the first few weeks, we had little idea where we were going. Alison had eventually taken us on a walk to the train station, but one guided trip didn't result in our smooth sailing. Matt knew we had to take steps leading up to the street before we got to a bridge. What he didn't know was that there were at least two sets of steps, each leading up to a different street. After getting hopelessly lost more than once, he finally figured it out. Eventually, he determined that it was roughly three hundred and fifty steps from our door to the correct flight of stairs. The stopping and starting we did confused him, and he had never been the greatest step counter.

Once inside the station, we grew adept at locating the ticket counter and asking for assistance. Matt found out that residents with disabilities could ride the trains and metro for free, but since he hadn't lived in France for three years, he wasn't technically eligible for the privilege. Sometimes, the employee asked us for a ticket, and sometimes they opened the gate for us to pass through without one.

I saw that Matt left it up to their discretion. It didn't concern me one way or the other since I never had to pay.

"*Bonjour,*" Matt said. We stood at the ticket counter of the train station. I'd taken him right to it this time. After weeks of practice, I had the routine down.

"I'd like a ticket to Chetley Station. And could you call there so someone can meet me and help me in the metro?"

"*Bien sur, monsieur,* and here's your ticket."

Matt put his change into his wallet. "And could you please call for someone to escort me to the train?"

"Bien sur, just a minute and I will."

I wasn't the only one who had gotten our routine down. Matt was asking for help like never before. A metro employee almost always came to meet us now and helped us through the labyrinth of hallways from train to metro.

There were times when no one showed up even after Matt had asked, and on those occasions he would stand still on the platform and wait. When the next train rolled in and dispensed passengers, Matt waved or called out until one of them offered us help.

It wasn't like in Rio where all we had to do was stand there. Sometimes several trains came and went before the kind soul we were waiting for arrived. But, sooner or later, someone always appeared. Matt had learned to be patient. He didn't even try to steer us through Chetley Station on our own. I was relieved—no more scary moments watching his foot probe the edge of a train platform. Now I could relax until our assistance came.

I was proud of my human. He'd figured out a way that worked.

The weeks passed. Matt's French got better, but his morale got worse. The trips to Paris were long and exhausting. Alison and he were on fragile terms. She wanted him to do half the dusting and vacuuming in the apartment. I could have told her that cleaning wasn't his strong suit.

His Rio friends now living in Paris were supportive, but there was only so much they could do for him. They had busy lives and demanding work schedules. He wanted to integrate himself more into French society, but how? He didn't have a scholarship to pay for any studies, and he had no job. His efforts to teach English had fallen flat. He had given flyers to Alison to distribute at her school, and he had asked his friends to spread the word. But, so far, nothing. After talking about his predicament with Marc one evening, his friend offered to help.

"I'll check with my supervisor at work. I think I can persuade her to meet with you. The company has a policy of helping minorities and, you know, underprivileged people. Maybe she can offer you some work. Your English skills have gotta count for something."

We had been in France for about a month now, and my human was already talking with friends and family about going home. He missed Rio for all the same reasons as in the past. And now, Rita had been added to the top of the list. They had been exchanging e-mails since he left—nothing terribly romantic, just a friendly keeping in touch. But I knew through his music that he felt something for her.

Part of him, I sensed, felt silly for ever having left Brazil. I wondered why we didn't just go back. Something else seemed to be keeping him in France. Was he holding out for the interview with Marc's company? No, that wasn't it. What was it?

Chapter 53

One Last Trick

O ne morning I watched as Matt strapped his guitar to his back before we left Alison's apartment. He had never taken it with us to Paris before, but now, off we trod in the direction of the train station. I hadn't heard him make any arrangements for a gig. He didn't have plans to meet up with anyone, at least, not that I knew of. I was puzzled.

Matt walked with more confidence than he had on previous days. His steps were purposeful, his demeanor light and upbeat. I guessed his enthusiasm stemmed from the instrument resting snugly behind him. He did love being the traveling musician.

"You play?" asked the train station employee who led us onto the platform.

"I do."

"Oh, are you going to play in Paris?"

"Yes, I am."

"Do you have a band?" she asked.

"No."

"Ah, you play alone."

This was the most conversation he had managed with her in a while, and she seemed dutifully impressed by his music connection. I hoped she'd ask him where exactly he planned to play, but she didn't.

We got off the train at Chetley Station. Matt had been so busy strutting his musician's stuff earlier that he hadn't bothered to ask for an escort to meet us. But he didn't seem at all fazed. He stopped abruptly on the platform and, before the exiting passengers had disappeared, called out in a clear, confident voice.

"Excuse-moi!"

"Oui?" A young, perfumed woman with blonde hair walking by us responded. Matt asked her for help transferring to line four. He didn't specify what kind of help, and she generously guided us all the way to our metro car. Maybe she had been taken by his musician's image. Maybe she was just being nice.

We got off the metro and found our way up some steps and into a long, narrow hallway. Its ceiling was high, causing the clicks and taps of shoes to echo loudly through the corridor. Without warning, Matt told me to halt. He then took two steps over to the far wall of the hall and sat down. I stood there, unsure of what exactly he was doing. Then, as he unzipped his guitar case, I understood. He was going to sing for handouts—to busk, as his musician friends called it.

It didn't make sense, and yet it all made sense now. Without a permit to play in one of the metro areas designated for musicians, Matt had remembered this corridor as a good alternative. The high ceiling and narrow walls would amplify his guitar and voice. This spot was a convergence of at least two metro lines, and there was a constant flow of people coming and going. The permit was a detail he'd chosen to overlook.

I lay down on the cold, hard floor next to Matt. He was nervous as he withdrew his guitar from its case. He sat there for a minute or two, the guitar in his lap, fighting his fear. Finally, he began to play.

The notes spilled out like pennies into a rippling pond, the reverberating sounds loud enough to be heard even over the roar of the metro cars below. It was, I think, exactly as he'd hoped. After a few minutes, he dared to open his mouth and sing. Almost miraculously, his voice projected through the air with an unnatural strength. It sounded loudest and loveliest at the top of its range. The heavy amplification provided by the hallway forgave any quavering and masked any strain. He was a magnificent tenor. His falsetto, too, carried in ghostly echoes through the hall. The music was beautiful, soulful and cried out to be heard.

I think he sang every song he knew, pausing only briefly to catch his breath. When he ran out of material, he started making up melodies. They were repetitive, but he only needed five or ten seconds of material since that was the longest anyone would hear him.

An hour or so later, he was breathless, and his voice was beginning to sound strained. Then, when it looked as if he'd played his last tune, I heard the clink of metal on metal. A shabbily dressed man had dropped a coin into Matt's guitar case as he passed by. Someone responding to his music? Someone contributing to my dinner? It wasn't clear, but what was certain was that the simple act had brightened Matt's spirits. He played his cover of "Imagine" one more time.

Matt saved the coins in a pouch of his guitar case. Later, he presented them to Marc for an official count.

"Wow, there's at least five euros here." His friend looked at the small pile in admiration.

Matt laughed, then calculated aloud that minus the train ticket he had bought, he had made between two and three euros. Well, it wasn't about the money, he said to Marc. It was the joy of the experience.

We returned again and again to our music spot where coins rained into Matt's guitar case. I saw his enthusiasm spark at each new clink. The notes of his guitar rang out with clarity, and he sang with passion. Gradually, however, behind the music, I began to make out something else. It was a desperate, anxious voice.

Notice me! Please, just listen! The voice became quiet, momentarily satisfied, after each sound of coins. Then, it started up again. *Pay attention, just for a second!* As I lay next to Matt listening to the music, I wondered if this unsettling voice was his.

Days turned to weeks. We continued our performances in the metro, but I saw Matt's joy beginning to fade. Even the sound of money did little to cheer him. The floor was uncomfortable. I felt his fingers numb in the chill of the station. And then there was the problem of going to the bathroom. I could relieve myself on the sidewalk outside the entrance, but Matt didn't have such an option. Going into a restaurant required first, finding one, and then, buying something. The cheapest item available, he discovered, was a coffee costing four euros. And I knew Matt wasn't about to blow his earnings so soon. He simply had to hold it until he got home at the end of the afternoon.

Matt stopped taking his coins to Marc for a count. He just threw them into his pocket at the end of his playing time, which, I noticed, came earlier and earlier. On the train ride home, his shoulders slumped against the seat, his mood somber.

I was content to support my human in whatever project he invested his energy. I wasn't exactly enthralled by his metro shows, but if he enjoyed them, they were worth it to me. As time passed and it became clear that they were losing their appeal, I began to wonder. Couldn't he just give it a rest and cut us both a break? Surely there were other ways he could share his music and make some money. Panhandling, the metro, even Paris—they were all dragging him down. Considering these ideas one night, I fell asleep and had a particularly vivid dream.

I walk, on a moonlit evening, along the river, Marne. It's the same route that Matt and I take into Paris, only he's nowhere to be seen.

Out of harness, I'm free to sniff. I trace the fresh, intoxicating scent of a dachshund. I follow her trail down the path, marking as I go. Suddenly, I catch another scent. Matt's scent. Soon, my ears perk at the familiar sound of his guitar playing. I spot him sitting near the edge of the river, hunched over his instrument. I stop in front of him, and now I can make out the words to his song.

"*Gonna be a great musician in my day—language speaker, world traveler. Loved by many! You'll see, you'll see. Loved by all. Just wait and see.*"

I don't like these lyrics. They have a grasping quality, not Matt's usual style. I begin to feel anxious and ill at ease. At last the song is over. I shake myself, my metal dog tags jingling.

"Merci, monsieur," Matt says, his head turned in my direction.

"It's me, Gilly!" My voice comes out sounding human, and for once, I can project my feelings as words. I press my nose against his hand. "Why'd you leave the house without me?"

"Hi, Gilly!" Matt strokes my head. "Sorry, boy, I just, I just need to get people to hear my music. How else am I gonna be a great musician, you know?"

"Maybe you could get some sleep first," I say, lying down at his feet.

"Gilly, we didn't come all the way to Paris just to sleep! This is a city of great artists, and if I'm gonna be one myself, I gotta get cracking."

"You're doing this the hard way," I say, sadly. "If you could just relax a little . . ."

"Relax? Yeah, that's easy for you to say. You're a dog."

The hair on the back of my neck rises as I reflect, for a second, on the freakishness of this conversation.

"It's different for humans, Gilly. We have to work at stuff, push ourselves, or we don't get anywhere. You think I wouldn't rather be back in Brazil hanging out at the beach? Well, I would, but no one ever became a great musician at the beach."

I look at him for a long moment. His thin frame sits cross-legged on the ground, his guitar still in his lap, his hand curved around its neck. I'm overcome with compassion for this human, my human.

"Matt, you are a great musician. Really. I just wish you could believe it."

He smiles, glowing. "Thanks, Guildenstern. I appreciate that. Even if you are a little biased, you know, being my dog and all, it's still nice to hear."

I scratch my ear. "Good. Can we go back to Brazil and visit the beach now?"

Matt laughs and strums an open chord. "Nope, sorry. We have more work to do. But, hey, there's a river right here. Watch my guitar 'cause I'm gonna take a little swim."

Before I can protest, Matt has put down his guitar and is wading into the murky, foul-smelling water. I try to call him back, but I suddenly feel very, very heavy. He's submerged in the water now, and I have the horrible sense that this water isn't good for him—not like Brazil's refreshing pools.

"Come back," I call as he begins to drift downstream. He shows no sign of hearing me.

I woke up from the dream, a yelp caught in my throat. I lay beside the bed where Matt slept soundly, his breathing deep and even. I could still recognize the harsh odor of the Marne in my nostrils, and I shook myself off and found a more comfortable position on the carpet. Finally, I managed to fall back to sleep.

We made more trips to Paris. Matt continued his French lessons and his metro performances. The weather got better. We spent more time just walking outside along the river together in the sunshine. Matt let me out of my harness and I had a chance to sniff the scents of other dogs to my heart's content.

Then, the meeting Marc had promised for Matt with his supervisor materialized. It turned out to be little more than an informational interview during which the well-intentioned woman told him about agencies for the blind in Paris—but no job.

This proved to be the final nail in the coffin of our Paris experience. Although we had been in France just over two months, Matt told his family and friends that the city was too expensive and that he was booking a flight home. I heard resignation in his voice and beneath that a hint of relief.

I didn't like to see Matt's projects go awry; but, if it contributed to getting us out of France, it was a necessary evil. The walks along the river were nice, but they were nothing compared to the blissful beach romps that were waiting for me back in Brazil.

Chapter 54

Fireworks

R afael greeted us at the airport in Rio with hugs as warm and affectionate as he had given some months before when we said goodbye. I leaped up and down just at seeing him again. My love for this great friend hadn't lessened a bit during my time in the United States and France.

With his help, we moved back into the penthouse in Ipanema where we had lived with Gabriel and August. Once again, the apartment was home to three male bachelors. Just like the old days, there were wild parties on the weekends. And just like the old days, I really enjoyed them. They often involved food handouts, or at the very least, the taste of spilled beer. Rita enjoyed them, too. She and Matt had picked up their courtship where they'd left off, and she and her friends came to the frenetic affairs on Saturday nights.

Rita was the most enthusiastic partygoer I'd ever seen. While she was normally shy and reserved around people she didn't know, at a party she drank until she became jovial, spontaneous, and totally uninhibited. This was the side of her Matt had kissed on their first encounter in Lapa. It was the side of her that, the more he saw, the more he disliked.

"Don't you think you drank too much?" he'd ask her as she lay in bed with a terrible headache. "Why don't you limit yourself to two drinks?"

I remembered Matt's enthusiastic drinking in college and smiled to myself as I considered the irony that he was now dispensing tips on staying sober.

Rita would agree with his ideas—in theory. But by the next party, she would insist on "just one more" until she had repeated the old pattern: spilled drinks, blackouts, nights being sick, days being hung over. During one party Rita got drunk and, walking out with some friends, tripped on a step and fell. The result was a black eye and other bruises.

Matt became incensed by her drinking. He gave her long, boring lectures on the importance of taking responsibility for herself. Rita would listen politely and explain that the drinks were stronger than usual or that her friends had talked her into it.

New Year's Eve came. The couple helped organize a dinner party in the penthouse, and it was a great success. Matt ate and drank contentedly, I got a nice assortment of scraps from the floor, and Rita, in animated conversation with her friends, remained fairly sober. Then, around ten o'clock, the group of Brazilians and gringos decided to go to the beach in Copacabana to see the New Year's Eve fireworks. Matt was reluctant, but Rita insisted. The event was world famous, she said, one of the largest of its kind. Finally, Matt agreed.

Outside the apartment, the city's wildly festive atmosphere reminded me of Carnival. We walked the thirty minutes or so through Ipanema's crowded, noisy streets into the thronging chaos of Copacabana. As we approached the mobbed beach, the group from the dinner party fragmented into twos and threes. Matt, Rita, and I found ourselves among strangers on the sand.

"We have to find the others!" Rita shouted over the noise.

"No, we're better off just staying put."

I recognized my human's stress at the confusion of so much noise, so many people. Rita frantically dialed numbers on her cell phone. Then, with an air of frustration, she gave up.

"I've never spent New Year's Eve away from my friends. How could they just leave us like this?"

Matt, who now sat next to me in the sand stroking my fur, wasn't any happier. "Just enjoy the fireworks."

Rita bought a caipirinha and sat down next to us. "You should see all the flowers. Everybody has some. They throw them into the sea at midnight. It's supposed to honor Iemanja—she's the Queen of the Ocean."

She finished her drink, bought another, and then continued her instruction on the Brazilian culture of New Year's.

"Almost everybody's wearing white. It's traditional, for peace and good luck for the new year."

Well, I thought with satisfaction. *I fit right in.*

Rita took a healthy sip of her drink. "But colors mean some-thing, too. Red's for passion—you have some red on your shirt, *amor,*" she said. When Matt said nothing, she went on. "Yellow's for happiness, pink's for love—" She broke off to buy another caipirinha from a passing beach vendor.

At last, the fireworks began. They exploded magnificently over the water in brilliant shimmers and thunderous cracks. The specta-tors roared with approval and applauded.

Sitting in the sand, Matt remained silent throughout the show. I lay next to him, equally mute, though much more peaceful. I realized the flowers, the colors, and the fireworks were all lost on him. He was bored. And as soon as the show ended, with an extravagant finale, he stood up. "Okay, ready to go?"

"Fine, just let me finish my drink."

Rita was sipping from her last purchase. Suddenly, several friends from our dinner party called to her. She answered excitedly, and we went to meet them. As she began talking with one young woman, I could hear her speech beginning to slur. Matt murmured to her that it was time to go, but she ignored him. Someone handed her another drink.

"Rita, let's go!" he said angrily.

"I'm having fun!"

"You've had enough fun tonight!" He reached over, found her drink, and threw it into the sand.

"Hey! Why'd ya do that?"

"You're drunk!"

"Everybody gets drunk on New Year's!"

"Let's go." He determinedly grasped her shoulder. She let him turn her away from the group, and we slowly made our way to the street. She weaved and bobbed under his grip.

"Which way?" he asked.

Her reply was too slurred to be understood.

"Excuse me," Matt called to a passerby. "Which way is Ipanema?"

He guided Rita through the crowded streets. She stayed on her feet and kept him on the sidewalk. I followed behind them as we awkwardly made our way, stopping several more times to ask directions. We finally arrived at our building and went inside. When we reached the elevator, Rita uttered something unintelligible. As Matt released his grip on her shoulder to press the elevator button, she collapsed onto the floor.

He said nothing until later the next day when she was sober. "I'm not trying to threaten you, but I just want you to know the truth. I think your drinking's really unattractive, and it's not good for either of us. If you keep acting like this, I don't want to be your boyfriend anymore. I'm sorry. That's just how I feel."

Rita was apologetic. "I don't want to lose you," she said tearfully. "It's just, it's hard to stop. When I'm at a party, I want to relax and have a good time, but I feel really awkward if I don't drink." Then, with more tears, she agreed to stop drinking whenever Matt asked her to.

We began going to Niteroi to visit Rita at her family's home on the weekends his housemates had parties. The two took up, in my opinion, a more productive hobby. They learned to cook. Rita's mom showed her how to make some traditional Brazilian dishes, and Rita found more recipes online. When Matt and I visited, she showed him how to make some of the heavenly-smelling foods. She seemed to enjoy being Matt's cooking teacher as much as she did the actual cooking itself. I think it tickled her that he tried to follow her in this domestic task since Brazilian men rarely ventured into this "woman's domain." Of course, I was totally on board. Matt, more than Rita, was much more likely to drop bits of food.

The truth is, Rita seemed to enjoy doing just about everything that Matt liked. She began reading to him, sometimes for hours. They completed a whole series of stories about a place called Narnia. Rita's voice was smooth and melodic, and her Portuguese lent the passages an exotic flavor I found pleasing, even if I didn't understand all the words. Matt would listen, his body turned towards her, the picture of attention and enjoyment.

After the Narnia stories, they moved on to a huge volume on the history of bossa nova and then a book by someone called Machado de Asis. All of these they read at Matt's urging. I thought, at first, that Rita delighted in the books and the act of reading simply because Matt did. But, I came to realize from their discussions that she had a quick mind and a similar appreciation for literature and learning.

Then Matt asked her to read from *A Course in Miracles*. He tried to explain its importance to him and how it had helped change his outlook on life. So she began reading it aloud from a Portuguese translation they found online. During the third session, she stopped at the end of a section. "I feel like I'm being brainwashed!"

"Oh. Well, yeah, in a way it is a sort of brainwashing. It's cleaning out all of the gunk in our minds and helping us to focus on what's real. Try reading just a little more, okay?"

So, she continued. After a few more pages, she broke off midsentence. "It just keeps saying the same things over and over again! I don't think I can take any more!"

"All right, all right, let's pick something else to read."

If Matt was unsettled that Rita couldn't bear to read his beloved *Course in Miracles,* he didn't show it. This was, I thought, a big change from years earlier when he had broken up with Amanda after their argument over the concept of sacrifice. He had grown since then, it seemed to me. Maybe his spirituality now had less to do with words in a book and more to do with his way of life. Or, maybe he was just so smitten with Rita that he could forgive her for not seeing the value of his personal bible. Either way, I was glad the two were staying together.

I had grown to like Rita more and more with the passing months. She was generous, fun-loving, and constantly told me how beautiful I was. And she had the charming habit of including me in a conversation. For instance, she would make a remark to Matt, then say, "Right, Gilly?" Matt never asked me if anything was right. Even if Rita did assume that the answer was always "Right, Rita!" at least she had the decency to ask.

Then there were the times that she seemed able to anticipate my thoughts and feelings even better than my human. Matt had the irritating habit of saying, "Gilly's been lying around all day and needs some exercise. Let's take him for a walk." Rita would say, "Gilly doesn't think that's a problem at all. He says if you wanna take a walk, go right ahead." Matt would argue, but Rita and I both knew that it was wishful thinking on his part.

I saw Rita growing, too. Since she'd promised to follow Matt's guidance on her drinking at parties, she had cut back. She still enjoyed it, but she was becoming more careful. They'd begun hosting gatherings at the penthouse that included people bringing food to share, reading poetry, and playing music. I benefited from these get-togethers, too, as it almost always meant better handouts. It was a win-win-win.

Chapter 55

Sacolés

Matt had returned to teaching English; although, his success at finding students this time around didn't compare to the year before. With the few students he taught, he struggled to pay the bills without dipping into his savings.

One sunny day in January, we were sitting in the sand of Itacoatiara with Rita. We could hear the calls of beach vendors who walked up and down, attempting to entice hungry and thirsty sunbathers. The most common items were sandwiches and a kind of iced tea called mate. But, some vendors sold *sacolés*. These were frozen treats: small tubes of plastic containing fruit juices, iced chocolate milk, or any variety of flavored ice. They sold for one to two reais.

"Sacolé da fruta!" I saw a stocky vendor trudging across the sand near us. Rita bought a strawberry and cream sacolé, giving Matt some to try. They ate it by biting a hole in the plastic, pushing out the frozen food and sucking on it, just like you would a popsicle. I watched hungrily, licking my lips. Sadly, Matt didn't feel like sharing.

"Que delícia!"

I wished he wouldn't rub it in like that. Still, I was glad that despite his struggling English-teaching career, he could still afford the simple pleasure of a sacolé on the beach.

Rita looked thoughtful for a few moments. "My mom used to make these all the time when we were kids."

"Oh yeah? How'd she do it?" As Matt continued slurping the cold sugary treat right in front of me, Rita launched into a detailed description of how to mix ice with the desired ingredients in a blender, pour the liquid into bags and tie them, and then put them in the freezer to harden.

"I wonder how much it costs to make them."

I looked at Matt with curiosity. *Uh oh. What was he thinking?* Together, the two humans began the calculations and came up with thirty cents per sacolé—more or less. I saw the wheels in my human's head turning, and I hoped the resulting idea didn't involve me.

But, of course, it did. Matt persuaded Rita to help him make sacolés at the penthouse apartment.

Several days later, with fresh fruits from her parents' yard, Rita and Matt spent the afternoon in the kitchen. They made four flavors: mango, coconut, orange juice, and chocolate. That evening, while the sacolés hardened in the freezer, Rita designed a sign for my harness. *"Sacolés do Gilly,"* it read, with a few decorative paw prints for effect.

It was a typical sweltering summer Saturday in Rio. People from all over the city flocked to Ipanema, some riding an hour or more on the bus to reach our neighborhood. Matt was bursting with excitement. Everything was falling into place, he told Rita gleefully. Mid-morning, the three of us walked the four blocks from the apartment to the beach. I wore the sign and it hung prominently from the left side of my harness. Rita carried the insulated bag. Matt practiced calling out as we reached the last street before the beach.

"Sacolés do Gilly!" He repeated the call, experimenting with his tone and pitch. "Whadaya think?" he asked Rita.

"I think you should wait until we actually get to the beach." She seemed more than a little embarrassed by the production.

"Is this for real?" A woman stood next to us waiting to cross the street.

"Oh, yeah," Matt said. "They're great sacolés. We made them ourselves."

She bought two with mango flavor.

"See?" Matt was triumphant. "And you wanted me to wait 'til we got to the beach."

"Sacolés do Gilly," Matt called, loudly. We trudged through the sand. Everyone stared, and some laughed out loud.

"Are you actually selling sacolés?"

A man wearing a barely visible swimsuit stopped as we met him walking along the shoreline. Matt insisted that we were, but our prospective client didn't buy any. We continued our trek.

"Do you want me to carry the bag for a while?"

Rita had insisted on lugging it over her shoulder since we left the apartment. "No," she said, firmly.

"Do you wanna try calling to the people?"

"No!" This reply was definitely more adamant.

We made our way to Apoador, the large rock separating Ipanema from Copacabana. Not one more person had bought a sacolé. Matt's calls become less robust, more plaintive. I panted. Rita perspired under the hot sun.

"Let's walk back to where we started and then quit," she said. Matt agreed, his disappointment showing.

"I don't understand it. People are looking at us, right?"

"Yeah, but I think a lot of them think it's a joke."

I certainly didn't think it was a joke. There was nothing funny about having to walk up and down the beach in these sweltering conditions. Finally, the two left me in the shade of someone's beach umbrella with the bag while they took a dip in the water. After a short while they returned, refreshed and renewed.

"Why do you think no one believed us?" Matt asked as we began a slow walk back home.

"Well, we don't exactly look like people who would be selling sacolés."

"What do you mean?"

"The real vendors are usually older, retired people who don't have much money. And they never have fat Labradors with signs."

"He's not fat," Matt protested good-naturedly.

My human had a thirst for new experiences and a craving to try different things. This was one of his most endearing qualities. But, as he was learning, all new experiences were not equal, and many that he found interesting once didn't merit repeating. We took the unsold sacolés back to the penthouse where Matt told the story of his failed entrepreneurism.

"So, they're in the freezer. Help yourselves."

Matt's friends adopted the practice of leaving some reais on top of the freezer to pay for the sacolés they consumed. It made Matt smile as he put the coins into his wallet. He might not have made a profit on the venture, but he definitely felt his housemates' love.

Chapter 56

Rita's Bed

As we spent more time at the house in Niteroi, Matt and I got to know even more about Rita and her family relationships.

"Mom, where's my hairbrush?" she called one evening as she got ready to go out with Matt and me to a party.

"Who knows?" Arminda replied. "Why don't you look in the bathroom?"

"I just did!" Rita all but screamed her answer. "Joao Carlos took it, I just know it! That little shit is always taking my things!"

Joao Carlos, Rita's younger brother, wasn't home at the time. As I lay in the corner of the living room and observed Rita slamming drawers open and closed, I thought that it was probably just as well.

"Calm down," Matt said. "I'm sure it'll turn up."

"No, it won't!" she said, fiercely. "He hid it from me. He does this all the time!"

A few minutes later, Arminda discovered the hairbrush in the bedroom that Joao Carlos and Rita shared.

"See? What did I tell you!" Rita said, taking the brush from her mom.

"It was on his bed. If he hid it, he didn't do it very well," her mom said.

After the party in Niteroi, Rita, Matt, and I took the hour and a half bus ride back to our apartment in Rio. As the vehicle rumbled through the darkened streets of two cities, my tired companions discussed how they could spend future nights together at Rita's house and avoid the long trip back to Rio.

"First I have to get my mom to convince my dad. He'll probably think it's bad that we'd be sleeping in the same bed." Rita frowned. "My mom is really traditional, too. A few years ago, she cried when I told her I wasn't a virgin anymore."

From the floor I watched Matt's weary face brighten in a smile. "You're not a virgin? Why didn't you tell me!"

Rita laughed and hit his arm affectionately. "Yeah, she said I wouldn't be able to wear a white dress at my wedding." She paused, thoughtfully. "But, she likes you. She might even make Joao Carlos sleep on the couch. Then we could have the bedroom to ourselves. I always sleep in the living room with my mattress on the floor so I don't have to share a room with him, but the bedroom's just as much mine as his. My bed is in there, after all."

A few days later, Rita broke the good news along with the bad. Matt was allowed to spend the night at her house, but they would have to share her mattress on the living room floor.

"Joao Carlos refuses to give up the bedroom, and my mom won't make him." Rita grimaced. "It's not fair. The little twerp has had it to himself for years and now he thinks it's his."

"Hey, at least we can stay at your house together."

The three of us began spending some of our nights in Niteroi. I was quite happy with the arrangement. Lying on the floor in the living room, I could usually get my head on a corner of the mattress. It made a nice pillow. Matt and Rita, however, seemed less comfortable.

"Stop, they'll hear us," Rita whispered as they lay in bed late one night.

"Are you sure?" Matt asked, disappointment in his voice.

"At least wait until my dad starts snoring."

Soon, the dull roar of Joao's snores was accompanied by a rustle of blankets and heavy breathing. I sighed and moved my head out of harm's way.

We spent more and more time at Rita's. Her younger cousins who lived in adjacent houses on the family property were always dropping by for visits. Sometimes Matt let them groom me or take me for walks. Sometimes, he would play his guitar for them in the soft shade of the jabuticaba tree. This cool spot became one of my favorite places to take naps, and the prime spot for Matt to do yoga. Rita's uncles and aunts who lived on the property became accustomed to seeing him bent into his curious contortions.

During bedtime, the symphony of heavy snores and labored breathing of humans at play continued. Then, one night, the usual routine was broken by a new sound. My ears pricked. Footsteps. A shadowy figure appeared in the living room and moved toward the bed where Matt and Rita continued their game under the covers.

"Sssshhhhh!" I felt alarm course through the two as Rita looked up and made eye contact with her younger brother. He lingered there, his gaze fixed on her, the scent of condemnation in the air. Then, just as quickly, he was gone.

"Oh, shit!" Rita said. "He was just waiting to catch us."

"Jeez, that was awkward. Do you think he'll tell?"

"Probably."

She was right, as it turned out. The incident didn't get Matt and me banned from the house, but it did get Rita a long and furious talking-to from her mom. Her dad, it appeared, hadn't been advised of the scandal. Or, if he had, he never let on.

After some days, and recovered from the humiliation of the incident, Rita decided that this was outright war. She vowed that nothing would stop her from taking back her part of the bedroom.

"If Joao Carlos comes in and sees us sleeping in my bed, he'll just have to deal with it. He can take his mattress and go to the living room, just like I've had to do all this time."

That evening, with her brother out of the house, Matt and Rita lugged her mattress from the living room into the bedroom. I followed them into the small space barely large enough for the two beds and understood why Rita had opted for the floor in another room. They began to position the mattress over her bed frame.

"Wait a minute," Rita said. "The bed boards are missing. This is ridiculous!" She looked around the room, under the other bed, and in the closet, but the boards that once supported her mattress on the bed frame were nowhere to be found. "I can't believe this! They took my bed boards!" She was actually shaking with outrage. After a moment, I saw her tears.

"Who?" Matt asked, gently.

"Leonardo and Carla!" she wailed, the tears coming now in full force. Matt and I had visited with Rita's older brother and his girlfriend more than a few times. They were renting a place together down the street. "I know it was them," Rita said in between sobs. "Leonardo asked me if he could have my bed boards for his house, and I said no. So he just took them anyway! He just took them from me and said nothing!" She kicked the empty bed frame, almost beside herself. I had never smelled so much despair and loathing from Rita as I did in that moment.

"I'm sorry, love." Matt put out a cautious hand to her. He seemed truly affected.

"I hate them so much!" she cried. "I have nothing—nothing in this whole house but a mattress on the floor."

Matt put his arm around her as she continued to sob. After a long moment, he said, "They're just bed boards. We don't need them, anyway. Let's go back to Rio. We can sleep at my place tonight."

But, we didn't go back. We slept that night on the living room floor after Rita, calmer but still fiercely indignant, told her mom what had happened.

Arminda was moved. "I'm sorry," she said, compassion in her voice. "They just don't understand what they did."

So we went on sleeping in the makeshift bedroom of the small house. I was happy to keep using their thin mattress as a pillow. For the record, I never once brought up not having a bed myself. And, if

Rita's mom became aware that the humans quietly continued to indulge in late-night playtime on the floor of her living room, she didn't say so.

Chapter 57

Change in the Wind

The months passed. I noticed Matt becoming dimly aware that I was slowing down, not that I'd ever been that fast to begin with. It was gradual, but I knew it was happening. When Matt would decide to go for a walk, I'd watch him grab the harness and leash, and I'd know what was coming.

"Gil-lee." He'd begin to call me, and I'd begin to consider getting up. After several more calls of "Gill-leee", and with Matt's voice rising in insistence, I would finally stand and shake myself vigorously. "Come on, Gilly!" he'd say, trying to convey urgency. He'd slap his thigh and clap his hands. Sometimes he'd even holler, "Gilly, fire, fire!"

I never bought it for a second. The only one of his tricks that I occasionally fell for was when he opened the front door and walked through, slowly closing it behind him.

"Bye, Gilly," he'd call, in a sad, far-away tone. After waiting a few seconds, he'd fling the door open again, and I would amble over to him just to make sure he didn't actually leave without me.

It wasn't that I didn't like Matt or didn't want to help him; it was just a matter of inertia. I had learned that a Labrador at rest tends to remain at rest, and this was in proportion to the Labrador's age. At least, so it seemed to me. I was seven going on eight, easing comfortably into middle age. At this point, I had so thoroughly perfected my ability to economize my effort, that some days the acts of sleeping, eating, and breathing were more than enough to completely occupy my energies. Retirement seemed like the only practical solution. Unfortunately, Matt was slow in getting the message. So I decided to give him some more clues.

Sometimes, when I was on the bus with Matt and Rita, I'd wriggle under their seats. When it was time to get off, I'd use the bottom edge of the bench to help me back out of my harness's leather straps and emerge, unencumbered. More than once, we'd be ready to exit when a passenger would see my harness and rush to return it. One time, the bus was already picking up speed as it drove away before a good samaritan frantically persuaded the driver to stop, open the doors, and allow him to return my harness. Matt and Rita were shocked and relieved, but all the stranger got from me was a deep sigh and a weary look. I wondered when my human was ever going to catch on.

Eventually, he did.

But, my looming retirement was not the only change reaching a critical point. Matt's courtship with Rita was now almost to the one-year mark. Long past was the honeymoon phase in which disagreements were swept under the rug. As each had experienced the other's dark side, it became clear that they had the strength to see through it to the beauty underneath.

It was more than just the ability to forgive each other that hinted at a lasting relationship. Their strengths were complimentary. Rita was passionate, attentive, and generous. Matt was rational, flexible, appreciative. They both loved art and culture; they both reveled in nature and pets. By late March, Matt had made up his mind that Rita was the girl for him to marry, and I whole-heartedly approved. She doted on me, gave me great massages, and always looked out for my well-being. I knew she would take good care of my human, too.

However, I wasn't the only one Matt looked to for approval. He cared little about the trappings and traditions of a formal wedding, but it was important to him that his family supported his decision. The problem was that none of them had met Rita. Even if they had, none of them spoke Portuguese, and Rita's English was minimal. He had applied for a tourist visa for Rita so that she could visit his family in the United States, but the consulate had rejected the application. He figured she didn't fit the economic profile required by the American government. Her father was a butcher, her mother a housewife. Her internship through the university in Rio paid almost nothing.

"So, anything else new?" Matt's mom asked. He and I were on the penthouse porch, catching up on family affairs via Skype.

"Well, yeah, actually, there is."

"Oh? Well, I'm all ears."

He took a deep breath. "Uh, I think I'm going to ask Rita to marry me."

And it's about time!

"Wow! That really is something new." His mom's voice sounded surprised.

"Actually, it's only kinda new. You know we've been dating for a while, and I really think she's the one. I wanted to introduce her to everyone in the family first, but, I guess that's not gonna happen."

"I know you wanted to bring her for a visit, but, well, this is more than I expected!"

I had the advantage of seeing Matt's mom through the video feed on his computer, and even from thousands of miles away, I could see her eyes sparkling with unshed tears.

"I still want you all to meet her, Mom. It'll just have to wait until after we're married." His hands gripped the edges of his computer. There was a moment of silence.

She's super! You'll love her, I wanted to say. *She gives great belly rubs.*

"Married. Well, you're certainly old enough."

"Yeah, I think so." Matt was 27. So was Rita.

"Well, I know you love her. And, from everything you've said, it sounds like you two get along." His mom paused for a second. "I guess I just wonder if she's someone who'll stick by you no matter how tough things get."

"Yeah, she definitely is, Mom. She's truly devoted to me and Gilly."

"I'm glad, honey. And I'm happy for you, really. I just can't believe you're getting married!"

At that, I saw smiles break out on both faces. As the conversation took a nostalgic turn, I rolled over onto my side. Humans could be so long-winded.

Once he had bought the ring, Matt needed to decide how to propose. Easter was just two weeks away, and Rita loved chocolate. He considered hiding the ring inside a chocolate egg, but after talking to friends, he scrapped the idea. It was at worst, risky and at best, messy, they said. I thought the idea sounded delicious, but nobody asked my opinion. It was a surprise, then, when Matt's focus shifted in my direction. I was the perfect package, he told his mom, through which to deliver the ring. Adorable and heart-warming, no one could refuse my Labrador charms. The gesture had symbolic significance as well, he explained. Not only would Rita be receiving a promise of marriage, she would be gaining my companionship.

On the Sunday after Easter, Matt and Rita were in her family's living room eating dinner. I lay out on the porch, resting in the cool evening breeze. Rita's dad was in the bedroom watching soccer on TV and her mom was in the kitchen. As I groggily listened to Rita and Arminda loudly exchanging bits of family gossip, I became aware of Matt, stealthily creeping out the door, headed in my direction.

"Hi, Guildenstern," he whispered.

Why are you crawling on the floor, and what's with the whispering? I gazed at him inquiringly.

As if he understood my questions, he said, "You are one lucky dog, Gil. You're going to be a ring bearer."

I wasn't sure what he meant, but patience was one of my virtues. And I soon got an inkling of his plan as he proceeded to pull a ribbon and a jewelry box out of his pocket. Then, with fumbling fingers, he tied the ribbon around my neck, securing the small box along with it. His hands were clammy as he pulled the bow tight.

"Amor, what're you doing?" Rita called.

"Uh, nothing, just saying hi to Gilly." He quickly went back inside.

From the living room, I heard Matt ask, "Aren't your parents going to eat?"

"Nah, they're both busy."

"Why doesn't your family ever have dinner together?"

"My dad likes to watch the game in the bedroom where it's more comfortable. Why does it matter, anyway?"

Matt gave up and went to the kitchen where Rita's mom was doing dishes. "Could you and Joao come into the living room for a minute?" he asked, his question drifting through the kitchen window to the veranda, where I still lay. Soon, the two filed in and sat down.

"Well, I just wanted to make sure," Matt began, clearing his throat, "uh, to make sure that it was okay with both of you that Gilly stays here while I go to the United States and get my new guide dog."

"Of course it's okay," Rita's mom said.

"Sure, we'll take good care of him," her dad added.

"Oh, and one more thing. Gilly has a present for Rita that I'd like you both to see. Gilly, come!" Matt called in a loud voice.

From my spot on the porch, my ears twitched. *It's so hot inside the house,* I thought.

"Gilly, come!" Matt repeated.

The porch was cool, with a nice breeze.

"Gilly!" chimed in Rita's mom, "come here, Gilly!"

She occasionally gave me bits of food. Slowly, I pulled myself onto all fours and ambled into the living room.

"Do you see the present?" Matt asked as I collapsed in the middle of the floor.

"There's a bow on him," Rita's dad said.

"Are you sure he has something?" Rita peered closely at my crumpled form.

"Yeah, he's supposed to." Matt knelt down and searched my body for the box. It was gone.

After a careful inspection of the porch, Rita found the box. She and Matt returned to the living room where she opened it and found the new ring. Any semblance of a magical moment had been undone, but Matt shook off his obvious dismay. He formally declared his love for Rita and asked her parents for their blessing. They granted it without hesitation. Rita, in turn, accepted her ring and sealed the engagement with a long kiss.

In another minute, it was over. Rita wore her ring, Joao went back to the game, and Arminda returned to the dishes. I, thankfully, was allowed to go back to the porch. In the living room, Matt sighed. It hadn't gone as well as he'd hoped, I knew. Still, it was done. Rita, I noticed, spent the rest of the evening taking frequent glances at her shiny new gift.

"So, you like it?"

"Yes!" she said, emphatically. I saw it was going to take some time for her to get over the excitement of the ring and come around to realizing that I was her greatest gift of all.

Chapter 58

Good-bye

That April passed quickly. Not long after the engagement, Matt, Rita and I were in the bedroom at the penthouse. They were sitting on the bed, talking. I lay on the floor in the doorway, my muzzle in the bedroom, my rump in the hall. I drifted in and out of naps, paying little attention to their conversation. Still, I sensed a slight tension. It wasn't the kind of mounting electricity that built up before they had a fight. It was a mild anxiousness, a gentle sadness. Then, Matt went to the closet and brought out something I hadn't seen in a long time. A suitcase.

Immediately, I was off the floor and going over to investigate the dusty object. I sniffed it curiously, and the memory of farewells and busy airports, long flights and greetings rushed in. I'd known this was coming, of course. I'd overheard lots of conversations. But, it was one thing to understand abstractly, and quite another thing to live the experience. Matt was going back to the United States to train with a new guide dog. I was staying in Brazil with Rita while he was gone. That was clear. Now, what began to sink in as I watched them put clothes into Matt's suitcase, was that he was leaving without me.

We had been separated before. I thought fleetingly of my Florida vacation with Cousin Ben when Matt went to Brazil for the first time. It had been hard saying good-bye then, but not as hard as now. We had grown more attached to each other over these last few years. Even Matt's practice of leaving me at home while he went out at night had stopped.

We were always together, and we both preferred it that way. Having Matt close by enabled me to keep him out of trouble and ensured a steady supply of kibble. Having me close allowed him to share in the warmth and attention people gave such a handsome Labrador. No matter how slowly I responded to his calls, he took me out with him. He showed me interesting places to smell, and if he didn't, I caught quick sniffs of them when he wasn't paying attention. We had a good thing, my human and I.

Matt spent his last night at Rita's house. His luggage sat ready in the corner, along with his guitar and backpack. The next day, Rita's relatives dropped in to say good-bye and wish him a good trip. The three of us took one last stroll down the familiar dirt road in front of her parents' house. Matt didn't bother to put the harness on me, letting me sniff freely in the weeds along both sides.

"He might as well get used to it. He won't have to guide me anymore."

And that's when the full weight of what was about to happen came to rest. It wasn't just that Matt was going away for our longest separation ever. It was that when he came back, things wouldn't be the same. He wouldn't be my responsibility. Another dog would accompany him on the bus, to his classes, to the beach, and into restaurants. I would stay at home, free to sleep and sniff and economize effort as much as I wanted. But I would no longer be his guide.

Back at the house, I lay next to him as we waited for the taxi to arrive. He stroked my soft, velvety ears with tenderness, and I breathed deeply in contentment. Then, the cab pulled up. He grabbed his backpack and a suitcase, and Rita got the second suitcase and his guitar. They hauled the luggage through the front gate. I followed them out into the street, hoping Matt would reconsider this momentous decision.

"No, Gilly!" Rita said. "Back inside!"

"Come on, Gilly!" Rita's mom called from the yard. Reluctantly, I passed back through the gate and then turned around to watch.

"Do you wanna say bye to Gilly one last time?" Rita asked Matt.

"No, that's okay." He shut the cab door. It was too much, I knew. He wanted to get this departure over with as quickly as possible. Matt didn't like showing emotion.

I watched Rita walk around and get in the other side of the taxi. I knew she was going to the airport to see him off. As they moved away, and the distance between us grew wider and wider, I felt sadness wash over me. I wondered if it was Matt's or mine.

"Come on, Gilly," Rita's mom called as she went up the walkway back to the house. I didn't follow her. I needed some time to be alone. My gaze remained on the gate as if by force of will it would open again, and Matt would come back. The minutes passed.

It was silly, I knew. There was no reason to be sad. I was an older dog now, and it was time for me to rest. Matt needed someone who was as eager to move and explore as he was, someone who would go to him on the second or third call instead of the fifth or sixth, someone whose training was fresh and who could respond easily to whatever lay ahead.

This retirement, as dramatic a life change as it seemed, was only superficial. I knew this instinctively even while I continued to stare mournfully at the gate. Emotions, routines, and life situations came and went. But, through it all I knew there endured and flourished something much greater, something that I couldn't define in dog or human terms. Something so simple, so awesome, so inspiring that it was all that mattered and all there really was. I loved my human, and my human loved me.

Epilogue

T he days passed, and I eased into retirement with my Brazilian family. I got my kibble from Rita, bones from her dad's butcher shop, and table scraps from her mom. I often smiled to myself, thinking about what a fit Matt would throw if he knew.

It was a good life. Still, I felt vaguely incomplete. Part of me was far, far away. I dreamed often of my human. I saw him flying home to the United States, training with a dog, a younger dog, not nearly as good-looking as I was, but full of vitality. I saw them return to Pittsburgh, learn the old route around the neighborhood, and visit with friends and relatives. I saw Matt at his computer, typing away. I recognized my name on the screen, and I felt my presence in his thoughts. He missed me, that was clear, and I think writing about me helped him.

The weeks turned into months. On my birthday, Rita's dad brought me an enormous cow bone, which I would've eaten in one sitting if I had been allowed. Later, Rita brought me to the telephone.

"Guildenstern!"

I pricked my ears and wagged my tail at the sound of Matt's voice.

"Happy birthday, Guildenstern! You're an eight-year-old dog! I miss you so much, boy! I can't wait to come back and see you!"

My tail slowed its wag. It was good to hear him, but I wanted to smell him, feel him nearby, taste the kibble that he measured out into my bowl. Rita put the phone to her ear and finished the conversation. All in due time, I told myself, lying down on the living room floor with a *humph*. Just a few more naps, a few more dreams, a few more stolen bananas, a few more walks in the street with Rita.

Before I knew it, he would be back. There was really nothing I could do to speed things up. Luckily, doing nothing was my specialty.

One early August morning, Rita woke up before sunrise, full of nervous excitement. She had told me the night before, as she'd caressed my soft fur, that Matt was on his way back. I'd looked deeply into her eyes. There was no need to say anything for she knew exactly how I felt. That morning, I kept an ear trained on the street, listening for the idling vehicle that would bring him back to me. Soon enough, it came.

I was at the gate in an instant. I could hear his voice. I could smell him, too. And there was someone else.

The gate opened. "Guildenstern!"

I leaped up in the air once, twice, three times. I was so overjoyed that I barely took stock of the dog at my human's side. He wore a harness like I'd worn, though it was made of plastic, not leather.

Matt removed the harness. "Achilles, this is Gilly."

Achilles. He was a skinny, excitable canine, barely out of his puppyhood. The frenetic youngster raced around behind me, trying to exert dominance. I sat down quickly to avoid his foolishness.

"He's trying to mount Gilly!" Rita exclaimed in horror.

"Achilles, no!"

The new dog backed off and went about sniffing the yard. I'd known things would be different, and this just confirmed it.

Well, I thought, *at least Matt is back.*

Things were different; that's for sure. A week later the engaged couple gathered up Matt's suitcases and Rita's things and moved out. Their new apartment, only a short walk down the road from the family's home, was part of a long, squat, stone building. It was the tiniest efficiency imaginable. And while Matt wanted to keep both Achilles and me with them, the landlady was adamant that only one guide dog was allowed. Matt complained about the woman's insensitivity and her hard-headed rule enforcing, but there was nothing he could do. I was a little more stoic. It was only a short walk between the two places. He could visit me all the time.

And that's exactly what he did. Every day, before and after the English classes he had started giving again, Matt would come to see me. He would groom me under the jabuticaba tree and brush my teeth with the chicken-flavored toothpaste I liked so much. On the weekends he and Rita would take me out of retirement so I could go to the beach with them. With my harness back on, I would ride the buses and hike the trails at Itacoatiara again. And when I got back home with the scent of forest and beach on me, Achilles would go nuts with jealousy.

After a rainy spring and a scorchingly hot summer, I enjoyed the mild tropical fall and winter months. Matt and Rita continued to function as a team, living together in their tiny, one-room house. In December they got married in a small ceremony in town. Then, as Rita entered her final semester at the university, Matt began talking about his latest plans. He wanted to work on a master's program in the United States. He said it would be good for Rita to experience another culture and to learn English. Reluctant at first, she began to warm up to the idea.

"Will Gilly be able to come with us?" she asked one night, stroking my back. They had snuck me over to the apartment under cover of darkness and would return me to her parents' house early the next morning—hopefully before the landlady caught on.

"Of course."

"But how? You can't take two guide dogs with you on the plane."

Matt had obviously thought about this because he answered without hesitation. "Well, I'll take Achilles first. Then I'll fly back to Brazil to get Gilly. If he wears the harness, he can go on the plane with me. It'll be two trips, but it'll be totally worth it."

I thumped my tail, feeling Matt's happiness at this thought. I wasn't so sure, though.

Some time later, I'm not sure how long, Matt and Rita left for the United States. I began sleeping a lot more after that, even more than usual. I dreamed of Matt. I saw him walking with Rita and Achilles in unfamiliar neighborhoods, laughing and chatting with people I didn't know. But more often, he and I were together, like we had been for so many years. I saw us on our first solos at guide dog school. I was wet behind the ears and Matt was painfully young and unsure of himself. I saw us walking down the street together at Oberlin College, my human laboriously counting steps so we could find our way home. I dreamed of Matt and Sylvia and exploring the trails of Frick Park with crazy Kassandra. In my dreams, I didn't feel like an old dog at all. In my dreams, time was irrelevant.

In my waking life, I continued to eat kibble and bones. Sometimes, Rita's mom gave me baths, and sometimes Rita's cousins took me on walks, though the trips grew shorter and shorter. I felt like a very old dog then. My right front leg was getting swollen and hard. It smelled like something rotting.

It's tough to say how much time passed. In some ways it seemed like a lot. Days and nights followed each other in an endless sequence. In other ways, though, it seemed like no time at all. My waking life took on a hazy quality and my dreams became richer and more alive than ever.

Then, he was back. I awoke from a dream in which I was luxuriating in a first-class belly rub and found the real Matt, rubbing me all over and repeating my name excitedly. I wagged my tail in an ecstatic greeting and tried to get up, but fell back down. Standing was difficult.

Matt touched my right leg, which had become enormous. "Oh my God, Gilly," he murmured. "I had no idea."

I didn't see what was so bad. It was just a dying leg. I had three others. Standing up on my own was too much work anyway. I liked having Rita's dad lift me up so I could do my business in the yard.

And with Matt back, I had more help. Those next few days, he was with me constantly. There was a bittersweetness in him I'd never sensed before. He gave me lots of belly rubs and even let me sleep on the mattress in the living room with Rita and him. Then a woman came to look at my leg, a woman I'd seen before. She was the vet who signed the forms that Matt needed to take me back to the United States. She gave him one of those forms, and he thanked her.

"How are we gonna get him on the plane?" Rita asked. "He can't walk by himself."

"We'll use a cart or something."

"Well, we'd better find one fast. Our flight is in two days."

They spent all the next day scouring the Internet and making phone calls. Apparently, Labrador-sized carts that could be wheeled through an airport and onto a plane were hard to come by in the city of Niteroi. I listened to their worried, confused discussions as I lay near Matt's feet in the living room.

"Maybe it's better that we leave him here," sighed Rita late that afternoon. "You heard what the vet said. Even if we have his leg amputated, he won't last much longer. The cancer's in his whole body."

"I know, Rita, I know. But how can we just leave him here? After all we've been through together? I'd rather have him spend his last days with us than . . ." His voice sounded strained.

On the floor, I gnawed at my annoyingly hard and dead leg. Even turning over to lie on my side was an effort now, almost more than I cared to muster. It didn't matter so much where I was lying anymore. The living room, the yard, Brazil, the United States, it was all running together.

Matt and Rita left the house early the next morning. Their suitcases were out and in a state of mid-pack. They told Rita's mom that they were going to get a wagon and would be back by lunch. They weren't, though. It was early evening before they came home. Matt was carrying a large skateboard. He put it down next to where I lay on the porch. I wagged my tail in greeting and then lifted my head quizzically as Matt measured my form and then compared the skateboard with his hands.

I looked at Matt inquiringly. Did he really think I would fit on that?

I heard Rita fuming to her mom. They'd been all over the city. There were no wagons in Niteroi, and this was the best they could do. Their flight was in two hours, and how were they ever going to make it in time?

"Come on, Rita. Help me, please."

Rita came to join us on the porch. "It's not going to work," she said, but she bent down and helped Matt lift me onto the skateboard. I lay awkwardly. My legs dangled over the side and onto the ground. Matt ran his hands over me and frowned.

"I told you it wouldn't work. He doesn't fit."

Matt said nothing. He just squatted next to me as I lay on the skateboard. A long moment passed. Finally, with Rita's help, he lifted me back onto the ground.

I sighed and closed my eyes. I was too old for skateboarding. Matt would just have to accept that.

After a few last frantic minutes of packing, I watched them come onto the porch with suitcases trailing behind them. Matt bent down and gave me a gentle pat.

"Bye, Gilly." He smelled of sadness and confusion. He still didn't understand.

It was some time after they left. How much I couldn't say. The day was warm and bright like many others, and yet something told me this one was different. I lay on the porch, only dimly aware of my surroundings. Suddenly, there was a familiar presence at my side.

"Gilly! Remember me?"

Of course I did. I lifted my head, my tail wagging weakly. Rafael's large, gentle hands stroked me. It was good to have him here. He was so loving.

Adriana was next to him then, saying my name and petting me. "You poor thing. You poor, poor thing." Then she faded in to the background, replaced by another woman.

"It's okay, Gilly," Rafael whispered. "It won't hurt at all."

I felt a prick then. The other woman, I realized, was the vet. Suddenly I became sleepy, so very sleepy. I closed my eyes and shuddered. I began to dream.

A phone is ringing. Rita's mom answers it. She talks for a moment, then calls Rafael and passes it to him.

"Hi Mathews," he says.

On the other end, Matt is both nervous and somber. "Hi."

"It's done. There was no pain at all. He went straight to heaven."

"Oh," is all Matt says. He exhales.

Rafael begins to talk about how kind the vet was, how easy it was for me.

On the other end of the phone line, Matt sinks into a leather chair next to Achilles, who lies on the floor nearby. Rita sits on a couch, watching. Her expression is concerned.

"I'm so glad you were there. I'm so glad it was you with him. Gilly loved you so much," Matt says to Rafael. He hangs up the phone and tells Rita what happened. She begins to cry. Matt doesn't though. He just sits there looking empty and lost.

Finally, Matt goes into another room and closes the door. He picks up his guitar and begins to play. Tears fill his eyes, and as he continues plucking the guitar strings, they spill onto his face. He opens his mouth as if to sing, and instead, his body shakes. The guitar becomes silent.

I watch him cry for a while. I want to comfort him as I have so many times before. But, my soft fur, the warmth of my body, and the rise and fall of my breath are gone. All I can do is experience an overflowing love for him. That's all I have left.

After a while Matt stops crying and begins playing again. This time he sings, and a song I've never heard before takes shape. It's beautiful! I hear in it his great sadness and, beneath that a glimmer of understanding. On some level, it seems, my human knows I'm still with him.

And that's the end of the story. Only it's not, really. Matt and Rita and Achilles go on, and I go on with them. Sometimes, when Matt is asleep, he dreams of me, and we play tug just like old times, and he gives me belly rubs and calls me fat. And other times, when his sleep is deepest, we forget about each other and remember that we are one.

About the Author

Matt VanFossan is a graduate of Oberlin College and of the University of Santa Monica's master's program in spiritual psychology. A counselor and a musician, he is currently living in Santa Monica, California with his wife, Rita, and guide dog, Achilles. To learn more about his work and music, visit www.guidingforlife.com.

Have an opinion? Post a review of this book to your favorite site and let others know about Gilly's story.

7855645R00193

Made in the USA
San Bernardino, CA
19 January 2014